UNCERTAIN GLORY

UNCERTAIN GLORY
Lee's Generalship Re-Examined

John D. McKenzie

HIPPOCRENE BOOKS
New York

For information, address:

HIPPOCRENE BOOKS, INC.

171 Madison Avenue

New York, NY 10016

Library of Congress Cataloging-in-Publication Data

McKenzie, John D.

Uncertain glory : Lee's generalship re-examined / John D. McKenzie

p. cm.

Includes bibliographical references and index.

ISBN 0-7818-0502-3

1. Lee, Robert E. (Robert Edward), 1807-1870—Military leadership. 2. United States—History—Civil War. 1861-1865—Campaigns. 3. Strategy—History—19th century. 4. Confederate States of America—History, Military. I. Title

E467.1.L4M48 1996   96-32522

973.7'42—dc20   CIP

Maps by Beth Queman

Printed in the United States of America.

NOTE: All of the maps are sketched from maps appearing in:
Atlas to Accompany the Official Records of the Union And Confederate Armies.
Washington: Government Printing Office, 1891-1895. (New York: Crown Publishers reprint, 1978.)

KEY TO MAPS

Legend

I I I I	Unfinished Railroad
++++	Railroad
——	Road
~~	River/Creek/Run
~~^	Entrenchment
)(	Ford
– –	Trail
—<—	Bridge
° ~ °	Woods
.:ı	City
⌐⊤⌐	Confederate Line
⊔⊔⊔	Union Line
❶ Ⓐ	Reference Numbers and Letters

	Union	Confederate
Infantry	■	☐
Cavalry	◢	◹

Contents

Maps

Acknowledgments

Many people have contributed to my writing of this book, and I regret not being able to mention all of them. My father, Henry John McKenzie, made at least two important contributions: he insisted that I receive an excellent education, and he took me to Gettysburg as a teenager where my interest in the Civil War was ignited. My wife, Betty, deserves much of any credit the book receives; besides continuous support and encouragement, she has proofread over and over and corrected my sometimes erratic spelling and grammar. Our children, Anne and John, Jr., have also given continuous support and help.

Without Alan T. Nolan, this book could never have been written. Alan acted as a diligent mentor steering me through the many pitfalls of writing a Civil War historical book and getting it published. Beside much constructive criticism, Alan never wavered from pushing me to <u>finish the book</u> regardless of how discouraging circumstances might be. A friend of long standing, Charles H. Everill, has had experience in newspaper editing; he used these skills for many hours unselfishly editing and suggesting changes in how I expressed my ideas. The book is far better than it would have been without his efforts.

A number of copies of an early draft of this book were sent to a few publishers, including Hippocrene, only to be rejected, sometimes with a few suggestions. I received an unsolicited letter from Ken Gallagher of Combined Books who urged me to continue my efforts in the writing of Civil War history and told me that my submittal to Hippocrene had been a "near miss." This encouraged me to re-write the book and re-submit it to Hippocrene which subsequently sent me a contract to publish it. At Hippocrene, Jacek Galazka, George Blagowidow and Jennifer Pigeon have been supportive of a first-time author and wonderful to work with. Coincidentally, Combined Books was assigned by Hippocrene to produce the book, and Ken Gallagher and Bob Pigeon became its editors, and Toni Bauer its production editor. All are excellent at what they do, have been good to work with and have contributed greatly to the final book. Beth Queman drew the excellent maps which add much to the understanding of the book.

My thanks to all these people and others not mentioned, and I must point out that any shortcomings in the book are mine alone!

Foreword

by Alan T. Nolan

Civil War writing tends to be marked by a sameness, the reiteration by one writer of what prior writers have said. Only rarely does a book contain original insights and analysis that test the conventional opinions. John McKenzie's book is just that kind of challenging book. This is not to say that McKenzie disagrees with the consensus view of every Civil War military leader or event. It is to say that he views the leaders and events without the conventional biases, favorable or unfavorable, of the commonly-held opinions and proceeds to his own thoughtful discussion. Sometimes his conclusions are consistent with the commonly-held opinions. Sometimes they are not. As suggested by the title, McKenzie's most pronounced departure from convention has to do with General Robert E. Lee. Most military writers, North and South, then and now, identify Lee as a military genius.

The traditional opinion is that Lee was a superior strategist and tactician. According to the tradition, Lee's defeat was not the result of any error or inadequacy on his part. Notwithstanding his peerless leadership, his defeat was caused by overwhelming Northern manpower. Because of the section's manpower differential, Lee's defeat was inevitable. The tradition does not inquire whether Lee's manpower problems, which were endemic, should have directed him away from the costly strategic and tactical offensives which marked his leadership at least until 1864 and which, because of his large and disproportionate casualties,

15

progressively limited the viability of his army. The tradition does not inquire concerning the likely consequences of a defensive grand strategy. McKenzie believes that Lee's offensive strategic sense was a mistake and that his failure resulted from this offensive, rather than defensive, approach to the war.

McKenzie's thesis regarding Lee requires his consideration of the issue of why the Confederacy lost the war. The theory of the inevitable loss of the Lost Cause has, at least implicitly, protected Lee from an inquiry into the validity of his offensive strategic judgment. If the Confederate cause was from the beginning simply a forlorn hope, the criteria in the evaluation of Lee's military leadership are lowered because advancing the objective of winning the war is read out of the case. On the other hand, if it is believed that the war could have been won, Lee must be evaluated in terms of whether he helped or hurt the chance of victory. McKenzie rejects the notion that the Confederacy's loss of the war was a foregone conclusion. In this respect, McKenzie accurately notes that but for Mobile Bay, Atlanta and Sheridan's victories in the Shenandoah, the 1864 election risked Lincoln's defeat and the possibility of independence for the South. The Confederacy could therefore have won. This conclusion permits McKenzie's analysis of Lee's responsibility for Confederate failure.

Another myth associated with Lee's reputation attributes his defeats to his lieutenants' failures. Gettysburg is the principal example of this phenomenon. Stuart, A.P. Hill, Ewell and Longstreet are blamed by Lee partisans for the defeat there. This scapegoating has created another exemption from responsibility for Lee. McKenzie rejects the rationalizations based on blaming others for what happened to Lee. Therefore Lee's decisions and activities are the point of analysis.

McKenzie's thesis also requires a discussion of the strategy of the war as a whole, both Northern and Southern, and an analysis by McKenzie of Union army commanders. McKenzie notes that at the outset of the war the apparently most qualified senior officers of the army, including Lee and the two Johnstons, went

South, which required the North to develop during the war general officers of high capacity. According to McKenzie, this was done and he cites the examples of Grant, Sherman, Thomas, Meade and Sheridan, several of whom he believes were superior to Lee.

McKenzie asserts that historians and commentators with a Confederate bias have controlled and dictated America's popular sense of the history of the war, at least until relatively recently. This phenomenon bears some responsibility for Lee's excellent reputation. McKenzie's book is offered as a corrective, a detailed and informed challenge of conventional wisdom. It is entitled to a wide audience.

Alan T. Nolan
Indianapolis
August 1, 1996

PREFACE

*I*n 1939 when I was fifteen, my father and I went to the New York World's Fair, and on our way back, we stopped at Gettysburg. He dropped me off at the start-point of Pickett's attack; I walked up that long slope alone; then, he picked me up at the stone wall where the Confederate Brigadier General Lewis A. Armistead died in 1863. When I started that walk, my reaction looking up was: "Those soldiers were very brave." Looking down from the stone wall, my reaction was: "Those soldiers were crazy to have made that charge against such heavy fire."

In June 1944 while still a teen-ager, I went into Normandy as a member of the 82nd Airborne Division; then, I fought with these brave and sometime crazy paratroopers from Normandy to Berlin. After fighting in such places as the Ardennes and Heurtgen forests, I developed a strong empathy for the soldiers on both sides who fought in the Wilderness and other woods of Virginia in the 1860s. In Europe, I learned to recognize a killing field which soldiers could not expect to cross with any expectation of living, and as a non-commissioned officer, I learned to value highly the lives of the soldiers for whom I was responsible.

After World War II, I graduated form Purdue University, then earned a graduate degree at the Wharton School and began a career as a business executive. Because I traveled widely, I had the opportunity to visit Gettysburg several times between 1960 and 1994. I went back to Pickett's start-point, thoroughly toured the battlefield and began to doubt the skills of Rober E. Lee as a general. I simply could not accept the logic of his being an excellent general along with my recognition that the difficult ground over which he chose to have his soldiers charge was a hopeless killing ground. If it had been 1944 with our greater fire-power, a far smaller force would not have allowed one of Pickett's men to return to the start-line unhurt; even so, in 1863 with much poorer weapons, Union soldiers showed great efficiency by allowing only 44% of Pickett's men to return unhurt.

Reading Civil War history books became relaxation for me while performing demanding work. As I read Catton's great trilogy and Freeman's wonderfully literate seven books on Lee, my doubts about Lee increased. I was forced to the unpleasant conclusion that between 1870 and 1940, Southern historians conducted an enormous exercise in revising history by falsely enhancing and even manufacturing Lee's skills in generalship. It required the reading of hundreds of Civil war histories for me to confirm my doubts about Lee and begin to understand the reasons why Southern historians made these historical revisions.

This book therefore dares to criticize the performance of Robert E. Lee as a general. It is a book of analysis and logic; it does not purport to present new facts from the records of the Civil War. To the contrary, the author has studied many dusty tomes of that war, like the *Official Records* (OR)[1], and raises questions concerning the conclusions previous writers have drawn from these sources. The OR are the basic foundation of most previous historian's books on the Civil War. The OR have a number of severe failings that allow a historian to use them as he chooses in order to support his pre-conceived conclusions. These failings and the motivations of historians must be considered if a search for the truth about any Civil War person is to be made.

Three failings of the OR are most critical. First, there are gaps in coverage that prevent a full telling of some events. Usually these gaps result from documents having been lost, the death of a key participant, the failure of a subordinate to write a report or the superior having failed to approve and accept it. There are many examples of reports being lost, but one example of a suppressed report is Pickett's after-action report following his failed charge up Cemetery Ridge. It is known that Pickett wrote such a report, but Lee declined to accept it, and Pickett refused to revise it. No copy has been found.

A second failing is the tendency for the OR to tell about actions from a position of hindsight. Almost every battle was described by surviving officer-participants in after-action reports. Many such after-action reports are biased in favor of the writer's part in the action. Maybe 90% of the writer's statements were 90% accurate or more, but some bias is everywhere, and a significant number of these reports are outright falsehoods. It was not the duty of those who edited the OR to state opinions of what was true and what was false. Commanders-in-chief show occasional self-serving bias in their reports, but usually a higher degree of such bias is seen in the reports of commanders of corps, division and regiments. Motivation for exaggerations, omissions or falsehoods usually rested in a defense of their failures or their desire to place blame on someone else. Often this motivation to slant things in the report-writer's favor rested on a short-term desire to keep their commands or avoid a trial by court martial for their failure.

The third failing of the OR is the lack of records of execution orders. When attempting to find the actual orders a commanding general issued to individual subordinates, a historian can find only about 30% of them in the OR. Most of the orders recorded in the OR are General Orders issued to the total command which were widely distributed. There are two main reasons execution orders are missing: some were given verbally, but were not recorded; and some were written, handed to a courier to be delivered but both the copies and original were somehow lost. An example of a lost order that was known to have been given was that which Lee gave to Stuart directing him to move around the Union Army before the Battle of Gettysburg. There is much evidence that such an order was written by Lee and given to Stuart, but since it was lost, exactly what it said is unknown.

While it may not technically be a fault, it is very interesting to read the accounts of the same moments of a single battle as written by Union and the Confederate participants in their respective sections of the OR. In many instances of this kind, it is difficult to square these two reports with the fact that they describe the same action at the same time. Each officer on each side is obviously trying to state his case in the most favorable way possible for himself and his side, yet both reports cannot be literally true in all the details stated.

Beyond the OR, the next best sources of information about the Civil War are the contemporary papers and letters of the participants. These papers and letters are subject to similar bias, but often, they are at least as accurate as the OR. Dozens of the leading participants in the Civil War wrote memoirs after the war. Those of Grant, Sherman and Sheridan have been in print almost continuously since they were written in the 1880s. Unfortunately, Lee did not write his memoirs.

Memoirs suffer from several problems. For the most part they were written fifteen to thirty years after the events they describe, and most were written before the OR were published. This meant that each author had to depend on his memory and whatever copies of his own papers he retained as his main sources for his book. Over twenty years, some clouding of memory is to be expected. Worse, as a commander aged, he might selectively remember decisions and incidents in his favor that made him look better in the eyes of the reader. He might even forget those unfavorable things of his war experience or color them in the way he describes them. As an example, when Grant wrote his memoirs, he knew he still hated General Rosecrans, and he could not bring himself to reconsider many unfair criticisms he had made of Rosecrans's generalship, give him any praise or find anything at all to say in Rosecrans's favor. Clearly, Grant should have fairly recognized some of Rosecrans's virtues as a commander and set aside some of his hatred. If a writer of memoirs made some errors from bias or defective memory, it does not necessarily make him a bad person, a poor commander, dishonest or makes his memoirs a poor source of information. When using memoirs as a source, the historian must recognize that human nature is an important factor to be considered.

All of the above sources of information are best used to describe what happened in the fighting in the Civil War. Part of the OR is an excellent *Atlas of the Civil War* which is accurate and honest.

Thomas L. Livermore did an admirable job of accumulating and analyzing data on casualties in his *Numbers and Losses in the Civil War in America, 1861-65,* and while not perfect, it is the best source for such information. Maps, numbers of casualties, locations, battle movements and who commanded what units are factually stated. The then-current idea that to be a victor, a commander had to drive his opponent from the field, clouded what people thought about winning and losing. For instance, after fighting three days at Gettysburg, Lee stayed on the field for a fourth day; this allowed Lee and others to maintain a fiction that the North had not "won" the Battle of Gettysburg. The OR, memoirs and private papers are full of negative, back-biting statements about generals other than the writer. No one was immune to criticism!

Believable descriptions of what happened on almost every day of the Civil War are typically available. On the other hand, contemporary, unbiased and independent sources of information on the qualities of officers engaged in the war on both sides are almost non-existent. Almost every staff officer who joined in or overheard verbal exchanges between commanders, or verbal orders given, had an ax to grind since he was favorable to one man or the other. Results of battles and the performance of individual units are the best way to judge a commander; yet, Southern historians seem to prefer to ignore results in their evaluation of commanders.

All of these defects in source materials allow a historian to select snippets of information to suit his pre-conceptions and use them to build a picture of any general as he saw him, rather than how he actually was. Why would a historian do this? Southern writers were the children of the men who lost the Civil War, and they remained loyal to the South. This loyalty may have overcome their honesty and resulted in bias. Simply stated, Southerners were trying to win a war with their pens that their fathers had lost with their swords and guns. The pictures they drew of these men were intellectually dishonest, whether or not they were stated in good will. They took three actions in their writings: they exaggerated the skills and performance of their Southern icons like Lee; they trivialized the skills and performance of their Union opponents; and they belittled to the point of personal destruction any Southerner who dared to criticize their icons.

Lee was not immune to contemporary criticism by civilian editors, mothers and fathers of lost sons and subordinates during the war, but most believable were his own statements. As a lawyer would say: these statements were given against interest so they may be believed. After he lost the Battle of Gettysburg, much criticism was made of Lee, his subordinates and the Army of Northern Virginia for what was perceived as poor performance. Lee said everyone except him performed well so all blame should be placed on him. A month after the battle, on August 8, 1863, Lee included this statement in a report to President Davis:

> "... It is fair, however, to suppose that it [dissatisfaction among his officers and men] does exist, and success is so necessary to us that nothing should [not] be risked to secure it. I therefore, in all sincerity, request Your Excellency to take measures to supply my place [i.e., replace me]. I do this with the more earnestness because no one is more aware than myself of my inability for the duties of my position. I cannot even accomplish what I myself desire. How can I fulfill the expectations of others? ... "[2]

After the war, a romantic twist was added to these and similar statements by Lee. Such interpretations imply that Lee said these things only to protect others. Would this not be personal dishonesty? Personal dishonesty was not in Lee's character. Lee's health was failing; he had been suffering from attacks of high blood pressure and symptoms consistent with congestive heart failure for some time. He was becoming exhausted and had been under unbelievable and long-term stress. Why is it so difficult for Southerners to understand and accept that Lee was dissatisfied with his own performance? Very likely, the answer is that Southerners could not accept the simple words of their icon since that would destroy their preconceptions and wishful thinking about Lee.

That Lee is an icon of the war is beyond question. He was a man of his time, an aristocrat of fine physical stature, and he was highly intelligent. He demanded and readily received the voluntary loyalty of his men under terrible conditions. These were fine traits for any military leader, but was he the high quality strategist and tactician that was required to win a war?

In all American wars after the War of 1812, leadership development for the Federal Army has followed a similar pattern. This pattern has been characterized, with a few exceptions, by the fact that the leading generals at the start of each war fell by the wayside by war's end and were replaced by lower ranking previously unknown soldiers who succeeded in winning the war. The best known and respected soldiers in the Federal Army, men like Lee and the Johnstons, joined the Confederacy. Their leaving the Union Army left it with only three general officers, all of whom were too old or infirm to command an army in action in the field. Examples of soldiers who were unknown at the beginning of the Civil War and brought the Union eventual success were Grant, Sherman, Sheridan, Thomas and Meade. They replaced more well-known soldiers like McClellan, Halleck, Hooker and Burnside, all of whom failed as army commanders-in-chief. Similarly, in World War II such officers as Eisenhower, Patton and Bradley rose from relative obscurity to assume prominent roles in victory. Generally speaking, officers gain promotion in peace-time by political acquiescence and in war-time by performance in battle. Frequently, these two conditions produce leaders of very different characteristics.

At the beginning of 1861, the Federal Army consisted of 16,000 officers and men. Many of these men were adapted to garrison life and would prove of little value in fighting a real war. In addition, some West Point graduates or officers experienced in the Mexican War, who were not in the army, were spread around the nation in the civilian population. The North and South divided these few experienced men between them, and they trained several million men to fight in the war. Both sides began the Civil War with similar civilian-soldiers, farmers and shop-keepers; these were men from rural areas and small or large cities.

In the Civil War, the Federal Army faced a severe double problem: their hierarchy had many "peace-time happy" officers in place; and the Confederacy took many of the most respected officers from them. A substantial portion of what was left in higher ranks was poor or over-aged officers who could not be effective leaders of an army in war.

To be his general-in-chief, President Lincoln first tried George McClellan, a very bright West Point graduate, who had been his friend when both had worked for the Illinois Central Railroad before the war. This was Lincoln's only appointment of a crony to the highest army command. When McClellan failed, Lincoln followed a tedious trial-and-error selection process that led to Grant after fifteen months of additional failures. Lincoln followed this process under the worst possible conditions: battles were being fought and lost, and soldiers were dying.

On the Confederate side, President Davis followed a system of supporting his old cronies and continued this practice throughout the war. As the Confederate war effort faltered, he continued to support the men who were his first five appointments as full generals; he added three and made changes only in the last resort or as the result of death or wounds. Of these eight full generals appointed by the Confederacy, there is no doubt that Lee was the best.

From the standpoint of underlying strengths, how did the two sides compare? The North was greatly superior in potential numbers and industrial power. Probably on a well-founded assessment of its initial strength, the South acted as though it could win the war in its first year and did not have to consider a longer-term view. Basically, Northerners and Southerners were both adjusted to peaceful urban and pastoral existences and did not take to fighting easily or naturally.

All of these factors will be expanded upon in this book, but the tremendous potential power of the North would become the key to winning the war only if the South gave the North the time it needed to develop it. The armies of the North initially had little effective leadership, and many months would be required before excellent leaders could be found and then developed. The only reason the leadership of the Confederacy did not recognize the threat of the potential power of the Union probably was based on conceit. In fact, the South was given a respite of over two years before it would be required to fight a well-led Army of the Potomac, the most important army of the North.

History has numerous examples of poorly led huge armies being destroyed by much smaller but better led armies. If we accept the lessons of history that generalship is much more important than comparative strength in numbers, this raises an important question about Robert E. Lee: Does such a general, who defeated but failed to destroy a poorly led enemy although given many opportunities, deserve iconship based upon his own actions? The author will attempt to answer this question.

*   *   *

Another question the book addresses is: Was Lee's iconship built for him after the war by well-meaning Southerners who could not accept the realities of their defeat?

Beginning in the 1870s, Southern historians were far more active than their Northern counterparts in writing histories of the Civil War. They felt compelled to defend the Confederacy in its defeat, and they did a good job of revising the facts in the South's favor. As Margaret Mitchell said; "I was ten years old before I discovered that the South *had not won* the Civil War." Most Northerners wanted to forget the war and get on with their lives so by default they allowed Southern historians to gain control of how the history of the Civil War was to be written. After General Robert E. Lee died, he was placed on a pedestal and every effort was made to down grade his opponents in order to improve Lee's comparative reputation. It is the goal of this book to correct this misstatement of history which has been unfair both to Lee and to Union commanders.

Was Lee the hero-figure the Southern revisionists enshrined in the period 1870 through 1940? Lee began the Civil War with all promise of becoming its greatest general, but by the end of 1863, three much younger Union generals, Grant, Sherman and Sheridan had surpassed Lee's level of skill as a general. While their skills improved greatly with experience, did Lee's skills continue to improve with his experience?

Throughout the war, even as leadership of the North became stronger militarily, the South held to a misguided offensive strategy while another strategy was available to it that might have allowed it to win the war. There is very persuasive evidence that a more defensive Confederate posture would have worn down the North's resolve to continue the war and led to a political settlement favorable to the South.

While it may have been a misguided strategy to maintain the offensive under almost every circumstance, there was certainly no lack of valor, or courage on the part of Southern generals. Fifty-five percent of all Confederate generals were killed or wounded, and some were wounded many times. The South's pool of potentially high quality officers was smaller than that available to the North, and the Davis Administration remained satisfied with the generals it had until it was too late. Its losses of generals brought on a great need for more good generals, but its process of finding high quality generals was woefully inadequate. If it had been more efficient, its system might have led to the selection of better generals than those who actually led the Confederate Armies. Frequently, the lack of any efficient system and the high losses of generals and colonels caused inferior officers to be promoted because of necessity based on preference of previously held rank, not skill. From time to time, Lee railed against this policy.

In considering Lee, many have ignored these possibilities in their analysis of the Civil War. Did they choose to do this due to their Southern bias or because they sincerely believed that Lee was one of the great generals of world history and could not consider that he had any weaknesses?

Another possibility is that Lee well deserved his iconship but was thwarted by the poor leadership of Davis and poor support by his subordinates. The author will also address these propositions.

President Davis had commanded a regiment successfully in the Mexican War, and he had been U.S. Secretary of War for four years. He was convinced that he was the greatest military expert in the North or South. Although Davis was President of the Confederacy, his real wish was to be its general-in-chief. In spite of his background, his strategic decisions were mostly wrong, and his chain of command resembled a spider in a web with Davis as the spider. This organization was inefficient, difficult to manage and did not lead to cooperation between generals who were equals reporting to Davis.

Frequently, Lee is presented as Davis's principal military advisor, but how did Lee and Davis really relate to each other? Did Lee recognize Davis's strategic errors? Did Lee defer to Davis even when he saw he was wrong? Did Lee agree with most of Davis's strategic ideas? Did Lee join Davis in rejecting strategies that gave the Confederacy chances to win the war, supporting instead strategies aimed at only short-term limited objectives?

Popular fiction written in the South in the late nineteenth century presented the Civil War in a different perspective than its ghastly reality. It presented Southern officers as chivalrous knights going forth into battle against an overwhelming enemy, thus promoting the idea of "fighting gloriously against all odds for a great but predetermined Lost Cause." It seems this fictional idea greatly influenced Southern historical thought in later years.

The reader must consider whether this book is an exercise in historical revisionism, or not. The author believes the Southern historians were the revisionists of history with their building of the iconship of Lee and the edifice of the "Lost Cause."

The "Lost Cause" is an interesting concept that was thought of after the war. This is good since if it had been current before or during the war, it would have been an admission of a conscious decision by Southerners to sacrifice 175,000 of its citizens to a futile purpose. Its premise is that the South never had any chance to win the Civil War due to its inferiority in numbers and the industrial power of the North. A qualification of the concept is that with the best general of history available to them, Lee, the premise of the "Lost Cause" must be true if this icon could not win.

There are many arguments against the "Lost Cause," but the most important one concerns Lincoln's 1864 re-election efforts. The North had suffered over 50,000 casualties in May and June in Grant's Virginia Overland Campaign and his army was bogged down in a siege in front of Petersburg; many Northerners felt the war was too costly, victory was hopeless, and the goals of their war-effort were not worthwhile. Political experts believed Lincoln would be refused the nomination of the Republican Party, and even if he received that nomination, he could not be elected. Lincoln's defeat would have led to a negotiated peace, tantamount to a Confederate victory since in all likelihood it would have remained independent to control its own institutions, including slavery.

What turned the situation around for Lincoln? Three events appear to have been telling: Farragut's capture of Mobile in August; Sherman's capture of Atlanta in September; and Sheridan's victory in the Shenandoah Valley in October. If the situation turned in the August-October 1864 period from a likely Lincoln election defeat to a Lincoln victory, then the Southern cause was lost with Lincoln's victory in the election of 1864, not because of any predestined "Lost Cause."

*　　*　　*

On the Union side, Generals Grant, Sherman, Sheridan and others lived long enough to write extensive memoirs in addition to a vast amount of other military papers and letters. Their writing quality varies. To judge their accuracy, their memoirs can be compared with the writings of other participants, the reports they wrote soon after each action and material that was printed later in the *Official Records*. It is unfortunate for posterity that Lee was not a writer and that he died so soon after the war. He left extensive papers, but these were made up of military reports, letters and personal correspondence; and, in these, he never fully described his military or philosophical ideas.

*　　*　　*

Southerners dominated the writing of Civil War history for a hundred years after the war. In their good descriptions of the actual events they intermixed their own opinions. Within these opinions were excuses for many of Lee's mistakes. When a Southern general criticized Lee, he was vilified, and many laughed at his opinions. As the historical literature expanded, it repeated these excuses many times, and soon these statements became gospel. Hundreds of Civil War books regurgitate the same old snippets of the OR and the opinions of predecessors over and over again.

Southerners typically denigrated Northern generals in terms that have little to do with what they accomplished: "Grant was a drunkard and a butcher." Yet Lee killed a greater percentage of his soldiers in action than Grant did, and Grant was never drunk while action was going on. "Sherman was 'crazy' and burned Southern cities." There is no doubt that Sherman was high-strung and did suffer a nervous breakdown early in the war, but he was one of the most intelligent and sensitive generals of the war. Neither side was immune to atrocities, and it was unfair to single out any general as being the "best atrocity-maker." There is no evidence that Sherman ever ordered any atrocity and much evidence that he tried to prevent them. "Sheridan was not intelligent but was uncouth and a bully." The record shows that Sheridan was promoted through the ranks from captain to major general and army commander on the sole basis of his own performance and competence. Sheridan knew how to win battles. He had the intellect to gain entrance into West Point when he had no patronage, and the fact that his military decisions were always well thought out and clever illustrated a high level of intelligence.

None of these denigrating evaluations and opinions were based on the OR or independent, unbiased sources, but rather a desire to build up its own by tearing down their enemies. Over the years, the repetition of these value-statements accomplished its purpose: they gained more weight in judging these Northern generals, and others, than the facts and their performance could give. It is hoped that this book can correct these biases and help to give these men their honest due.

*   *   *

While the major portion of Civil War literature continued to restate itself, in a few areas some new thinking began after 1930.

Recent studies in other areas have brought forth some new ideas about the Civil War. Alexander[3] has written an honest and unbiased book on "Stonewall" Jackson and his military genius. By necessity, Alexander made a careful study of the relationship between Lee and Jackson. Alexander concludes that Lee and Davis rejected superior strategic suggestions by Jackson on at least four occasions, and that these rejections probably cost the Confederacy the loss of the war.

In 1995, Nesbitt[4] wrote a thorough study of Stuart's orders and actions before and during the Battle of Gettysburg. One of the Southern historians' excuses for Lee's failure was to allege that Stuart had taken the Confederate cavalry on an unauthorized "glory" ride around the Army of the Potomac, leaving Lee blind and unsupported by cavalry. In a scholarly work supported by many contemporary references, Nesbitt concludes that: in leaving Lee, Stuart acted under Lee's specific orders; over half of the total number of cavalry were left with Lee and Lee was satisfied with this; Stuart and Lee *were* in frequent contact with each other while Stuart was gone; and Lee did not criticize Stuart in any way for his actions after the battle.

The quality of Lee's generalship has been considered by Fuller[5] in two excellent books in 1929 and 1932. He said he began his study of Lee and Grant believing Lee was one of history's great generals and ended it by concluding Grant deserved this praise and that Lee was a good but second-rank general. Fuller was easy for the Southern historians to dismiss since he was an eccentric Englishman, so: "How could an Englishman know anything about the American Civil War?" Nevertheless, Fuller made one of the most thorough and unbiased studies of the subject ever undertaken.

Other books critical of Lee have been written by Nolan,[6] Connelly[7] and others. These authors address the moral decisions made by Lee, and question the formation of the Lee "myth."

This book will deal with Lee, his military failures and the superior generalship of the Union commanders who were developed late in the Civil War. Hopefully, it will be fair. Hopefully, the qualities of the Union commanders will be shown in a more honest light than those provided by earlier historians.

CHRONOLOGY

1861

JANUARY

- South Carolina is first state to secede
- Five more states secede

FEBRUARY

- Confederate Constitution adopted
- Jefferson Davis inaugurated Provisional President of the Confederacy

MARCH

- Lincoln inaugurated

APRIL

- Lee resigns from Federal service, joins Virginia's army two days later
- Ft. Sumter fired upon and surrenders

JUNE

- First sizable engagement at Big Bethel
- Lee appointed full general, CSA

JULY

- The First Battle of Bull Run (Manassas I)
- McClellan made Federal commander in Virginia

SEPTEMBER

- McClellan and Rosecrans defeat Lee in West Virginia

NOVEMBER

- McClellan replaces Scott as Federal general-in-chief

1862

JANUARY

- Stanton confirmed as Secretary of War

FEBRUARY

- Grant takes Fts. Henry and Donelson

MARCH

- Battle of first ironclad ships: the *Monitor* and the *Merrimac*

APRIL

- McClellan begins Virginia peninsula campaign
- The Battle of Shiloh; Albert S. Johnston dies
- Farragut captures New Orleans

MAY

- Jackson victorious in Shenandoah Valley
- The Battle of Seven Pines (6 miles from Richmond); J.E. Johnston wounded

JUNE

- Lee succeeds J.E. Johnston in command of what would become the Army of Northern Virginia
- Memphis, Tennessee captured by the Union
- Halleck succeeds McClellan as general-in-chief
- Pope ordered to form new army to defend Washington
- The Seven Days Battles begin on the Peninsula

JULY

- McClellan retreats to Harrison's Landing on the James River

AUGUST

- The Second Battle of Bull Run (Manassas II)

SEPTEMBER

- McClellan given full command in Virginia
- Lee invades Maryland
- The Battle of Antietam
- Preliminary Emancipation Proclamation announced

NOVEMBER

- McClellan replaced by Burnside

DECEMBER

- The Battle of Fredericksburg

1863

JANUARY

- Emancipation Proclamation formalized
- Rosecrans wins at the Battle of Stones River
- Hooker replaces Burnside

MARCH

- Federal Draft Act approved

APRIL

- Hooker begins Chancellorsville campaign

MAY

- Lee wins the Battle of Chancellorsville
- Jackson dies from wounds

- Grant begins Vicksburg campaign

JUNE

- Lee invades Pennsylvania

JULY

- Meade defeats Lee at the Battle of Gettysburg
- Grant takes Vicksburg
- Rosecrans drives Bragg south of Tennessee River
- Lee safely retreats to Virginia

SEPTEMBER

- Longstreet is sent to reinforce Bragg
- Bragg defeats Rosecrans at the Battle of Chickamauga

NOVEMBER

- Grant defeats Bragg in battles around Chattanooga
- Mine Run campaign aborted in Virginia
- Bragg's resignation accepted

DECEMBER

- J.E. Johnston appointed commander in Georgia

1864

MARCH

- Grant commissioned lieutenant general and appointed general-in-chief

APRIL

- Sheridan joins Army of the Potomac in command of its Cavalry Corps

MAY

- Grant and the Army of the Potomac cross the Rapidan River
- The Battle of the Wilderness
- Sherman begins Atlanta campaign
- Sheridan defeats Stuart at Yellow Tavern; Stuart dies of wounds
- The Battles of Spotsylvania
- The Battle on the North Anna River

JUNE

- The Battle of Cold Harbor
- Grant crosses the James River
- Grant attacks Petersburg and is repulsed
- Siege of Petersburg begins
- Lee sends Early to Shenandoah Valley

JULY

- Early threatens Washington, then retreats
- Hood replaces J.E. Johnston in Georgia
- Battles around Atlanta
- Petersburg mine explosion and assault

AUGUST

- Sheridan appointed to command Shenandoah Valley operations
- The Battle of Mobile Bay
- Democrats nominate McClellan for President

SEPTEMBER

- Sherman takes Atlanta
- The Third Battle of Winchester in Shenandoah Valley
- The Battle of Fishers Hill

OCTOBER

- The Battle of Cedar Creek

NOVEMBER

- Sherman begins march to the sea
- Thomas sent to defend Tennessee
- The Battle of Franklin, Tennessee
- Lincoln re-elected

DECEMBER

- Sherman takes Savannah
- The Battle of Nashville

1865

FEBRUARY

- Sherman begins drive north through Carolinas
- Lee appointed general-in-chief
- J.E. Johnston restored to command in the Carolinas

MARCH

- Sheridan rejoins Grant
- The Battle of Bentonville, N.C.
- Confederate attack on Ft. Stedman

APRIL

- Sheridan attacks Lee's southern flank
- The Battle of Five Forks
- Evacuation of Richmond and Petersburg
- The Battle of Saylor's Creek
- Lee surrenders to Grant at Appomattox, Virginia
- Lincoln assassinated
- J.E. Johnston surrenders to Sherman in North Carolina

CHAPTER I

Conflicting Views of Robert E. Lee

What did Hannibal, Napoleon and Lee have in common?
They lost their wars and their countries; they were losers.
What did Scipio, Wellington and Grant have in common?
They were winners. Is it not a strange and dangerous logic
that some have used to rate the losers as being superior to
the winners?

*I*s it surprising that in the Southern Confederacy, views of Lee's performance and skill as a general vacillated widely throughout the Civil War years? When it is considered that Lee's first battles in West Virginia and his last in Virginia were defeats and failures, such reaction could be expected. When one considers the Battle of Antietam in the midst of his period of command which was, at best, a costly draw, along with the great casualties his battles brought about, it was a wonder that the criticism was so mild. The opinions stated in newspapers throughout the South varied from hero worship to giving him part of the blame for the loss of the war.

In Lee's initial fighting in what is now West Virginia, he was considered timid and too cautious to be effective. Federal Brigadier General William S. Rosecrans defeated Lee ignominiously in the West Virginia campaigns.[1] Lee then became a desk general as President Jefferson Davis's military assistant, performing menial tasks. This assignment was made particularly difficult since Davis pictured himself as a military genius based on his West Point education, a regimental command during the Mexican War and as a past U.S. Secretary of War. To be the Confederacy's general-in-chief rather than its president was Davis's real wish.

When General Joseph E. Johnston was wounded in the Seven Pines fighting, Major General Gustavus W. Smith, his second-in-command, replaced him. Almost at once, Smith suffered a physical paralysis, probably a stroke, and was unable to function. Davis ordered Lee to assume command of the Confederate army that was defending Richmond against McClellan's army on the Peninsula. The Battle of Seven Pines was still under way, only six miles east of Richmond, but Lee delayed joining his hard pressed command for some eight hours.[2] This delay has never been explained.

Immediately after the victories at the Second Battle of Manassas and Chancellorsville, most of the credit went to Lieutenant General Thomas J. "Stonewall" Jackson, not to Lee. The most costly single day of the war, the Battle of Antietam, was one that Lee should never have fought. After Antietam, Lee was severely criticized for the futility and enormous casualties and for missing the opportunity to severely damage his poorly-skilled opponent, Union Major General George B. McClellan.[3]

Lee was criticized during the war for his parochialism, that is, his loyalty to Virginia rather than the Confederacy as a whole. This was reflected in his choices of subordinate general officers of the Army of Northern Virginia. Only one non-Virginian, Lieutenant General James Longstreet, a Georgian, became a corps commander in this army and served throughout most of the war. By far the majority of other general officers were Virginians, although the army was made up of regiments from all of the Confederate states.[4]

In 1863, when the Confederates in Mississippi and Tennessee were hard pressed by Major Generals U.S. Grant and Rosecrans,

Davis was faced with a choice of where to send his limited manpower resources. He could continue in an offensive posture in Virginia, or he could go over to the defensive there and temporarily transfer some troops from the Army of Northern Virginia to Tennessee. Little threat then existed from the Army of the Potomac which had just been severely defeated at Chancellorsville. Such a move might have stopped, or slowed, Union advances in Mississippi and Tennessee. Lee pre-empted Davis's options by persuading him to approve Lee's decision to invade Pennsylvania which eliminated the possibility of sending Army of Northern Virginia troops west on a timely basis.[5] The Pennsylvania invasion which culminated at Gettysburg was ill-fated and poorly fought by Lee. The 28,000 men Lee lost at Gettysburg were thrown away to little purpose. At the time, Lee was severely criticized for these actions.

Lee was also criticized by his subordinate generals. For one, Major General D.H. Hill, Jackson's brother-in-law, criticized Lee for his strategy and actions in the Peninsula Campaign and at Antietam.[6] Lee seemed relieved when Hill was sent to North Carolina to lead the defense there. After Lee's death, Hill refused to comment on Lee, saying he had made his comments when Lee was at the height of his powers and to do so in 1885 would be unfair.

Major General George E. Pickett led "Pickett's Charge" at Gettysburg. Losing 54% of 10,500 men, Pickett wrote a scathing report of the attack, criticizing Lee's plan for the assault. Lee refused to accept Pickett's report, and he was ordered to re-write it. He never did, and the original report has been lost. After a post-war visit with Lee, Pickett told another officer: "That old man ... had my division massacred." This statement probably summarized the lost report.[7]

Unable to hide his great respect and love for Lee in his Memoirs, Longstreet gently criticized him for his overall strategy at Gettysburg and for Pickett's Charge in particular. Longstreet dutifully ordered an attack that he felt was hopeless. Longstreet felt strongly that Lee passed a great opportunity by not filing around the left flank of the Union army and placing the Army of Northern Virginia between the Army of the Potomac and Washington. This would have forced the Army of the Potomac to attack the Army of Northern Virginia under favorable circumstances to Lee. Another advantage of such a move was that it would be against Major General George G. Meade who had commanded the Army of the Potomac for only a few days, and Meade was a commander who never demonstrated himself to be very skillful in offensive movements.[8]

After the Civil War, Longstreet's mild disapproval of Lee's strategy, along with his renewing his friendship with Grant and joining the Republican Party, elicited overly strong reaction from Southern war historians: they found ways to blame Longstreet with everything that went wrong for the South in the war.

In his own military papers of the war, particularly those addressed to Davis, Lee was frequently self-critical. When his nephew, Fitzhugh Lee, wrote a biography of the general, he was unconsciously critical of Lee in several instances.[9]

Among Civil War generals whether Confederate or Union, Lee was responsible for a very high percentage of casualties among his troops. Of men engaged in each major battle he fought, he lost 19% on average. This contrasts to Grant's losses of 14.5% on the same basis.[10] This comparison makes Grant's reputation as a "butcher" seem very unfair. Lee often chose to fight to recover from a strategic defeat, a practice which proved costly and futile in almost all cases. Of many, the three best examples of this tendency were: Malvern Hill, Gettysburg and the Wilderness. These fights involved costly and purposeless frontal assaults by Lee.

From time immemorial, private soldiers have demonstrated they will accept high losses and any hardship and still follow their general steadfastly provided only that they are victorious. When Lee gave them no victories after Chancellorsville, the private soldiers began to vote their dissatisfaction in Lee with their feet as the desertion rate grew higher.[11]

In the five years between the end of the Civil War and Lee's death, Davis, Lee and General Braxton E. Bragg received most of the blame in the South for the loss of the war. Beginning with Lee's death in 1870, this perception began to change.

Southern historians apparently refused to accept or explain the Confederacy's loss by the real facts (these facts are more fully demonstrated later in this book): the South was badly beaten; the North produced several generals superior to Lee and all other Southern generals who survived the war; the South did not lose because of their fewer numbers; they lost because they followed a hopeless strategy; but they could have won the war except for their own critical errors in strategic choices before Lincoln's re-election in November 1864. The truth was too hard to accept or even discuss rationally, so they proceeded to re-write the history of the Civil War to suit their preferences. In short, Southerners tried to win a war with their pens they had lost with the sword.

Characteristically, Lee's orders were vague and left much to the judgment of his subordinates. He usually stated how and when a battle was to be started and pursued, but seldom managed a battle once it was under way. This left Lee out of the command system once the battle started, leaving to subordinates such decisions as whether to follow up success or how to meet adversity.

In his command system, Lee could only revise his plans at the end of the day or during an interruption in the fighting. Lee was far better qualified than his subordinates to make reactive decisions, but chose not to do so. Under Lee's command system, unlike the Northern system, the movement of troop units from one corps to another was almost impossible in the heat of battle. Since Lee did not write his own personal views, this left the field open for aides, associates, historians and others to state Lee's case for him. They used Lee's vague orders as a basis to change history to agree with their own bias. These later writers often wrote much in Lee's name that is questionable and uncharacteristic in view of what is otherwise known of his character, actions and personality.

This has led to a complete revision of Civil War history from fact to wishful Southern thinking. Probably, this revisionism initially arose from one motivation. Southerners were unwilling to accept the fact they had been soundly beaten, much less that they could have won except for their own poor choices. Further, the idea that the North ended the war with several generals superior to any the South had produced was far too repugnant for them to consider rationally. For several years after the war, the threat that radical elements in Northern politics might gain sufficient control to conduct show trials and hangings for such men as Davis and Lee was very real, and their silence protected them. It also kept the many Southern participants from expressing their opinions openly.

Some of Lee's biographers did not hesitate to change history or bend military rules. If Lee made an error and changing the clock fixed it, they changed the clock. This was easy to do since time for any location was based on the position of the sun at noon; there was then no such thing as Standard Time. If Lee made an error, they had no hesitation in placing all blame against a subordinate in spite of the well-accepted military rule that a commander-in-chief is responsible for results of the day, good or bad, including all of the acts, or lack thereof, of all his subordinates. They frequently placed blame elsewhere even when there was a clear record of Lee accepting full blame himself.

There are many examples of such incidents, but Pickett's Charge stands out. After the charge, Lee blamed himself. In this case, when Lee accepted full blame, Southern historians said the "paladin was doing the right thing" by accepting full blame, "but Longstreet was really at fault." Trying to maintain the proper military relationships while ignoring their own contradictory logic must have been very difficult. In most cases, the revisionists showed a preference to "make up history" while ignoring numerous sources that overwhelmingly supported a different idea.

Fortunately, such a web of misinformation is too hard to maintain and much of the truth shows through most of the time.

The revisionists who changed Lee from a great man, who tried to do his best but failed, to a saintly paladin have not done him good service since Lee, the man, is a far more real and attractive human being than Lee, the paladin and the statue.

One must conclude that Lee received deservedly mixed reviews on his skill as a general during the Civil War and before his death in 1870. During this time he was not an idol but was well respected as a man. After his death, Southern historians took advantage of Lee's lack of written record and many vague orders to re-cast him as "the greatest general ever" and the hero of the "Lost Cause." Their ideas in building this position substituted wishful fictions for historical fact. All this raised Lee to an undeserved level of expertise to the detriment of such generals as Jackson, Grant, Sherman and Sheridan.

CHAPTER II

The Basis of Lee's Pre-War Reputation

The Federal Army before the Civil War was dominated by Southerners. Almost all of the top pre-Civil War Federal Army assignments were held by Southerners, men like Cooper, Lee and A.S. and J.E. Johnston. While his high level of intelligence, skills and military bearing must be recognized, Robert E. Lee was a product of pre-war Southern favoritism.

*T*ypically, the pre-war reputations of Civil War generals were based on: graduation from West Point and their class standing, peace-time army breadth of experience and rank attained, combat experience in the Mexican War and the combined politics of the Army, the Federal Government and the War Department. Men who were creative, independent military thinkers are usually difficult to deal with in garrison; therefore, such men were often thought less of than those who accommodated themselves to the petty politics of a post. Soldiers often gained promotion as a result of their appearance, political acumen and becoming a superior's favorite. Once the Civil War started, some of these apparent qualifications proved important, some did not. Skills learned on-the-job in the early years of the war proved more important and propelled a few generals into high prominence.

West Point was the military foundation for most of the leading generals on both sides. At that time, it was the best engineering school in the country, perhaps in the world. From a military standpoint, West Point taught discipline, honor, drill, the use of weapons, company tactics and how to command a company sized unit. There were no command or staff schools to further a cadet's military education after he graduated from West Point. There were few lectures, nor was there much interest shown in larger military matters such as strategy, large-scale tactics or the numerous staff functions. Some cadets studied the works of Baron Jomini on Napoleon as a matter of personal interest, but classes on Jomini and other military thinkers were not offered as a part of the formal curriculum.

Since engineering was a very important subject taught, West Point graduates, whether they stayed in the army or not, contributed substantially to building the country's bridges, harbors, railroads, dams, roads and major construction projects. The graduates of the highest academic ranking at West Point were assigned to the Engineer Corps. Lee and George B. McClellan received such assignments; graduates like Grant, Sherman, Sheridan and the Southern Johnstons did not, although all later showed a high order of military skill.[1]

Most graduates' military education was furthered by experience on the frontier. This gave them practical experience in dealing with their men and their superiors, supplying their troops and planning minor operations. While one could learn a lot in a few years, garrison duty turned into boring repetition for most men of any intellect or imagination. Many turned to drink or resigned to rejoin civilian society.

As an exception, Philip H. Sheridan's six years of frontier experience illustrated what a young second lieutenant could learn if he applied himself. Three times he independently commanded small units of under 100 men facing well-armed Indians substantially out-numbering him. Knowing he could not attack them frontally without the loss of too many of his own men, he chose less direct methods of winning and thus kept the men's respect and loyalty. In each instance, he developed a strategy that won his goal without conflict, or he devised a flanking or rear attack and carried the day with few casualties to his force by being intelligent rather than brutal. While not in action, his responsibility was to build roads, to feed and supply large numbers of both his men and his Indian charges. This honed his engineering, quartermaster and logistic skills for later generalship.[2]

The Mexican War, in 1846-48, gave West Point graduates real experience in war. The distances over which things had to move made for difficult supply problems, and this improved their logistic skills. Dealing with responsibility while facing an armed enemy intent on killing them and their men, improved their skills in leadership, tactics and strategy. Most Civil War officers ranked below major during the Mexican War so they did not deal with the problems of higher commands and the wide scope of the war. The Mexican War was small and numbers were limited; experience there proved only slightly useful in the vast Civil War.

Many Mexican War veterans over-valued their experience which blinded them to the great changes that occurred in the 13 years between the Mexican and the Civil wars. In these 13 years, the Minie-ball rifled musket and the rifled cannon were developed. The Minie rifle could be aimed accurately at a range of 400 yards and was deadly beyond 600 yards. This was an enormous improvement when compared to an effective range of 100 yards for the smoothbore musket that was used in the Mexican and Napoleonic Wars.[3]

Similarly, rifled cannon were far superior to smooth-bore cannon in range and accuracy. In a leap forward in accuracy, they could actually hit specific targets a thousand yards away. These improvements forced changes in tactics that Mexican War veterans were very slow to accept and apply in the Civil War.[4]

Lee graduated second in the 1829 West Point class of 46 cadets. He was assigned to the Corps of Engineers and performed meritorious service. Part of the time he was occupied in improving the defenses of Fortress Monroe at the entrance to Chesapeake

Bay and in improving New York Harbor and its defenses. However, his greatest accomplishment involved planning a new shipping channel on the Mississippi River from St. Louis north to the Des Moines River. St. Louis was in danger of losing the river which was trying to cut a new channel through Illinois to the east; this would have made St. Louis a land-locked city. In addition, rapids to the north of the city interfered with commerce moving into the northern reaches of the Mississippi. Lieutenant Lee organized and supervised the surveying and analyses of these problems and made recommendations to solve them.[5] Later, he supervised part of the execution of his plans for the Mississippi. The Office of the Army Engineers in Washington was another of his assignments. In his assignments from 1829 to 1846, nothing was very helpful in training a general on the field of battle except that he improved his skill at building fortified positions.

Lee was assigned to General Winfield Scott's staff in the Mexican War. He showed skills in intelligence gathering and proved his courage. Scott believed in assigning tasks to division commanders and then sitting back and allowing them to complete them successfully or to fail, without interference. Lee concluded that this was the way a general should perform in battle, which proved a detriment to him during the Civil War. Command of a fighting unit in combat in the Mexican War would have been an experience of great value, but Lee did not have such an opportunity.

While a highly intelligent man, Lee's most important characteristic was his appearance and standing as a Virginia aristocrat. Lee was related to George Washington by marriage, and his father, "Light Horse Harry" Lee, was one of Washington's most skilled and dependable subordinates. Although Lee protested against favoritism in all its forms, he accepted his share. In the 1850's, Scott, a fellow Virginian, was general-in-chief of the U.S. Army, and other Southerners controlled the War Department. Without ever asking for it, Lee received partiality from Scott in the Mexican War and continued to receive favorable assignments until the Civil War started. Lee was appointed Superintendent of West Point. Later, he was assigned to an elite cavalry regiment in Texas as second-in-command to Albert Sidney Johnston, his first true experience in high command. Later, he succeeded Johnston in the command of the cavalry regiment.

Of the Virginia aristocrats at the start of the Civil War, Lee appeared to have the best qualifications to be a commander. While he did very well at West Point, his real experience after graduation was as an engineer which did little to teach him very much about leading men at war. His experience in the Mexican War was limited to being a staff officer for Scott. He never led a unit in battle or suffered casualties to the men he personally commanded. His short command of a regiment in the late 1850s was of minor value.

Lee looked and acted the soldier, was well thought of by those who had commanded him (mostly Southerners), was probably the best available soldier from Virginia; but it was not until his first actions in the Civil War that he learned what war was really like to a commander. Lee's pre-war career did not show him as a promising prospect to be commander-in-chief. In fact, no outstanding candidate for such a post was available to either side in April 1861 with the possible exception of Albert Sidney Johnston.

CHAPTER III

Strategic Choices

Thomas J. Jackson was a difficult but brilliant man, an implacable and merciless foe. A superior strategist and tactician, he recognized the South must quickly defeat a numerically superior enemy so he set traps and used his imagination, demonstrating his high level of skill when in independent command. He knew that brutal, frontal assaults against a foe that was increasing in relative size and improving in quality must eventually fail. Why did his superiors, Davis and Lee, use Jackson's strategic and tactical advice so seldom?

To understand the factors that brought about the final outcome of the Civil War, the defeat of the Confederacy, the nation-wide strategies that best fit the prospects to win the war for the Union or the Confederacy must be addressed and compared with the choices each side made. To win the war, the North had to invade and conquer the South, since allowing them to set up their own government without interference would probably result in the North losing the Civil War by default.

The Union Army's first general-in-chief, Lieutenant General Winfield Scott, developed a strategy when the war began: surround the Confederacy with a blockade of all commerce and strangle it. Events quickly proved that this strategy by itself could not be successful because the Union Army and Navy were not strong enough to implement it fully. Using only a blockade, the naval part of this strategy, might involve many years, or even decades. As the war went on, leaks in the blockade were never totally closed. In addition to what they produced internally, the South continued to receive enough arms and supplies from overseas to sustain their war effort for four years.

The concept of blockade did become an important part of the ultimate strategy that proved successful for the Union. The Union eventually used blockades and the military capture of Southern ports to make the export of cotton and the import of goods and supplies ever more difficult. They fought a combined campaign by the navy and army for the Mississippi River, splitting the Confederacy in two. They destroyed centers of manufacturing which seriously weakened the South's ability to produce war materials. Union armies struck at Southern field armies, exhausting their manpower, spirit and resources. Their eventual strategy, devised by Grant,[1] was to strike the Confederacy everywhere simultaneously. Of all these factors, exhaustion of the spirit and will to fight in the face of this massive Union effort eventually took its toll of defeat on the Confederacy.

The Northern commanders had to attack, and early Civil War experience proved attackers needed a greater than 3:1 advantage to assure success.[2] To make the situation worse, attackers almost always suffered a higher percentage of casualties than did defenders. This was a change from the experience of the Napoleonic and Mexican wars brought on by the improvements in ordnance that produced superior range and accuracy for the rifled muskets and cannon used in the Civil War. Most commanders on both sides were slow to recognize the new strategies and tactics which these changes demanded.

The most likely war-winning strategy for success for the Confederacy was that employed by their illustrious Virginia ancestor, General George Washington, against the British Army in the Revolution. The British had the numbers to overwhelm the small Colonial armies whenever and wherever they fought in the Revolutionary War.

Faced with a vast area to conquer, the British Army's only hope was to attack and destroy the small colonial armies; mere occupation of territory was not enough to insure victory. Washington's strategy of avoiding battles, along with the accompanying heavy losses, was carried out over seven long years, and this wore down the British Army. More importantly, the British people's and government's political will was seriously damaged by casualties, cost and the failure to defeat the upstart Colonists. The British abandoned the Colonies and negotiated peace when they were faced with the question: "Why should they continue to throw men and money away into a great, untamed wilderness?"

What are the comparisons between Washington's and Lee's wars? The Confederacy was also a vast territory. They also faced an enemy of enormous industrial strength that had much greater resources of treasure and manpower. The situation the North faced forced them to invade and conquer the South.

A similar strategy to Washington's of conserving military strength was available: fighting on the defensive except for occasional counter-offensive opportunities that promised certain success, giving up territory grudgingly, causing the Union to extend their supply lines and raiding them, taking advantage of their interior lines to move troops to their best advantage, prolonging the conflict, inflicting the maximum casualties on the Federal Army and wasting as much in Northern resources as possible. Would such a strategy have led the Union politicians to ask a similar question the British asked and arrive at a similar conclusion? When we consider that this almost happened in the summer and fall of 1864 in spite of the strategy the South chose, the chances of the South achieving a victory by default using such a strategy seem substantial.

If such a strategy had worked, consider what the political situation would have been if the Union Army had lost 50% more casualties from battle and disease while executing an even more aggressive strategy than it did, and if the Confederate Army had suffered 50% fewer casualties being more defensive. By September 1864, would Lincoln have been re-elected? Probably not, and the Democrat, McClellan, might have negotiated a peace that would have given the Confederacy its independence. In these circumstances, the Confederate Army would have been very strong indeed in 1864, perhaps strong enough to defeat the best the North could offer.

Contrary to the above ideas, the Confederate leaders accepted a strategy of attacking the Union invaders whenever they crossed into Confederate territory and even invading the North and neutral border-states. Through October 1863, the Confederate armies were on the tactical offensive in these major battles: Shiloh (Loss), Fair Oaks (Draw), Seven Days (Win), Manassas II (W), Perryville (L), Stones River (L), Chancellorsville (W), Gettysburg (L), and Chickamauga (W). Before Antietam (D), the Confederates had started a strategic offensive, invading the North, but during the actual battle, they were on the tactical defensive. At Fredericksburg (W) and Vicksburg (L) they were fully on the defensive. In these twelve battles, the Union had 809,456 men engaged, lost 113,160 (13.9%); the Confederacy had 622,265 engaged, lost 152,841 (24.6%).[3]

According to the combined records of both sides,[4] disease caused almost twice as many deaths (388,580), as deaths or mortal wounds in battle (204,000). Deaths from disease for Southern forces are probably understated since their records were less complete than those of the Federal Army. In this most terrible of our wars, deaths from other causes brought the total to 623,026 with a minimum of 471,427 wounded. Only at Fredericksburg did the Union Army lose a higher percentage of its forces engaged than did the Confederacy. By following this generally offensive strategy in these major battles and in many smaller ones, the Confederacy was inadvertently supporting the best strategy available to their Union foes while diligently following the worst strategy that was available to the Confederacy.

* * *

In the first year of the war, the Southern Army had a substantial advantage in leadership. It enlisted as full generals five of the eight leading officers in the U.S. Army. This temporary advantage eventually turned against the South. The Confederate leadership had chosen as its military leaders the top men in the U.S. Army, and organized its army with a full hierarchy of general officers.

The five full generals the Confederacy initially appointed were Samuel Cooper, Albert Sidney Johnston, Robert E. Lee, Joseph E. Johnston and Pierre G.T. Beauregard in this order of rank which was loosely based on their previous Federal Army rank. Cooper, a New Jersey renegade, proved to be a competent administrator and organizer but never led troops. A.S. Johnston died in 1862 at Shiloh, and Beauregard proved erratic and was not consistently valuable as a commander of troops. Lee and J.E. Johnston showed considerable leadership skills.

Of the three full generals the Confederacy added later, Braxton E. Bragg proved particularly ineffective, and John Bell Hood wasted huge numbers of soldiers in quixotic attacks until he destroyed his own army towards the end of the war. Nevertheless throughout the war, the Confederate leadership never considered replacing any of the initial five full generals from the whole pool of experienced general officers developed in the first 12 months of war. Those of the first five who survived and the three additional full generals remained principal military leaders in spite of their many exhibited failures.

Having no outstanding officers left who were young enough to serve in real war, the Union was forced to take an opposite course from the South. From a pool of about 100 officers who were appointed as major generals by the end of 1862 and who had shown their abilities in the field, a several-year selection process evolved that finally resulted in Grant, Sherman, Thomas, Meade and Sheridan becoming the North's principal military leaders. The highest rank any of these men held in the pre-war army was major. Each proved his generalship was as good or better than any Confederate general with the possible exception of Stonewall Jackson.

The South held this substantial advantage in leadership during the 12-24 month period before the Union's leadership selection process could be completed during 1863. Particularly in the East, the Union generals in command, McDowell, McClellan, Pope, Burnside and Hooker, along with many of their subordinate corps and division commanders, proved themselves to be inadequate commanders in battle. This was the period in which Southern commanders might have taken more advantage of these poor Union generals than they did if only Lee had shown greater skills. The longer the South waited for the Union to build up its leadership, numbers and armaments both in quality and quantity, the more certain became the Confederate defeat.

Jackson proposed a strategy to Davis and his military advisor, Lee, while the South still held its leadership advantage. Jackson suggested a strategy of swift strikes into the North at opportune times following Confederate victories or when a Union army commander placed himself at a disadvantage. His thought was to make such strikes at a major Northern city, like Baltimore or Philadelphia, and cut off the rail supply routes to Washington. He recommended that a Confederate army make such strikes when Union forces were occupied with an offensive effort or were too weak to defend against such a strike quickly. He foresaw that under these circumstances he could assume a strong defensive position of his choosing and force the Union army to attack him; he believed such attacks would lead to a Union defeat and be enormously costly in Northern blood and morale. In the face of this strategy, if it were successful, could the Union politicians and people stand the cost, or would they choose to retire from the war?

Specifically, Jackson made proposals of such limited offensives four times. After the First Battle of Manassas, he proposed to follow McDowell back into Washington with 5,000 "fresh troops" and take the place.[5] At that time, the Federal Army was beaten and Washington had not yet built any strong defenses; perhaps 5,000 fresh troops were not enough; but a determined attack might have ended the war. Davis, Lee and J.E. Johnston chose not to follow up their victory and rejected Jackson's plan. This reprieve allowed McClellan to take command and reorganize a beaten 30,000-man mob into the strong and well trained 130,000-man Army of the Potomac during the following six months.

After his victories over Fremont and Banks in the Shenandoah Valley and after McClellan had invaded the Peninsula, Jackson proposed to Davis and Lee that his army be reinforced to 40,000 men and that he make a drive to capture Baltimore.[6] His thought was that this would remove the threats to Richmond posed by McClellan on the Peninsula. Such an attack would, he believed, draw the two Union field armies to him and leave Washington open to attack and occupation by the main Confederate field army commanded by Lee. Davis and Lee, who apparently agreed with one another on most strategic matters, considered only immediate threats, not strategic opportunities and therefore turned Jackson down.

As McClellan advanced toward Richmond up the Virginia Peninsula, J.E. Johnston was severely wounded, and Lee replaced him in command. Lee proposed that Jackson join his army in the defense of Richmond. Jackson again proposed an alternative, a strike into the North, but Lee rejected his proposal. Jackson sent an emissary over Lee's head to Davis, but he also rejected the idea.[7] The fourth recommendation by Jackson was at the time McClellan abandoned the Virginia Peninsula; he saw the likelihood that the Army of the Potomac would be unable to perform in battle anywhere for a period of at least ten days. With the major Union army in the East voluntarily incapacitated, he saw this as a golden opportunity. He proposed a quick strike into Maryland or Pennsylvania by a three-division army, one small enough to move quickly, but big enough to hold a good defensive position.[8] This idea was rejected, but it caused Lee to decide upon the campaign that culminated at Antietam.

*   *   *

In spite of their reputations for aggressive strategies, when compared with those proposed by Jackson, Davis's and Lee's strategic ideas appear commonplace and somewhat timid. The difference was that Jackson saw war, or a battle, as a conflict between two intellects; numbers of soldiers were secondary to this higher conflict. Lee thought in terms of winning or losing territory, and somehow believed he could destroy a stronger enemy by assaulting him with brute force.

CHAPTER IV

Lee's First Command Experiences

When Lee was assigned to replace J.E. Johnston in command of the Confederate army defending Richmond,[1] his background was fortress building, staff-work and a small combat failure in West Virginia. The officers and men under his command looked forward to the return of J.E. Johnston once he recovered from his wounds.

Lee became commander of the armed forces of Virginia on April 23, 1861. He immediately showed great skill in organizing that state's war effort. Virginia was the most populous state of the Confederacy, and before West Virginia defected, it was huge in area, extending from the Atlantic Ocean almost to Cincinnati. Having a common border with many states that would be likely to remain loyal to the Union, Lee faced the reality of Virginia being invaded soon after the war began in earnest.

He immediately began to organize military units, to enlist officers from the state and from the Federal Army and to begin to train these troops to be useful in the defense of the state. His first concerns were for ordnance, military supplies and the threat of the Union Navy. While the Federal Army faced the same organizational problems he did, the Federal Navy was ready to fight. The James, York and Rappahannock rivers offered easy access for the Federal Navy to move heavily armed vessels and troop transports deep into Virginia, threatening Richmond and other important cities.

To meet the immediate naval threat, Lee built and manned batteries of artillery on the three major rivers and these proved successful in resisting this naval threat.[2] To establish a longer-term naval capability, Lee recognized the urgent need to capture and defend the Norfolk ship yard, the only major shipbuilding facility available to the Confederacy. By June he had secured the Norfolk facility, and in the process added to the state's very short supply of ordnance and gun powder.[3]

Harpers Ferry was a very important ordnance factory and armory for the pre-war United States, located on the south side of the Potomac in Virginia. This became a major target of Lee's strategy in these first weeks of the war. Besides holding a substantial amount of arms and powder, the armory had equipment used to manufacture rifled muskets and other arms. Lee sent Thomas J. Jackson to capture the armory which he successfully accomplished. Lee recognized that he could not hold the armory unless he took the hills on the Maryland side of the river, and Davis was fearful of upsetting the politics of Maryland, a state he still hoped would secede from the Union. Therefore, Lee ordered the removal of everything useful, and the rifle-making equipment was installed elsewhere.[4]

Lee's two months of organizational effort bore great dividends for the Confederacy.

* * *

Once the Confederacy was organized, President Davis appointed Lee as his principal military advisor. He participated in the decisions made prior to and after the First Battle of Bull Run (Manassas I). Problems arose quickly for Davis in western Virginia where the population did not have strong Southern sympathies. A small Union army under McClellan, assisted by Rosecrans, had invaded western Virginia in support of those who wished to secede from Virginia, and things were going against the Confederate contingent.

Davis sent Lee to recover the situation. Lee's first military command effort was a failure. His planning was poor, and he was not blessed with skillful or cooperative subordinates. Weather and road conditions were poor, but Lee proved to be hesitant and timid in his first action.[5] While this weak beginning threatened his military career before it really began, Lee showed rapid improvement in the following months. Even Lee's principal biographer, supporter and sometime apologist said: "His [Lee's] first campaign had ended ingloriously."[6]

After West Virginia was lost, Lee returned to Richmond where Davis assigned him to supervise the strengthening of the Confederacy's Atlantic coastal defenses. Lee was back in an element that was comfortable to him, an engineering assignment. Later, in June 1862, Lee was recalled to Richmond to again take up his position as Davis's military advisor. Whether or not it was deserved, he brought with him the reputation of a timid commander whose main interest was digging defenses. He had earned the nickname: "The King of Spades."

*   *   *

In April 1862, McClellan moved his newly re-organized Army of the Potomac to the Virginia Peninsula. Typical of his approach to all forthcoming battles, McClellan's advance up the Peninsula was slow and meticulous. Davis and others criticized the Confederate commander, J.E. Johnston, for not bringing McClellan to serious battle before his army moved into the suburbs of Richmond.

McClellan advanced to within six miles of Richmond. His supply base was at White House Landing (one of the Lee family estates) on the Pamunkey River, a tributary of the York River, on the north side of the Peninsula. The Richmond and York Railroad served his army from White House. The James River was closed to him because of the presence of the Confederate ironclad C.S.S. *Virginia*, a particularly powerful armored ship. The Chickahominy River, a deep, muddy and swampy stream, separated the Federal army into two parts.

At that time, most of the Federal army was north of the Chickahominy, but one corps, the Fourth, was isolated around Fair Oaks south of the river. On May 31st, Johnston decided to attack and destroy this corps. His subordinates failed to understand or follow Johnston's orders; the attack became confused and failed. That afternoon Johnston was severely wounded, and his second in command, Major General Gustavus W. Smith, succeeded him.

The night of May 31st, Lee and Davis, who had been observing the confused battle from a position that was under fire, rode back to Richmond and Davis told him to make preparations to take over command in Johnston's place. The next day he received the order along with requests from Smith for reinforcements. He ordered Major General Huger's division to move from Norfolk to support Smith. The Confederate high command was deeply concerned that a second Union army under McDowell was marching south to support McClellan, but on the day before he took command, Lee learned from Brigadier General J.E.B. Stuart that McDowell had stopped his march southward as a result of a perceived threat by Jackson on Washington following his victories in the Shenandoah Valley. Lee received his orders to join the army at 8:00 A.M. about the same time that Davis told Smith, who was in the midst of a mental and physical breakdown probably from a stroke, that Lee was superseding him.

The battle began again the morning of June 1st in spite of Lee's absence. The seriousness of the situation can be illustrated by the fact that the Union lines were five to six miles away from Richmond; cannon fire could be heard clearly in Davis's office; and if the Confederate lines broke, Federal pursuit could be in the capital in less than two hours. In spite of this seriousness, Lee delayed joining his command until 2:00 P.M., a delay that has never been explained.

Soon the battle bogged down in mud, and the two armies facing each other just west of Richmond went over to the defensive. "The King of Spades" put everybody on the Confederate side to work preparing defensive works. Most of Johnston's subordinates expressed discomfort in being under the command of a "staff officer like Lee." In the meanwhile, Lee began to devise a plan to make a strong counterattack against McClellan.

CHAPTER V

Battle Strategy, Tactics and Management

In the short period between the Mexican War and the Civil War, weapons, particularly rifles and artillery, were greatly improved. Tactics, military doctrine and strategic ideas remained those of fifteen to sixty years earlier. Few officers of 1860 had military ideas that were apace with the changes in ordnance. Those generals who adapted to these new conditions, and who were able to develop new tactics and doctrine to best accommodate the new opportunities offered, as well as the problems, proved by the end of the war to be the most successful.

Compared to a national strategy, battle strategy, management and tactics concern a specific battle against the general's main foe in his area of operations. How he plans to attack or defend against his foe is his battle strategy. What tactics does he plan to use; and, once the battle begins, how does he manage the battle as it unfolds? Does the general efficiently respond to threats against his army and take advantage of opportunities to follow up success and strike heavier blows against his enemy? Does the general conceive tactics that involve direct assaults against an enemy's strong positions, or does he try to find a way to out-flank, or otherwise attack, the enemy by a less costly, indirect method? Does he conserve or waste his manpower? Will he be prepared to fight effectively another day in the future, regardless of the outcome of the immediate battle? Does he recognize that fighting well today may avoid the necessity of fighting tomorrow?

The tactics that were used in the Napoleonic and Mexican wars strongly influenced those that were attempted in the Civil War. Napoleon was a workaholic who thought through every strategic and tactical detail of each campaign or battle in advance; then, once the battle started, he was expert at changing his plans to overcome errors or take advantage of opportunities. He always held a large reserve of his best troops ready to follow up any advantage or resist an enemy success. In the Mexican War, General Winfield S. Scott followed a different idea: he planned a battle, gave orders to his division commanders, and let them fight, making little adjustment changes himself. Unfortunately, Lee learned about being a commander-in-chief from Scott, and he thought it was his duty to plan a battle, determine when it should start, and get his divisions into the desired positions. Then, he let his subordinate commanders fight the battle with little interference.

Napoleon's basic unit of battle was the corps, which was made up of a number of divisions. Napoleon's armies were usually in the 30,000- to 50,000-man range but he eventually fought with armies of over 100,000 men. Armies used in the Mexican War were much smaller than Napoleon's in size; the basic battle unit there was not a corps but a division of about 4,000 men.

In the Civil War, armies were usually over 50,000 men in size and Union armies of over 100,000 were not uncommon. Sherman and Grant commanded army groups of 100,000, or more. The ideal tactical unit in the Civil War was a corps of 15,000 to 20,000 men, probably made up of three divisions. It took the Confederacy until late 1862 to organize corps and formally appoint corps commanders because their Congress organized their armies following a Mexican War model.[1]

The Union Army had a different problem: they established large numbers of small corps. Their inconsistency in organization led to much confusion. Sometimes they organized these small corps into "wings;" sometimes they called a 60,000-man army a corps and broke it down into "wings." Major General Don Carlos Buell's XIV Army Corps, with over 60,000 men, was so organized at the Battle of Perryville, after which the same organization was designated as the Army of the Cumberland made up of three corps. Until each side eliminated these confused organizational disadvantages, they frequently encountered command and responsibility problems that were costly. Examples are: Lee during the Seven Days battles and McClellan at Antietam.[2]

Massed artillery was used in front of infantry in both the Napoleonic and Mexican wars. Loaded with canister (cans which were full of 1-inch balls that would break apart when fired), the massed artillery blasted a hole in the defending ranks of infantry, and the infantry, or cavalry, then charged through the gaps. The defensive tactic against this artillery-infantry assault was for the defenders to form squares as self-supporting strong-points. The attackers would then try to reduce and capture each square using coordinated attacks by artillery, cavalry and infantry.

The limited, effective, aimed range of the smooth-bore musket, about 100 yards, meant the artillery could move into a position just over 100 yards from the enemy infantry without much concern that the artillery gunners would be hit. This gave the artillery a great advantage since the range for effective canister fire was about 200 yards. Counter-battery fire by defending artillery was the only defense against attacking artillery, and the short range and poor accuracy of the smooth-bore artillery limited this defensive tactic. In that stage of artillery development the attackers had an advantage because once the gap was blown in the enemy line, friendly infantry, or cavalry, had only 100 yards to charge to engage the enemy with sabers, musket fire or bayonet thrusts.

The Civil War brought these tactics to an abrupt end and few generals were able to adapt to the new situation with new tactics:

the main cause of change was the *Minie* rifle which was very accurate against a single soldier at a range of 300 yards and had a killing range of well over 600 yards. Following the same tactics described above meant that all the canoneers of artillery attacking from 100 yards would all be shot down before many artillery rounds could be fired. If the massed canons fell back to over 300 yards away where they were safer from rifled musket fire, their canister fire was no longer effective. Under these new conditions, the unsupported infantry had to charge 300 to 500 yards under heavy and effective fire to reach the enemy's line with only minor help from artillery. Such assaults were tried frequently and disastrously early in the war, but these old tactics had no chance of success in the new circumstances.[3]

When artillery was used to soften up a strong defensive position that had been enhanced with barricades and an infantry charge of over 500 yards was attempted, it was repulsed in the Civil War over 95% of the time. From over 100 examples of such failures, these two stand out: Pickett's Charge at Gettysburg and Grant's at Cold Harbor. In the few cases where a direct assault overcame a strong position, success resulted from other influences, such as: infiltration by night or use of nearby woods to gain a closer approach to the defenders, or as was the case at Missionary Ridge, the defensive position was very poorly designed, appearing to be strong but actually being extremely weak.[4]

New designs of artillery using rifling and other innovations caused these guns to fire shells or solid shot that rotated during their trajectory. This increased the range of artillery, but in addition, accuracy improved to the point that any visible target could be hit after the gun had fired only a few rounds. The result of this change was that artillery batteries had to be fired from behind hills or from other protected positions. On balance, this change was much in the favor of the defense.

With the onset of the Civil War, these changes allowed defensive tactics to gain ascendancy over offensive tactics. The use of barricades, trenches, defenses-in-depth, and other engineering design improvements made it almost impossible for either side to overcome the other's defenses provided they were well designed. Few generals on either side had the skill and imagination needed to develop effective offensive tactics.

With improvements in weapons, firepower, mobility and with much larger numbers of troops on both sides, the Mexican War no longer offered a viable basis for any battle management system. Scott's methods did not require an extensive staff to support the commander-in-chief. The changed conditions of the Civil War required an expansion of staff. Lee did not adapt to this changed requirement while the younger Union generals saw the needs and advantages and developed larger, more efficient support staffs.

*   *   *

At the start of the Civil War, generals on both sides faced a difficult situation. The attack doctrine they had to use, as described in their common military manuals, followed the Napoleonic and Mexican war models, and could not work against new Civil War weapons. During the war, infantry defenders continued to improve their situation with such things as repeating rifles and carbines, mines and grenades, and artillerymen continued to make improvements.

Since much improved offensive tactics were required if the Union were to win or if the Confederacy were to destroy the advancing Union armies, Jackson, Grant, Sherman and Sheridan were among the few generals who eventually became effective on the offensive.

CHAPTER VI

Lee Drives McClellan from the Virginia Peninsula in Some of the Bloodiest Fighting of the War

McClellan's military intelligence chief, Alan Pinkerton, told him Lee had 200,000 men, and McClellan believed him. In fact, both Lee and McClellan each had about 80,000, and Lee had the advantage of being in home territory on the defensive.[1] In addition, McClellan proved timid and indecisive. Although Lee successfully chased McClellan from the Virginia Peninsula, he was unable to destroy the Union army.

*A*fter the Seven Pines Battle, most of the Army of the Potomac was south of the Chickahominy River except for Major General FitzJohn Porter's V Corps of about 32,000 men which was isolated by the river about four miles north of it.

Lee developed a battle strategy to cut McClellan's main supply line from White House Landing by destroying the Richmond and York Railroad. He thought this would accomplish two aims: cut McClellan's main supply line, and draw Porter's corps out of its defenses to protect the railroad, thus placing him in a further isolated position in the open, where Lee could concentrate against and destroy his corps. To prevent McClellan from sending reinforcements to Porter, Lee planned the destruction of the bridges over the flooded Chickahominy. After destroying Porter, Lee planned to force the rest of the Union army to retreat from the suburbs of Richmond or face similar destruction.

It was a very good plan that began to go awry almost at once when two things happened. Union troops captured Norfolk Naval Yard, which caused the Confederates to scuttle the *Virginia* since it no longer had any base. This opened the James River to McClellan who could now use a superior supply line through Harrison's Landing rather than through White House Landing on the York,[2] and unknown to Lee, McClellan began to move his base to the James as soon as that river was opened.

In an attempt to gain his own intelligence about McClellan's positions, Brigadier General J.E.B. Stuart was assigned by Lee to reconnoiter the Union position. In a move he could brag about but which had little military value, Stuart and his cavalry rode completely around McClellan's army.[3] Completed June 15, 1862, Stuart's movement demonstrated the vulnerability of his White House Landing base to McClellan and he further accelerated his efforts to shift his base to Harrison's Landing on the James.

Lack of good intelligence information from his cavalry and scouts certainly limited Lee's knowledge; however, did he not have other sources? He had to know of the loss of Norfolk, the sinking of the *Virginia* and McClellan's efforts to move up the James. The conclusion that cutting the railroad to White House Landing was not a viable objective could have been made without additional knowledge from Stuart. Why did Lee not consider another strategy other than cutting the railroad and attacking Porter?

This intelligence mistake by Lee made his objective a false one since Porter's assignment was no longer to protect the Union base of supplies but to protect the Union army's north flank by establishing a defense line along the Chickahominy. Porter's planned response to an attack north of the river was to fight a rear-guard action and fall back across the Chickahominy using it as a line of defense.[4] Nevertheless, Lee continued to hold to his original plan and neglected better strategies.

Lee ordered Jackson to make a surprise return from the Shenandoah Valley. Lee instructed him to proceed to Mechanicsville where he would be on Porter's right (north) flank; then he was to move around Porter and against his rear. This position was so threatening that Porter only had to learn of Jackson's position, and he would have to retreat. It is true that Jackson was several hours late in gaining his position, but this had little to do with the prosecution of the plan.

The strategic plan failed when division commander Major General A.P. Hill, impatient with waiting for Jackson to make his move, could no longer contain his aggressiveness. He opened an attack on Porter's center.[5] Rather than calling a halt on the attack, Lee demonstrated his own tendency for direct assaults and supported Hill by ordering two other divisions to his aid in the attack. In the meanwhile, Porter had turned his defenses from a north-south line to an east-west line defending the bridges over the Chickahominy.

Lee was unable to realize that this shift of front by Porter was a sure signal that McClellan had successfully moved his base to the James, and that Jackson could outflank Porter easily by moving to take the Chickahominy bridge at Dispatch Station which should have trapped Porter north of the river and would have made Hill's bloody assaults completely unnecessary. Lee failed to understand that Porter's shift was also a sign that McClellan was in general retreat toward his new base at Harrison's Landing.[6]

Once McClellan's general retreat became obvious to all, the apparent best strategy for Lee was to pass McClellan's left flank and race him for Harrison's Landing or Evelynton Heights which was a dominant position overlooking McClellan's new base. Instead, Lee sent a far too weak force, Major General Theophilus T. Holmes's small 6,000-man division, to cut McClellan off, and the rest of his army followed the Union rear guard in four columns. Having set up no communications between the columns, their actions were not well coordinated.

Lee fought a costly and purposeless battle at Frayser's Farm, after which the Union army occupied and fortified Malvern Hill, a very strong defensive position. In his attack on Malvern Hill, a precursor to Pickett's charge, the Confederate army lost 20,000 real casualties (killed and wounded only, since all captured men were soon exchanged) against the Union army's loss of 10,000.[7] Whether intentionally or not, Lee became engaged in a war of attrition the Confederacy had no chance to win.

Evelynton Heights above Harrison's Landing remained unoccupied by either side until Stuart and his cavalry took them and placed one howitzer there. After minor shelling, the Union infantry drove him from the heights and fortified them.[8] Again, a major strategic opportunity was lost by Lee; if Stuart had not exposed the importance of the Heights, the inept McClellan would probably have allowed Lee to occupy them in force. Such an occupation would have reversed the tactical positions of the two armies, placing Lee in a stronger position than McClellan held at Malvern Hill. Such an occupation would probably have driven McClellan's troops back to Fortress Monroe or onto their ships in the James. Union losses in making such a movement would probably have been staggering.

Summarizing Lee's strategy in the Seven Days Campaign, Lee showed two fatal defects in his strategic vision: (1) a tendency to turn a good plan that promised a low cost of manpower into costly direct assaults and (2) inflexibility once he decided upon a course of action. Lee conceived the strategy of cutting the Union army off from its base at White House Landing; however, he did not order adequate scouting and intelligence-gathering operations so he did not know the Union army was in the porcess of abandoning its base at White House Landing. McClellan established a new base at Harrison's Landing on the James River and defended his right flank along the Chickahominy River.

CHAPTER VI

*   *   *

While Lee had developed a good plan to move a strong force behind the right of the Army of the Potomac, did the tactics he used support his plan? Jackson was a few hours late in turning the flank. Rather than insisting that all other commanders wait for Jackson to reach a dominating position behind the Union flank, A.P. Hill became impatient and Lee allowed the overly-aggressive general to attack Porter's corps at Mechanicsville using frontal assault tactics. Porter fell back to strong defensive positions along Beaver Dam Creek. At this point, the army's organizational structure failed, since Lee had a front of about 10 miles to manage personally with no trusted corps commanders to control local conditions.[9]

When Longstreet and D.H. Hill saw A.P. Hill's movement toward Mechanicsville, they concluded that he was in touch with Jackson who, they assumed, had turned the Union right flank. On this erroneous basis, they came to A.P. Hill's support and joined in the attack. Distant from the action without adequate staff officers to inform him of what was going on, it was too late for Lee to do anything but to support a change in tactics which he had not initiated. This frontal assault was costly and unnecessary, since a few hours later Porter became aware of Jackson's flanking movement which caused him to abandon his positions at no Confederate cost.

Unknown to Lee, at 5:00 P.M. on June 26th Jackson reached Hundley's Corner two hours late and out-flanked Porter's position.[10] Jackson heard firing from the direction of Mechanicsville and assumed Confederate forces were crossing north over the Chickahominy to join him. This caused Jackson to conclude that movement should be called off for the day, and he went into bivouac until morning. Earlier, Lee had also concluded that action should be stopped for the day, but he changed his mind and approved A.P. Hill's continuing the attack on the Beaver Dam line north of the Chickahominy that evening.[11]

The movements of Lee's army on June 26th illustrate clearly the inadequate organization and lack of staff and intelligence support he faced, which caused him to take many actions based on faulty assumptions. Lee did not know Jackson was only four miles from Mechanicsville and had out-flanked Porter by 5:00 P.M.; A.P. Hill made his first attack across the Meadow Bridge to the north of the Chickahominy without Lee's approval at 3:00 P.M.; D.H. Hill and Longstreet supported A.P. Hill's attack thinking he was in contact with Jackson without informing Lee in advance; Jackson thought the fighting for the day was over and went into bivouac; finally, Lee approved the continuing of an unnecessary frontal assault on Porter at Beaver Dam Creek. A.P. Hill's attack was one of the most bloody and useless of the war: he lost 1400 men to Porter's 360 in only a few minutes and then Porter retreated under Jackson's threat during the night. How can one imagine a more confused command system or a poorer tactical use of soldiers than existed in the Confederate army on June 26, 1862?

Lee continued to batter the Union rear guards in engagements at Gaines' Mill (June 27th), Savage's Station (June 29th) and Frayser's Farm (June 30th). All these engagements were made by parts of Lee's army against parts of McClellan's army. Although an opportunity was available, Lee made no attempt to concentrate against one of McClellan's parts and destroy it. He also made little effort to push around to the front of McClellan's formations to interfere with their easily reaching their objective on the James.

Early in the war, Lee showed that he was satisfied with the lesser objective, driving the Union forces away from Richmond. When McClellan assumed a strong defensive position on Malvern Hill, Lee again ordered inadequate reconnaissance and made a number of costly direct assaults against the Union positions. If destruction of his enemy had been in his mind, his best tactic would have been to hold his enemy there while cutting his lines of retreat to the river ports.

*   *   *

In summary, although Lee had driven the Federal army away from Richmond, his losses in the Seven Days Campaign were enormous. His system of battle management could not accommodate the great opportunities that arose for him to destroy a major portion of McClellan's army. In pointing out to the enemy the importance of Evelynton Heights and failing to discover and inform Lee of McClellan's change of base in a timely manner, Stuart might have missed chances to change the course of the war. Lee's unwillingness to discipline Stuart did not show him as a great general. Can it be concluded that Lee fought these engagements well? It is difficult to draw this conclusion!

Until his death in May 1864, Stuart followed a career which gained him much glory, but Lee allowed him to do things to the great detriment of the Army of Northern Virginia. Besides these events on the Peninsula, Stuart later misled Lee in the Antietam Campaign and behaved disastrously prior to Gettysburg when he followed Lee's orders to move around the Federal army prior to Gettysburg. However he left his poorest commander with Lee; this man failed and Lee was blinded as to the movements of the Army of the Potomac. Although Stuart created these problems, they were Lee's responsibility, and he made no move to discipline Stuart or to prevent re-occurrences of the problems. Lee's only strong expression of disapproval of Stuart was his decision not to promote him to lieutenant general when he eventually formed his Cavalry Corps.

One must conclude from his performance on the Virginia Peninsula that Lee made a number of mistakes in judgment and that his generalship was flawed. While many of his problems were associated with poor organization and some lack of good leadership above him, iconship does not yet appear to have been earned.

CHAPTER VII

Lee Follows Jackson's Strategy to Move the War from the Gates of Richmond

With McClellan's Army of the Potomac bottled up at Harrison's Landing, Lincoln organized the Union Army of Virginia under Major General John Pope. Jackson saw an opportunity to destroy Pope's force, and Lee tried to execute the plan. Lack of quick movement and Lee's failure to take advantage of this great opportunity doomed the plan to failure. This was one of many lost opportunities for the South to end the war in its favor.

A regional strategy is one which is aimed to place a commander's army at an advantage against his foe in the region for which he is responsible. Another aim of a regional strategy is to improve the commander's position to eliminate or reduce his own risks or to destroy or weaken the enemy forces he faces. A regional commander, such as Lee, is sometimes unable to execute the strategy he wishes because of the interference of his superiors. His opponent will also have much to do with his execution of strategic moves: a skillful opponent may block his every move with better counter-strategies, or a weak opponent may make the accomplishment of the commander's strategy easy to execute. McClellan was a good strategic thinker but consistently showed indecision and weakness in executing his plans.

In 1862, Lee had excellent support from Stonewall Jackson who had many original and sound strategic ideas. Unfortunately for the Confederacy, Jackson's strategic thoughts were seldom followed since Davis and Lee were more conventional and less aggressive in their strategic thinking, more aggressive tactically, and usually thought only of the immediate future and the risks at hand. They seldom tried to develop opportunities to destroy an enemy. Jackson produced strategies that could lead to a complete Confederate victory and always considered the long-term implications; Lee and Davis seemed to think in terms of winning and surviving a battle today, stopping the enemy while considering and reacting to future events as they came.

In his location on the Peninsula, McClellan was holding the strongest strategic position the Union army was able to attain until the summer of 1864. It was not necessary for McClellan to stay bottled up in his enclave at Harrison's Landing under the eye of a small part of Lee's army. McClellan had other options: he might have broken out; he might have crossed the James and taken Petersburg; or he might have moved by boat to another location on the Peninsula. He chose none of these options and timidly remained out of the war for months.

Dissatisfied with McClellan and concerned about a Confederate attack on Washington, Lincoln brought Major General Henry W. Halleck from the West to replace McClellan as general-in-chief of the Federal Army and Major General John Pope to command a new field army, the Army of Virginia. All the politicians feared a Confederate attack against Washington, and themselves, so Pope's army was positioned to protect Washington in McClellan's absence.

After the Seven Days Battles on the Peninsula with McClellan's exhausted army static at Harrison's Landing, Jackson made another proposal. He believed the Army of the Potomac was spent and would not be able to assume the offensive for many months. It was also known that McClellan, as advised by his intelligence chief, Alan Pinkerton, lived under the delusion that his

90,000-man army faced 200,000 Confederates while their actual numbers were closer to 60,000. Given these circumstances, Richmond was safe from attack, and the Confederate Army could supply a large field force with which to strike into Northern territory.

A quick strike would have devastating effect on the North before McClellan could move his army all the way from the James to fight Jackson's invading army. Beside drawing the Army of the Potomac away from the gates of Richmond, Jackson saw that this was a rare opportunity to win the war. Jackson's proposal was not a radical idea; it was similar to Napoleon's favorite strategy. Since the North had chosen to divide its forces, the strategy was to concentrate the bulk of the Southern forces against one part, overwhelm that part, destroy it while defending against the second part. Then he would turn against the second part with overwhelming force and destroy it too. Again, Lee and Davis rejected Jackson's idea because they were concerned McClellan would attack Richmond, and they chose to wait idly while McClellan rebuilt his army and Lincoln raised a new army under Pope to defend Washington.[1]

* * *

In all of the battles in which Jackson had independent command, he strove for these objectives: gain numerical superiority over his immediate enemy, attack and defeat parts of the enemy army in detail, find ways to attack him in flank or rear, minimize his own casualties and attempt to annihilate his opponent.[2] Only one other, and later, Civil War general consistently followed and sometimes achieved such objectives: Federal Major General Philip H. Sheridan, many of whose battles were similar in design and result to Jackson's. In July 1862 having failed to persuade his chiefs of his strategy to penetrate the North, Jackson abandoned that idea and adopted a secondary alternative:

find a strategy to destroy all, or large parts, of the main Federal army in the East, the Army of the Potomac.

As the Civil War progressed, Lee's concept of a national strategy became exposed as being weak and based on wishful thinking, not military action and reality. He had failed to support Jackson's possible war-ending ideas to invade the North when Union armies and leadership were weak. Since these Union armies were stronger in numbers and their leadership was improving as 1862 progressed, the opportunity for real results from invasion were no longer as viable by the latter part of 1862 as they had been previously. This would be clearly demonstrated by Lee's failures at Antietam and Gettysburg.

*   *   *

With McClellan still holed up at Harrison's Landing, Lee sent Jackson with 21,000 men north to defend the Virginia Central Railroad from the Shenandoah Valley to Richmond. Jackson drew Nathaniel Banks' corps into battle and defeated him severely at Cedar Mountain. At about the same time, Halleck ordered McClellan to abandon the Peninsula and return to Washington. This gave Lee an unparalleled strategic opportunity. Since McClellan's army would take over 10 days to embark, travel to the vicinity of Washington and re-deploy, Halleck had voluntarily taken the largest Union field army out of any possible combat role. During this 10-day period Pope's army of 45,000 men could be attacked by a larger Confederate army if Lee could concentrate his full army against it.[3]

Pope was established in a defensive position along the upper Rapidan River. Jackson proposed that on August 16, 1862 the now fully concentrated Confederate Army of Northern Virginia cross the Rapidan and strike to the left rear of Pope's army. This would cut Pope off from Washington and his supplies, subsequently leading to his being surrounded and destroyed, or at the least, he would be seriously damaged in the peninsula between the Rapidan and Rappahannock rivers.

Lee and Jackson saw the opportunity differently: Lee thought of the territory involved and saw it as an opportunity to drive Pope out of northern Virginia; Jackson saw an opportunity to destroy Pope's army against the Rapidan and then attack McClellan's army in detail as it arrived on the scene a few units at a time. The opportunity, as Jackson saw it, would disappear if they delayed, and Lee delayed the advance until the 20th for what seemed to be minor reasons.[4] Given the opportunity by Lee's delay, Pope recognized his peril and retreated to relative safety north of the Rappahannock River.

Lee's mind seemed fixed on the lesser strategy of cutting Pope's railroad supply line. On August 22nd, Stuart captured papers indicating that Pope's army would be reinforced to 120,000 men within five to ten days. After the impatient Jackson had been restrained by Lee for two days, on the 24th Lee ordered Jackson to move around Pope's right (west) flank and cut the railroad, thinking that this would cause Pope to rush back to protect his supply line.[5]

Jackson seized the opportunity to enlarge upon Lee's strategy. A move north around the west side of the Bull Run Mountains would allow him to turn east through Thorofare Gap and capture Manassas Junction 25 miles behind Pope and only 18 miles from Alexandria. First, Jackson eliminated any easy movement by Pope toward Manassas Junction by going to Bristol Station and destroying the railroad bridge over Broad Run. This made it impossible for Pope to use the railroad so he had to move indirectly, south, east and then north, to reach the Manassas area.

Having placed Pope at a disadvantage, Jackson moved by forced marches to capture Pope's main supply depot at Manassas Junction. Taking what his men could use, he burned the rest.[6] Upon receiving word of Jackson's successful movement, the remainder of Lee's army broke contact with Pope's army along the

Rappahannock and began to follow Jackson's route to Manassas Junction.

Jackson then made plans for Pope's inevitable attack. Jackson understood that Pope would arrive overly confident of his more than 2:1 advantage against Jackson's single corps and sure of being able to defeat him. Recognizing the substantial advantage defenders had over attackers, Jackson occupied a position he had previously scouted which was very strong defensively from which he planned to use new tactics. He placed a portion of his men along an unfinished railroad near Bull Run which offered them a naturally fortified position; he strengthened the position in greater depth with two echelons of defenders behind the line that could concentrate immediately against any enemy penetration.[7]

With only 21,000 men, Jackson hoped to draw Pope's 45,000 into an assault on his strong position where the Union force would have to advance across open, flat fields against withering fire that they could not effectively return (a killing ground). He expected Longstreet, Lee and the rest of the Army of Northern Virginia to arrive soon after Pope's initial attack was spent. This would offer the rest of Lee's army the opportunity to attack the open flank of a worn-out army, and together they could drive Pope's army against Bull Run and destroy it.[8]

*　　*　　*

At the Second Battle of Bull Run, Jackson's strategy had placed Pope's army in severe danger on August 29, 1862, but due to lack of support, this turned out to be a day of lost opportunity for the Confederacy. Jackson's effort to wear down Pope's larger force was very effective during the morning while he successfully repulsed their repeated attacks. Although outnumbered 2:1, Jackson was confident he could hold Pope in place in front of his defenses until Lee and Longstreet arrived; once concentrated, the Army of Northern Virginia would still not outnumber Pope's exhausted army, 48,527 Confederates to 75,696 Federals.[9] If there was ever a demonstration that a smaller army following a superior strategy could defeat a much larger, poorly led army, this was it. The opportunity to destroy or greatly cripple Pope's Army of Virginia was ripe.

About noon, Lee and Longstreet arrived on the scene, while Pope was still immersed in the idea of destroying Jackson's weaker force, not realizing that only a 2:1 advantage in numbers left the attackers in severe peril of defeat. Pope had taken no steps to protect his undefended left flank. Longstreet's corps was in position for an attack that would probably have split the Union army, rolling it up and driving it into Bull Run where few easy crossings were available.

Although he said he regretted his decision later, Lee allowed Longstreet's corps to remain idle all afternoon and Jackson continued to hold his line while absorbing a pounding. Once Lee met with Jackson, he saw the opportunity that had existed for hours and ordered the assault, but it was too late for that day.[10] Pope took no steps to protect his left flank and ignored the threat of a 25,000-man corps which was positioned to crush him. It is difficult to choose which field commander made the greater blunder, Lee or Pope. To show the efficiency of Jackson's defenses, it was estimated that he lost only 3,000 men to Pope's 8,000 on the 29th.

In Lee's defense, he was still dealing with a severe organizational deficiency of which he was aware but had no power to correct. In addition, plans seldom work out well which are originated by a subordinate but are unknown to his superior. At Manassas II the battle plan was Jackson's, and it failed; however, if each general had adequate staff officers who could communicate each commander's ideas to the other, Pope's army could have been destroyed. In fact, neither Lee nor Jackson had superior staffs, and Jackson's almost paranoid desire for complete secrecy about his plans made matters much worse. It is to Lee's credit that he recognized some of the organizational problems of the Army of

1. The Second Battle of Manassas — Lee's Lost Opportunity

Bull Run Mtns.

Unfinished Railroad

Centerville

Thoroughfare Gap

Haymarket

Bull Run Mtns.

Bull Run

Manassas Railroad

Warrenton Pike

Manassas Station

Artwork by Beth Queman

0 1 2 3 4 Miles

1. Jackson strongly entrenches along unfinished railroad.
2. Pope's forces attack Jackson.
3. Porter's corps separated from Pope.
4. Heintzelman's corps.
5. Reno's corps.
6. Pope's Headquarters.
7. Longstreet's position, well before sunset August 28th.
8. Opportunity to split Pope's force and drive him back into Bull Run.

Northern Virginia and was taking steps to try to remedy these faults.

August 30th presented Lee with another tactical opportunity. He lined up Longstreet's "corps" to the right of Jackson's. Pope's left flank was still exposed, but Lee decided to hold the defensive until he saw what the Federals decided to do.[11] Clearly, the proper tactic was for Longstreet to attack the weak right of Pope's army in strength.

Jackson removed most of his men from the works along the

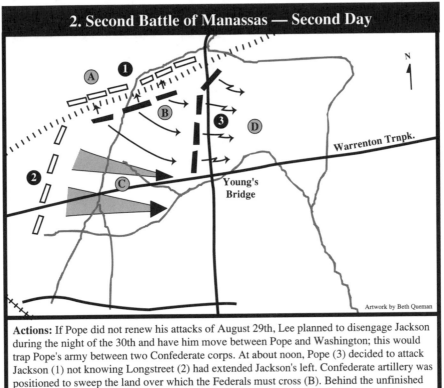

2. Second Battle of Manassas — Second Day

Young's
Bridge

Warrenton Trnpk.

N

Artwork by Beth Queman

Actions: If Pope did not renew his attacks of August 29th, Lee planned to disengage Jackson during the night of the 30th and have him move between Pope and Washington; this would trap Pope's army between two Confederate corps. At about noon, Pope (3) decided to attack Jackson (1) not knowing Longstreet (2) had extended Jackson's left. Confederate artillery was positioned to sweep the land over which the Federals must cross (B). Behind the unfinished railroad, Jackson's line held, and the artillery fire was very damaging. Longstreet counter-attacked (C) from the flank, and Pope's army retreated across Bull Run towards Washington. Lee's attempts to move around Pope's army and trap it failed. This was an overwhelming victory for Lee, but it only drove Pope's army from the field.

railroad and hid them in the woods about a hundred yards behind his real defensive position. This avoided exposure to preparatory artillery fire; and then, when the Federals moved, his plan was for his men to rush forward to his first battle line of defense and occupy the works while a second line remained sheltered in the woods. In addition, the Confederates placed 36 cannon in an infiladed position on the right of their lines; these cannon swept all of the ground over which the Federals would have to cross when they attacked.

Little happened until mid-afternoon when Pope ordered a general attack. After numerous unsuccessful assaults, Pope's army was broken up and fled north in retreat. At this point, Lee ordered a general attack, but nightfall stopped the effort, and Pope's army escaped. In the two days, real casualties were about 9,100 for the Confederates and almost 10,200 for the Federals.[12] Jackson's battle strategy and tactics, if they had been fully implemented, had set up conditions for the destruction of Pope's army; but Lee passed up an annihilation opportunity for a lesser victory.

Did Lee learn from observing Pope's futile assaults against Jackson's strong defensive position?

CHAPTER VIII

Antietam: A Confederate Disaster and a Huge Lost Opportunity for the Union

After the Confederate debacle at Antietam (it cannot be glossed over as anything less than that), Lee wrote to Davis: "Since my last letter to you of the 18th, finding the enemy indisposed to make an attack on that day, and our position being a bad one to hold with the river in the rear, I determined to cross the army to the Virginia side."[1] Nothing was different in his situation from three days before except that Lee had lost 13,700 out of his 51,800-man army and accomplished nothing for their loss. One might ask why Lee made his decision after and not before the Battle of Antietam.

*I*n 1862, the organizational structures of the opposing armies were rapidly changing for the better after a difficult trial-and-error process. In the fighting on the Peninsula, each division commander had reported directly to Lee, and each ran his division more or less as an "independent little army." If two divisions were to act in concert, the command of the combination was treated as a temporary arrangement and was given to the senior of the two commanders, regardless of their relative abilities.

Lee recognized the problems of running a large army with this overly complex structure and wished to change it, but Confederate law did not allow the formation of corps and the assignment of permanent corps commanders. Before Antietam, Lee informally assigned Jackson and Longstreet as commanders of two groups of divisions; later the Confederate Congress confirmed his action by passing legislation that allowed for these groups to be called corps. This led to the Army of Northern Virginia being organized with only the two corps commanders reporting to Lee with all division commanders reporting to the assigned corps commanders.[2]

Both sides were also trying to make their artillery organization more effective. The old system was that the available artillery was divided equally between brigades, and each brigade commander controlled the artillery assigned to him. From a technical standpoint, artillery had frequently been shown in battle to be much more effective when concentrated into a larger coordinated force under higher command. Before Antietam, Lee was in the process of removing artillery from brigade control by assigning a battalion of artillery to each corps and assigning reserve artillery units to corps and division command for increased effect.[3]

In trying to develop a more efficient organization, Lee was far ahead of McClellan. After McClellan was restored to command of the Army of the Potomac following Manassas II, and Pope had been banished to Oregon, the army was made up of the corps that Pope had commanded and those from his own army that Lincoln had released from Washington guard duty to form a mobile army. He had seven corps commanders, some of whom had only a few days of command. There was unresolved conflict between those corps commanders who had served under Pope or McClellan; and at the time, the Army of the Potomac's most experienced and respected corps commander, Porter, had been relieved until he could stand Court Martial for insubordination to Pope.[4]

McClellan placed Burnside in charge of his left wing which consisted of IX Corps under Major General Jesse Reno and I

Corps under Major General Joseph Hooker. He did not form center or right wings, and I Corps was detached from Burnside and fought on the far right. Reno was killed in the South Mountain fighting before Antietam, and Burnside replaced him in command of IX Corps, which fought on the far left at Antietam. Burnside was still classified as a wing commander.[5] It is difficult to imagine such an ill-thought organization for an army just in advance of going into a major battle.

McClellan was also attempting to concentrate his artillery, but most of it was still under division command. He appointed an army artillery commander, Brigadier General Henry Hunt, but he was given no tactical command authority nor could he influence the performance of the army's artillery during battle.[6]

In September 1862, Lee finally decided to strike into Union territory. His ideas and Jackson's were very different. Jackson wanted to capture a major northern city, Baltimore or Philadelphia, believing either would be poorly defended since McClellan would be forced by the politicians to concentrate on protecting Washington. He proposed to assume a defensive position as strong as the one he had held during Manassas II, confident that he had demonstrated that the Union army could not drive him from it. Planning to become an open sore in Union territory, he expected the Northern populace to demand that their leaders negotiate peace.[7]

Lee's concept was more simplistic and naive: he expected to invade the North with no designated military objective, avoid battle, live off the land, recruit troops from Southern sympathizers in Maryland, and once he had brought the war to the North, Davis was to use this "strong" position to offer peace based on Southern independence. It seems unlikely that such a vague plan could have accomplished much even if he had executed it well. No Southerner knew that Lincoln had prepared the Emancipation Proclamation and was only waiting for any Union victory to release it. Lincoln believed that its release would add strong moral fiber to the Union cause and change the basis of the war.

Lee's army crossed the Potomac near Leesburg into Maryland, south of Frederick, from September 4 to 6, 1862. Contrary to Lee's expectations, the Union garrisons at Martinsburg and Harpers Ferry were ordered to hold their places. Lee became concerned about these forces, about 15,000 men in all, being in his rear and near his supply lines. Against the advice of his chief subordinates, Jackson and Longstreet, who believed these troops were garrison-oriented, not accustomed to taking the offensive and therefore of no significant threat, he chose to divide his small army of 55,000 into four parts and capture these garrisons.[8]

These moves succeeded, but his detailed order, General Order No. 191, dividing the army, and describing his objectives, fell into the hands of McClellan. Lee soon learned of this breach of security from a Confederate sympathizer. Lee's initial reaction was to realize that the campaign into the North was lost before it started, and he ordered the various segments of his army to fall back to the south side of the Potomac.[9]

The fatal flaw and shallow strategic insight Lee had exhibited during the Seven Days now caused him to issue orders that cost the Confederacy a major strategic defeat and possibly the eventual loss of the war. As soon as he knew his order had reached McClellan's hands, Lee knew his strategic advantage had been irrevocably lost. Nevertheless, he changed his mind about crossing the Potomac when his tendency to fight even when unfavorably positioned, as opposed to a judicious retreat, made him fight to try to recover a lost strategic advantage. This concept was impossible; he had only two choices: to retreat across the Potomac with his army whole, or to cross the Potomac later with his army greatly diminished by a fruitless battle. Lee chose the latter alternative.

In his report to Davis of September 19th after the battle, Lee reported the successful crossing of the Army of Northern Virginia into Virginia at Boteler's Ford. Lee also wrote: "Since my last letter to you of the 18th, finding the enemy indisposed to make an attack on that day, and our position being a bad one to hold with

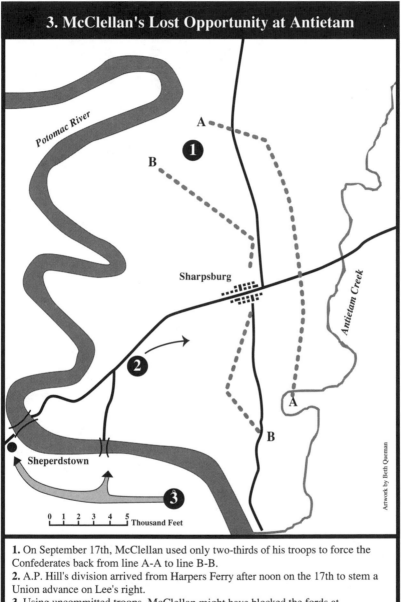

3. McClellan's Lost Opportunity at Antietam

Potomac River

A

B

1

Sharpsburg

Antietam Creek

2

A

B

3

Sheperdstown

0 1 2 3 4 5
Thousand Feet

Artwork by Beth Queman

1. On September 17th, McClellan used only two-thirds of his troops to force the Confederates back from line A-A to line B-B.
2. A.P. Hill's division arrived from Harpers Ferry after noon on the 17th to stem a Union advance on Lee's right.
3. Using uncommitted troops, McClellan might have blocked the fords at Shepherdstown. This would have blocked A.P. Hill from joining Lee's army and trapped it. This action would have led to a strategic Union triumph.

97

the river in the rear, I determined to cross the army to the Virginia side."[10]

Except for the men he had lost, the position and situation were the same on the 19th as they had been on the 17th when Lee chose to fight. This was an admission by Lee that the strategy he followed on the 17th was wrong in light of his better thinking on the 19th. In fact, it took Jackson's and Longstreet's strongest persuasion to keep Lee from attacking McClellan on the 18th.[11]

McClellan did not show much skill as a strategist at Antietam. His best plan before the battle started would have been to hold Lee's front in place along Antietam Creek with all or most of 80,000 men while sending 50,000 or more south of the Potomac to block all the fords that were available for Lee's retreat. If McClellan had established these positions, it would have been only a matter of time until Lee found himself surrounded and in severe trouble. He would have had to go over to the offensive to fight his way out of the pocket. At worst, he would have had to surrender his army; at best, he would have suffered greater losses than he could have inflicted on the Union army.

*   *   *

Comparing the strengths of the Army of Northern Virginia and the Army of the Potomac on September 1, 1862, it must be concluded that the Army of Northern Virginia was generally superior in quality in spite of its smaller numbers. Lee, its commander-in-chief, was far superior to McClellan as a strategist, tactician and leader. Lee's informal change in organization to a two-corps structure made the Army of Northern Virginia more controllable tactically than the Army of the Potomac. Used to marching faster and harder, the Army of Northern Virginia had greater mobility than the Army of the Potomac. Lee's "corps commanders," Jackson and Longstreet, were much superior soldiers to any of McClellan's corps commanders, most of whom had little experience in corps command.

The artillery of the Army of Northern Virginia was more concentrated and effective in its use than that of the Army of the Potomac although the latter had more cannon, which were of better quality. The staff organization of both sides remained inadequate, but McClellan's intelligence, which fallaciously informed him the Confederate army was larger than his, was poor to the point of being damaging. Only in numbers, 130,000 to 55,000, did the Union army have a clear advantage, but McClellan negated much of this advantage by leaving 50,000 men completely out of the fight at Antietam.[12]

After Lee's army crossed the Potomac, his Special Order No. 191, issued September 9th, fell into McClellan's hands on the 13th. This order told McClellan that Lee had divided his army and in the Sharpsburg-Boonsboro-Hagerstown area he only had about 30,000 men in all. Of these, he had only his cavalry and 6,500 men under D.H. Hill, to defend the South Mountain passes against 65,000 Federal soldiers advancing from Frederick.[13]

Not believing his good fortune and thinking Order No. 191 might be a trick directed against him, McClellan helped Lee's situation by delaying any movement for almost a day after he read Lee's order while he thought about all the possible alternative actions he might follow. Aggressive movement was his best immediate choice, and he might have thought of moving some force to the south side of the Potomac to keep Lee from concentrating his army at Sharpsburg.

With its great advantage in numbers, the Army of the Potomac fought its way through the South Mountain passes against determined Confederate rear guards but took a full day to do so. When he learned his order had been captured, Lee concluded that the best tactic was to withdraw to the south side of the-Potomac; however, he changed his mind when he learned his army should be fully concentrated at Sharpsburg by the 16th or 17th.[14]

Lee saw Sharpsburg as a position he should hold in Maryland to satisfy some vague strategic purpose he never enunciated. While it was the only position in Union territory that he had the opportunity to hold, it had great tactical disadvantages to Lee and it served no strategic purpose. Sharpsburg was part of a rough peninsula within the meanders of the Potomac River; thus a line along Antietam Creek was somewhat protected on each flank by that river. Bridges over the Potomac had been destroyed and only one good crossing was available behind him.

Even if it could be concentrated, Lee's army had only 55,000 men against McClellan's 130,000, and natural features did not add strength to his positions along Antietam Creek. His disadvantageous ratio of 1:2.4 was slightly favorable to Lee over McClellan as long as he maintained a defensive stance. McClellan did not enjoy the 3:1 ratio that would give reasonable assurance that a good offensive commander would win,[15] and he was not a good offensive commander. To further dilute his ratio of advantage, McClellan would leave 50,000 men unengaged so the engaged ratio was only 1:1.3 against Lee. McClellan did not use these 50,000 men as a ready reserve, he just left them idle.

The superior mobility of the Army of Northern Virginia that had stood Lee in good stead in previous actions was negated by the position Lee chose for the battle. It offered little potential for a successful counter-offensive because the closed flanks of the position eliminated any possibility for Lee to perform a turning movement. Lee chose to fight a stand-up, face-to-face battle that he could not win but might easily lose. The only question that remained was how severe Lee's losses would be, and whether McClellan would prove to be a poor enough general to allow Lee to escape with a draw.

Looking at it from a Confederate viewpoint, McClellan was their ideal foe. His slow, meticulous and predictable approach had eliminated an opportunity to wipe out Lee's Sharpsburg position when he had only 24,000 men in place on September 15th. He actually allowed Lee to concentrate his forces, and this mitigated the severity of Lee's losses. The Battle of Antietam (Sharpsburg) was fought on September 17th and was the bloodiest one-day battle of the war. Lee showed poor strategic vision to have fought it at all, but his defensive tactical skills, which were far stronger than the offensive skills of McClellan, saved him.

At Antietam, Lee remained on the defensive and made no vainglorious assaults. He fought a single tactical battle moving troops to meet all Union penetrations. His final such movement was by A.P. Hill's division which arrived on the scene from Harpers Ferry at the last moment to stop the deep penetration by IX Corps of Lee's left after it had forced a crossing of Antietam Creek at Burnside's Bridge.[16] McClellan fought a series of uncoordinated battles sending different corps on the attack several hours apart. He supported none of these attacks with reserves and continued to leave his strongest unit, 50,000 men, out of the fight.

Tactically, Lee and his generals did well to avoid annihilation even though being on the defensive with the numbers engaged was in their favor. They would have faced a disaster if Grant or Sherman or Sheridan, in their primes, had faced them that day rather than McClellan. As it was, the Confederates lost 10,300 in killed and wounded and the Federals who were consistently on the attack lost 12,400.[17]

Lee wanted to fight a second day which would have brought sure and final disaster, but Longstreet and Jackson persuaded him of the folly of such action. After the battle, everyone on the Federal side was sorely disappointed. Wires had gone out announcing "Lee's annihilation after he was trapped against the flooded Potomac."[18] A massive attack by the Army of the Potomac on the 18th had every expectation of success and fulfilling the words of the optimistic wires, instead, McClellan passively allowed Lee's army to cross the Potomac to safety on the 19th.

After being unable to convince McClellan to make offensive movements, Lincoln despaired of his efforts and replaced him on November 9, 1862 with Major General Ambrose E. Burnside who proved to be even more inefficient than McClellan. Strangely, McClellan had finally developed a good offensive strategy, but he was too late. He planned to drive between Jackson's Corps at

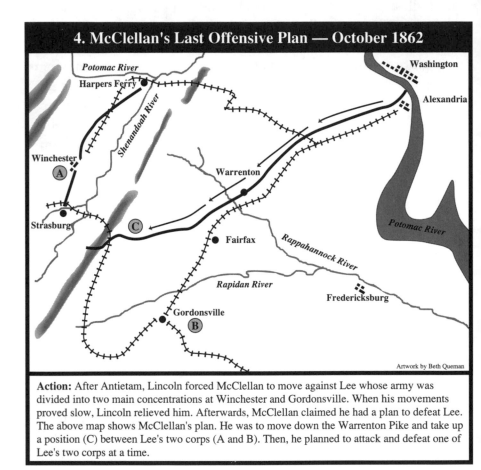

4. McClellan's Last Offensive Plan — October 1862

Artwork by Beth Queman

Action: After Antietam, Lincoln forced McClellan to move against Lee whose army was divided into two main concentrations at Winchester and Gordonsville. When his movements proved slow, Lincoln relieved him. Afterwards, McClellan claimed he had a plan to defeat Lee. The above map shows McClellan's plan. He was to move down the Warrenton Pike and take up a position (C) between Lee's two corps (A and B). Then, he planned to attack and defeat one of Lee's two corps at a time.

Winchester and Longstreet's at Gordonsville. With his great advantage in numbers, such a strategy might have proved successful although there is little reason to believe that McClellan had suddenly become a good, aggressive leader. Such a strategy seems to have had better chances of success than that followed by Burnside later that year at Fredericksburg.

*   *   *

After Antietam, Lincoln concluded that since the drawn battle had ended with Lee's retreat, it justified his issuing the Emancipation Proclamation and issuing a decree suspending *habeas corpus*. The Emancipation Proclamation changed the war from one to save the Union to a crusade to abolish slavery.[19]

This was both a political and strategic triumph because in one blow it gave the North moral ascendancy over the South and stopped the almost successful Confederate efforts in Britain, France and other foreign countries to gain their recognition and support. In addition, since a small minority of plantation owners owned the great majority of the slaves and a majority in the South cared little about slavery, this action was expected to drive a wedge between these factions in the South. The suspension of *habeas corpus* produced a less democratic legal system which dealt more harshly with Confederate sympathizers and those opposing the war effort but had little other effect. From a strategic standpoint, these actions by Lincoln, which arose directly from Davis's and Lee's strategic weaknesses, were devastating to the Confederacy.

* * *

Strategically and in spite of the Union armies having more soldiers, during the first seven months of following Lee's methods of waging war, the cost to the South was *more* real casualties (killed and wounded) than to the North—44,000 to 41,200.[20] With only a third of the white population that the North had, the South could not win a war of attrition, and Lee's actions seemed to support his desire to fight a war of attrition. The only factor the North needed to win the war was time to develop improved leadership. Several excellent leaders were learning their trade and would soon be ready for assignments as generals-in-chief.

What was Lee's "report card" like after seven months of command?

1. He had driven the Union army away from Richmond.
2. He had entered into a war of attrition he could not win.

3. He had followed commonplace strategies compared with those more decisive ones Jackson had suggested.

4. He had shown great skill fighting on the defensive.

5. He had shown little skill in fighting offensive battles but had shown a proclivity to do so.

6. His invasion of the North had failed miserably.

7. He had shown little strategic vision, choosing only to react to the next problem imposed upon him by his enemies.

8. He had cost his country huge casualties for little advantage.

CHAPTER IX

Fredericksburg, Where Lee Won but Missed a Great Strategic Opportunity

In December 1862 at the Battle of Fredericksburg, Lee defined himself as a general satisfied with accomplishing only limited objectives when he chose to defend the Rappahannock line. The over-eager and incompetent Burnside, driven by Lincoln to accomplish anything, was ripe to be ambushed. By rejecting Jackson's plan to draw Burnside into a deep and perhaps fatal trap, Lee passed up a chance to take strong action that could have changed the outcome of the war. Such chances were rare. Unlike Jackson, Lee was not efficient in recognizing real and enormous stategic opportunities.

*I*n late 1862, both sides were trying to recover from the huge battles of August and September, Manassas II, Antietam and South Mountain where both sides combined lost about 50,000 men; the 26,000 Americans lost at Antietam was more than in any other one-day battle of the war.[1] During that fall, the two corps of the Confederate army occupied two areas: one around Winchester in the Shenandoah Valley and the other about 80 miles away around Gordonsville on the Rapidan River.

On the Union side, Major General Ambrose E. Burnside had

replaced McClellan as commander of the Army of the Potomac. Burnside was an unimaginative general who had questioned his own abilities to command the army when he was first offered it earlier in the war. On this point he was correct, but he did not prove right about many other things. He apparently took the command to prevent it from being given to Hooker whom he thoroughly hated. The single thing he could be depended upon to do was to blindly follow the orders of his superiors whether such orders were strategically sound or not, and he proved not to be skillful in executing any orders. His Confederate opponents knew Burnside well enough from the pre-war army to be convinced that they could take full advantage of his very limited abilities and many faults.

In November Burnside was under heavy pressure from Lincoln to act so he decided to assemble the Army of the Potomac opposite Fredericksburg, cross the Rappahannock and drive south around the right flank of the Army of Northern Virginia. Rapidity of movement and using great security to maintain the secrecy of his moves were the principal requirements for his plan to be successful. Lee's cavalry accurately identified Burnside's intentions just after his move began, and Lee ordered Jackson's corps in the Valley and Longstreet's near Gordonsville to move rapidly east to Fredericksburg. The Army of the Potomac moved sluggishly so the Army of Northern Virginia won the race and occupied strong defensive positions on Marye's Heights above Fredericksburg.

Slowly, Burnside prepared to assault these defenses, fully disclosing the details of his intentions as he proceeded. Jackson foresaw that the Union forces could not win such an assault, but he believed winning a defensive battle and then going back to the positions both armies had held before would serve no good strategic purpose for the Confederacy. He believed that whatever casualties the South suffered would only involve wasting the lives of good men for no good purpose.[2]

Knowing Burnside's determination to attack under almost any circumstances, Jackson proposed an alternative strategy to Lee

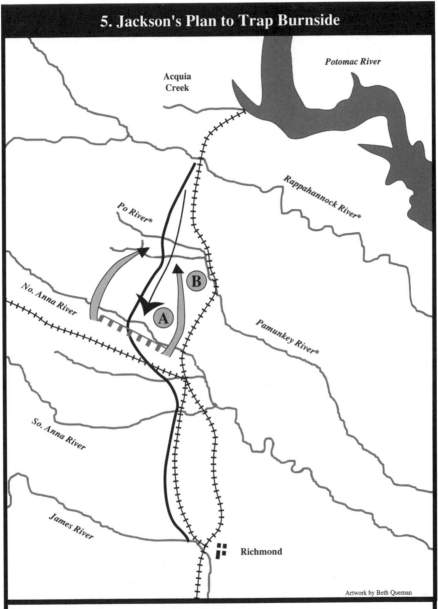

5. Jackson's Plan to Trap Burnside

Potomac River

Acquia
Creek

Po River*

Rappahannock River*

No. Anna River

B

A

Pamunkey River*

So. Anna River

James River

Richmond

Artwork by Beth Queman

A. Jackson planned to draw Burnside to the North Anna River where a strong defensive position was established.
B. After Burnside's attack was spent, assaults around each of his flanks would be made with reserves.
C. Bridges over the rivers marked with asterisks (*) would be destroyed by cavalry; these rivers could not easily be forded.

which would elicit a Union attack but also had the potential to destroy the Army of the Potomac. He had selected a defensive position on the North Anna River and he proposed that the Army of Northern Virginia retreat grudgingly to this position. He was sure Burnside, under Lincoln's prodding, would follow the Confederates to the North Anna, and Jackson thought Burnside was not intelligent enough to realize that he was marching into a trap in time to avoid disaster.

Under Jackson's plan, engineers would be ordered to build strong fortifications secretly along the south bank of the North Anna before the troops arrived; and, when the Lee's army finished its slow but orderly retreat, it would occupy the strong defenses and defend them with vigor. A major advantage of the North Anna position was that it was chosen so that the attackers would have little flank protection; thus when their attack was spent, flanking counter-attacks by a reserve of fresh Confederate troops might surround and destroy all or part of Burnside's army.[3]

Jackson would make the Army of the Potomac's retreat more difficult by sending Stuart's cavalry around them to destroy bridges over the Po and Rappahannock rivers which could be forded in only a few places. He believed this could result in the total destruction of the Army of the Potomac as an effective force either in the fighting along the North Anna or in the ensuing chase.

The Fredericksburg position had no such potential advantage to the Confederates once they successfully withheld the Federal assault. Even if routed at Fredericksburg, the Union army could defend the line of the Rappahannock from which it had less than 12 miles to retreat by rail or road to Aquia Creek, a tributary of the Potomac River, where it could be reinforced or evacuated by Union gunboats. However, if routed at the North Anna position, the beaten army would have 37 miles to travel to Aquia Creek, and it would have to cross the deep Po and Rappahannock rivers while under attack by pursuing Confederates.

Lee refused to accept Jackson's strategy. This rejection may have been based on an unwillingness to give up Virginia territory even temporarily in baiting a trap. It is also possible that the rejection was based on Davis's insistence on fighting only a perimeter war. Another possibility was that Lee thought the Northern people had had enough after Antietam, and they were tired of heavy losses and would soon sue for peace after another failure. If the latter was his reasoning, it is strange he did not consider these things about his own people. It is also possible that at that time Lee, himself, was tired of the slaughter and wanted to minimize it.

The Battle of Fredericksburg was won by Lee where he lost 5,300 casualties to the Union's 12,700.[4] Afterwards, both armies retained the same strategic position they had before the battle. The Union gained slightly in generalship when Hooker replaced Burnside. The Confederacy gained nothing strategically for their "victory," but Lee had passed up the possible war-ending opportunity Jackson had offered.

*   *   *

As usual when he held the defensive, Lee and his subordinates performed excellently and used sound tactics at Fredericksburg. Jackson said: "My men have sometimes failed to *take* a position, but to *defend one*, never!"[5] Nevertheless, their position faced a threat that could have led to a Confederate defeat if the Union leadership were more efficient. Meade's division attacked up a marshy, wooded draw and reached the crest. Although Meade saw the opportunity that this weak point in the Confederate defenses offered, the opening successful thrust against it was not strong enough, was not supported and was easily isolated and thrown back.[6]

Burnside had planned a general assault against a wide area that included the draw but did not see the importance the draw offered as an unusual opportunity. A more skillful army commander should have recognized the opportunity offered by the draw and allocated reserves to support a main attack against it. As things worked out, the attack up the draw surprised the Confederate defenders who scrambled to put together a force to drive it back; it was a close-run repulse. Against a coordinated attack up the draw supported by Union reserves, such a defensive response would not have been successful, and the battle might have been lost.

A flanking attack against Jackson's left was attempted early in the afternoon, but it was repulsed much more easily than that up the draw.[7] It was at this point in the battle that Burnside decided brute strength could dislodge the defenders from any position they held no matter how strong. From noon on, numerous assaults were ordered up-hill across open land against Marye's Heights on Lee's left.[8] These positions were the strongest that the Confederates held.

The Confederates occupied positions along a stone wall with a sunken road behind it, an ideal natural defensive position. In front of the stone wall, the Union attackers had to advance under flanking and direct fire from all of Longstreet's corps artillery. It was on this field where Longstreet responded to Lee's concern about the number of men Burnside was drawing up to charge the position: "General, if you put every man now on the other side of the Potomac in that field to approach me over the same line, and give me plenty of ammunition, I will kill them all before they reach my line."[9] At the same time, Longstreet's chief of artillery, Edward Porter Alexander assured Longstreet that: "A chicken could not cross that field when we open on it."[10] Burnside's attacks continued until evening when he gave up the attempt, but only after six more unsupported assaults were made on an almost impregnable position.

Lee had won the battle but had gained no real strategic advantage in doing so. His lost 5,000 men, mostly seasoned veterans, would be very difficult for the Confederacy to replace if their shrinking reserves of manpower who wished to and were qualified to fight are considered. On the Union side, replacements were available from the North's larger manpower reserves. The

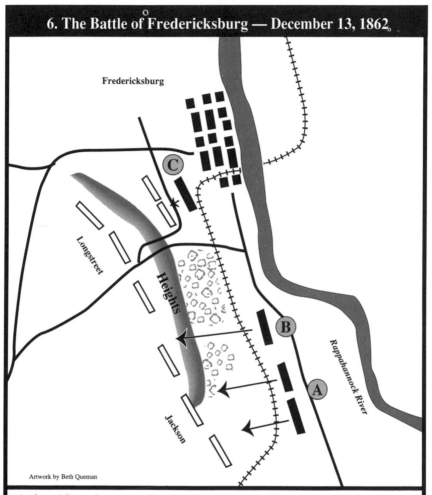

6. The Battle of Fredericksburg — December 13, 1862

Fredericksburg

C

Longstreet

Heights

B

A

Jackson

Rappahannock River

Artwork by Beth Queman

Action: After a slow preparation that allowed Lee to build strong defensive postions along the slopes of the heights west of Fredericksburg, Burnside began to make poorly coordinated assaults on December 13th. His first attacks (A) were made against Jackson's positions and these were repulsed. Meade led an attack up a wooded draw (B) and gained the heights, but he was repulsed with difficulty. In the afternoon, the Army of the Potomac made numerous assaults against Longstreet on the left of the Confederate defenses. About six assaults (C) in all were made against the strongest point of the defenses along the sunken road and the protecting stone wall into fierce artillery and musket fire. The day at Fredericksburg was the most disastrous of the war to the Army of the Potomac, and it was one of Lee's easiest victories.

men of the Army of the Potomac were very tough: they would shrug their shoulders, lick their wounds, replace their losses and make ready to fight again under their next commander.

CHAPTER X

Chancellorsville: The Confederacy's Last Chance to Achieve a Military Victory

At Chancellorsville, Union Major General Joseph Hooker devised a brilliant plan to crush Lee and the Army of Northern Virginia, but his nerve failed him, which prevented the successful execution of the plan. Faced with total destruction, Lee and Jackson mounted an equally brilliant counter-attack. The mortal wounding of Jackson caused the counter-attack to fall far short of his goals, since his subordinates were unable to complete it. The great victory became a Pyrrhic one with huge Confederate losses, and the final Southern opportunity for military victory failed, leaving political collapse in the North as the only possibility for a Confederate victory.

The Battle of Chancellorsville was one of the most complex in the Civil War. Strategically, each side attempted a wide turning movement aimed at destroying the other side's army. In this battle major action occurred, sometimes simultaneously, around Fredericksburg and Chancellorsville, points that are about ten miles apart. Massive maneuvers were made over an area 26 miles by 20 miles.[1]

Hooker was a more skillful commander than Burnside although this would not be much of a compliment. Hooker was unable to understand a battle in its widest scope; he appeared to be able to understand what he could actually see around him; but he could not deal with events very far beyond his vision. This limitation made it impossible for him to command his large army over the large field of the Battle of Chancellorsville. His political naivete interfered with his relations with his civilian superiors. He openly criticized Lincoln and Stanton as well as Burnside when the latter commanded the Army of the Potomac, along with most other prominent Union generals, but he felt this was unimportant since he was "right" in his own eyes.

Going into the Battle of Chancellorsville, Hooker had 133,000 soldiers and 428 pieces of artillery; Lee had 60,000 men and 170 cannons; further, the Union artillery was significantly superior in quality to that of the South. Hooker originated an excellent plan to use his numerical superiority to outflank and surround Lee. On April 29, 1863 he began a wide turning movement when he moved about 54,000 men over Kelly's Ford on the Rappahannock and then over Ely and Germanna fords on the Rapidan, ten miles in back of Lee's left flank. He stationed Sedgwick with about 40,000 men at Fredericksburg, and he left 36,000 men under Couch in a reserve north of the river midway between his two forces.[2]

At first Confederate scouts believed this was a Union detachment on the way to occupy the Shenandoah Valley, since Kelly's Ford was so far away from Confederate positions. When Hooker's right wing crossed the Rapidan, Lee held the center position between the two parts (Hooker's and Sedgwick's) of the Army of the Potomac which threatened to surround him. Lee apparently did not realize Hooker had more than 54,000 men, and depending on how Hooker used his reserve, each part of his force could be numerically stronger than Lee's whole army. The center position was one of Napoleon's favorites in battle since it allowed him the use of interior lines to concentrate against and defeat one part of the enemy even if it had superior numbers overall while holding the other at bay with a much smaller force.

When Lee saw that only I and VI Corps, under Sedgwick's overall command, were crossing the Rappahannock in front of Fredericksburg on April 29th, he correctly concluded that this was not a large enough force to be the Union army's main effort. He also concluded that Hooker must be trying to turn his left flank, and this was soon confirmed by reports from Stuart's cavalry and Lee's extensive spy system. Lee left one division (10,000 men) under Early to defend the heights.[3] Hooker's orders to Sedgwick were to cross the river and advance against the Confederate positions, threatening them, but he was not to make a full-scale attack unless he was certain he could win. Hooker's orders were vague; and, he was too far away and his communication system was too poor to change them; thus, Sedgwick did not follow up an opportunity to capture the heights easily and threaten the rear of Lee's main force.

Leaving Darius Couch's reserve at Bank's Ford, Hooker's portion of the Army of the Potomac, the II, V, XI and XII Corps, moved west and crossed the Rappahannock at Kelly's Ford. Then, they crossed the Rapidan at Germanna and Ely's fords. Hooker planned to advance along the south bank of the river and open both Bank's and U.S. fords for easier communications with Sedgwick's force. They succeeded in opening U.S. Ford but were not able to reach Bank's Ford. This seemingly small failure eventually doomed Hooker's effort.[4]

Before 6:00 A.M. on April 30th, Lee's forces had moved west from Marye's Heights and were dug in along a line on both sides of Zoan Church. Jackson had arrived at about 11:00 A.M. and immediately ordered an advance by Brigadier General Lafayette McLaws westward along the Orange Turnpike while Brigadier General Richard H. Anderson was to advance along the Orange Plank Road. McLaws drove Sykes's corps back and Anderson advanced unopposed, soon outflanking Sykes.[5]

Hooker had stated his expectations in advance: "Our enemy

must either ingloriously flee or come out of his defenses and give us a battle on our own ground where certain destruction awaits him."[6] Believing he controlled the fate of Lee's army, Hooker was astonished when Jackson attacked him in the open fields east of Chancellorsville and drove his advancing forces back into the heavy woods of the Wilderness.

Having made a brilliant strategic move to gain a good position from which he could conduct a strong offensive, Hooker's retreat placed the Army of the Potomac on the defensive in a much poorer position than that from which it had been driven during the battle that had occurred around Zoan Church. In view of his enormous advantage in numbers, 133,000 to 60,000, and the army's success in gaining such a tactically strong position, Hooker's decision to go over to the defensive shattered the morale of his officers and men. They knew the army's prospect had changed from a promising offensive scheme which promised likely victory to waiting for what Lee would do. Hooker had given the initiative up to Lee whom they feared and respected.[7] In effect, Hooker had voluntarily given up offensive operations, and he was now waiting for Lee to attack him. Candidly, Hooker later said: "I lost confidence in Joe Hooker."

Once again Hooker's retreat showed that a battle is usually won by the general who can influence the mind of his opponent, not by brutal charges. Jackson's unexpected spoiling attack had turned Hooker into a beaten general early in this major battle. For both sides, the question remaining was whether Hooker would prove able to recover his nerve in time to take advantage of the strong position he still held and use it as a base from which to win the battle.

As Lee and Jackson met on cracker boxes around a campfire in the pre-dawn hours of May 2, 1863, they discussed the alternative strategies available and reduced them to one: their only alternative was to attack Hooker's right flank. A frontal assault against Hooker's larger and defensively well prepared army in its very strong wooded position was impossible and his left flank, his main escape route over U.S. Ford, was strongly protected all the way to the river. Lee's thorough cavalry scouts had determined that Hooker's right flank was "in the air," that is, this flank was not protected by any strong terrain feature such as a hill, river or lake or by strongly manned defensive works. The only viable movement that could be made was obvious: there was no need for either general to think of it in a flash of insight.[8]

The question they had to decide was how many men should make the move. Jackson proposed to take his whole corps, 26,000 men, leaving Lee with only about 17,000 to hold against Hooker's front. Lee said "go ahead."[9] For the fourth time since the fighting on the Peninsula, Jackson gave Lee the opportunity to destroy the Army of the Potomac. This was the only time Lee accepted Jackson's plan, and most importantly, Lee left it up to Jackson to decide how and where to strike Hooker's right.

The greatest risk for Lee in making the flanking attack was that Hooker might discover the move before the attack was ready and order part of his army to move deeply between Jackson's force and those that remained with Lee. Hooker could then turn to face each force and first destroy the weaker and then concentrate against the stronger. This was a risk of real and final Confederate disaster which Lee clearly recognized; he alone accepted full responsibility for the risk and expected full credit for any success. Jackson's only responsibility in the situation was to make the flanking attack successfully.

It took most of the day of May 2nd for Jackson to move around the Army of the Potomac since the move could only be successful if Hooker did not make preparations to meet it. Complete secrecy was the only way to guarantee that such preparations could not be made. Secrecy proved to be inadequate because as Jackson moved down the Furnace Road toward Catharine Furnace, Union artillery observers in the treetops at Hazel Grove saw his marching troops. Rifled artillery from over 2,000 yards away opened fire and Stuart's horse artillery answered in an artillery duel that continued for 45 minutes.

Jackson detached the 3rd Georgia Regiment to protect his flank, but he kept his main body moving quickly away from where they had been observed. Sickles's III Corps, which had crossed U.S. Ford on May 1st, were the troops that made a sortie against Jackson. Sickles reported to Hooker: "...a continuous column - infantry, artillery, trains and ambulances - observed for three hours moving apparently in a southerly direction toward Orange Court House...The movement indicated a retreat on Gordonsville or an attack upon our right flank...."[10] Sickles sent forces south to interrupt the movement; but by the time they arrived, Jackson's main force had moved on. Sickles's men continued searching until 6:30 P.M. when they learned of Jackson's attack and retreated to join Hooker's main force.

The Army of the Potomac was dug in along the Orange Turnpike facing south. At Dowdell's Tavern, the largest part formed a salient pointing south around Chancellorsville. Across the base of the salient, Bullock Road led to Chambers from which the road continued to U.S. Ford; Meade's V Corps protected the route to U.S. Ford.

At about 5:00 P.M., Jackson ordered his attack to begin eastwardly along the Orange Turnpike behind the Union position. His lead brigades were ordered not to stop their movement under any circumstances. Jackson's attack on the right flank of Oliver O. Howard's XI Corps was four brigades wide with seven behind them, 26,000 men in all. It was centered around the Orange Turnpike, near to which Howard had set his lines. Only a very small weakly fortified return about 400 feet long protected his right flank. Jackson's front was over 5,000 feet wide so the return was totally inadequate to give the Federals any protection against the kind of attack that fell upon them. The attackers quickly overwhelmed Howard's flank and rear, and then they rolled up his force for a mile within a half hour.[11]

Repeatedly, Howard set up defense lines perpendicular to the road, but Jackson's men overran all of them. Brigadier General Alfred H. Colquitt, on the right flank of the attack, incorrectly

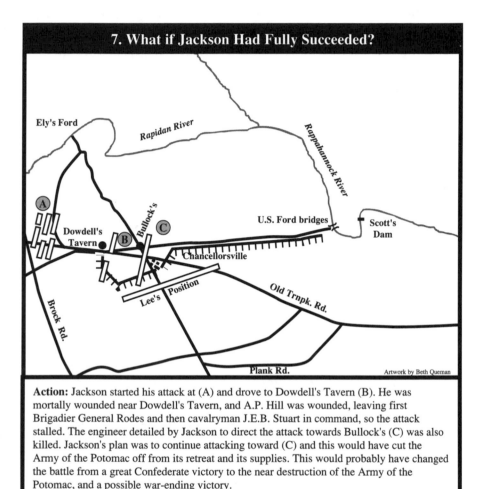

7. What if Jackson Had Fully Succeeded?

Artwork by Beth Queman

Action: Jackson started his attack at (A) and drove to Dowdell's Tavern (B). He was mortally wounded near Dowdell's Tavern, and A.P. Hill was wounded, leaving first Brigadier General Rodes and then cavalryman J.E.B. Stuart in command, so the attack stalled. The engineer detailed by Jackson to direct the attack towards Bullock's (C) was also killed. Jackson's plan was to continue attacking toward (C) and this would have cut the Army of the Potomac off from its retreat and its supplies. This would probably have changed the battle from a great Confederate victory to the near destruction of the Army of the Potomac, and a possible war-ending victory.

felt a Union attack was imminent against his right flank, and he disobeyed Jackson's order to "stop at nothing." Eventually, this action slowed the advance and intermingled the Confederate units. Without Colquitt's halt, the results might have been even more devastating to the Union army than they proved to be. At 7:15 P.M., Rodes's division halted only a mile and a half from the Federal center and only a half mile from the Bullock Road at Chambers which was Hooker's main line of retreat toward U.S. Ford. [12]

If he were to destroy Hooker's army, Jackson knew he must reach all three of these critical objectives: Hazel Grove and Fairview Hills, where he could place artillery that would dominate the Union positions, and Chambers, possession of which would cut off retreat for the Army of the Potomac.

Insistent that the attack continue into the night until the three objectives were achieved, Jackson and a party of his staff scouted toward Chambers. Just prior to this move, Union Brigadier General Alfred Pleasonton, who commanded a brigade of cavalry, made a rare mounted charge against the Confederate infantry. The Union cavalry charge and the general confusion always present in an ongoing attack, combined with the dusk of early evening, caused the Confederate infantrymen to mistake Jackson and his party for another Union cavalry force, and they fired into them.[13]

Jackson was hit three times, and one wound through his upper arm that shattered the bone was severe. A.P. Hill, his second in command, was wounded and put out of action a few minutes later. No Confederate infantry commander ranking above brigadier general remained who was strong enough and experienced enough to sustain a night attack. As tragic as Jackson's loss was at the time, the critical loss was Captain J. Keith Boswell who was killed instantly. Boswell was the engineering officer Jackson had detailed to lead the corps to Chambers. With neither Boswell or Jackson, no one was prepared to continue the attack without a pause to regroup and think things over. In addition, no one knew that Chambers was the key objective. The senior officer on the scene, Brigadier General Robert E. Rodes, halted at 7:15 to reorganize and the assault was never resumed; this pause, when it happened, eliminated the possibility of Jackson's hoped-for decisive success from the action.[14]

After the Confederate assault ground to a halt on the night of May 2nd, the Union forces strengthened their defenses. They were still 75,000 men on the defense against less than 40,000 attackers, and the Confederates were split into two forces. Once Jackson's hammer-blow had run its course and without his strong leadership, the Confederate opportunity to annihilate Hooker's wing of the Army of the Potomac was forever lost. Now under Stuart's command, Jackson's corps eventually joined Lee's force, and Hooker remained on the defensive behind strong entrenchments.

On May 3rd, Sedgwick attacked Early and succeeded in moving around his left flank threatening Lee's rear. Lee left only 6,000 men in front of Hooker's 75,000 and turned on Sedgwick. He drove Sedgwick back over the Rappahannock as Hooker, now mentally beaten and suffering from a head wound, remained inactive behind his fortifications. After Sedgwick was defeated, Hooker also retreated to the north side of the river.[15]

*　　*　　*

Behind the action on the ground, Chancellorsville was a battle between the intelligence resources of Lee and Hooker. Since they were in Confederate territory, Lee had spies everywhere behind the Federal lines, and Stuart's cavalry did an outstanding job of scouting Union army movements. The politically minded Union generals made many breaches of security when they bragged to newspaper reporters about their ideas and plans, and the Northern newspapers printed almost everything. Lee received newspapers from Washington, Baltimore and Philadelphia a day after they were printed which allowed him to know much of what the other side was thinking. Southern generals were more security minded, and Confederate newspapers were far more careful about what they printed.

After McClellan lost command, Alan Pinkerton resigned as the Army of the Potomac's intelligence chief because he felt McClellan had been unfairly treated. Although Pinkerton's intelligence service had been poor, Burnside and Hooker had developed no effective replacement. To make matters worse, Hooker sent 80% of his cavalry on a raid toward Richmond so he did not have enough cavalry left to do adequate scouting. If this raid had been directed against Lee's major supply depot at Guinea Station, it might well have affected the outcome of the battle. As it was, the raid accomplished no useful purpose in support of Hooker's actions. Hooker was in unfriendly territory so Union spies were scarce. The Army of the Potomac had one advantage, three balloons tethered 1,000 feet above the heights on the north side of the Rappahannock.[16]

These "aeronauts" reported Lee was moving most of his forces westward from the works above Fredericksburg. Hooker read this as an intent by Lee to attack him so he stopped his advance near Zoan Church and formed a defense line there. Sedgwick also received this report that Lee's main force was moving west, but he failed to take advantage of the information by attacking Early strongly and then falling on Lee's rear.

Jackson's flanking movement was too far away for the aeronauts to see. Ironically, the aeronaut corps was disbanded after Chancellorsville and the balloons were sold as government surplus. This decision was made on the advice of Major General Daniel Butterfield, Hooker's chief-of-staff, who declared them to be of no value. The importance of the Round Tops at Gettysburg for observation purposes showed how useful balloons could have been there. The abandonment of balloons was one of the Union army's most short-sighted decisions of the Civil War.

In another irony, Lee's otherwise excellent intelligence sources did not do well in counting the numbers in each of Hooker's separate forces or his whole strength. As the battle moved forward, Lee continued to believe that Hooker had about 75,000 men in all and thought Hooker's detachment that crossed the Rapidan consisted of only 15,000 to 25,000 men. The moves he made that were based on this poor information might not have been made if he had known Hooker had 133,000 men available to him. He might have decided the moves he actually made later were too reckless.

Based on the intelligence Hooker had, Jackson's flanking movement should not have come as a surprise. The records show

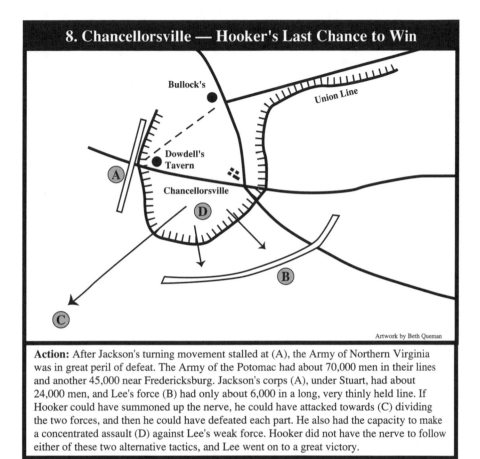

8. Chancellorsville — Hooker's Last Chance to Win

Bullock's

Union Line

Dowdell's
Tavern

A

Chancellorsville

D

B

C

Artwork by Beth Queman

Action: After Jackson's turning movement stalled at (A), the Army of Northern Virginia was in great peril of defeat. The Army of the Potomac had about 70,000 men in their lines and another 45,000 near Fredericksburg. Jackson's corps (A), under Stuart, had about 24,000 men, and Lee's force (B) had only about 6,000 in a long, very thinly held line. If Hooker could have summoned up the nerve, he could have attacked towards (C) dividing the two forces, and then he could have defeated each part. He also had the capacity to make a concentrated assault (D) against Lee's weak force. Hooker did not have the nerve to follow either of these two alternative tactics, and Lee went on to a great victory.

that at least ten sightings or reconnaissances by Union officers were made on the 2nd that identified Jackson's column moving across the Union front. Sickles had spotted Jackson's corps which was accurately described as to its size and movement in a southwestward direction. He reported this to Hooker, stating it might be a movement against the Union right flank. Howard sent cavalry to scout to the west of his right flank, and they found a large force of Confederate cavalry on their flank and rear.[17] He asked Hooker why they would be there except to screen an attacking force? Self-delusion reigned as Hooker assured Howard that the Confederate cavalry was screening a general Confederate retreat toward Gordonsville.

In other words, Hooker began the battle believing Lee would retreat once he saw that his army had crossed the Rapidan in force in two places. No matter what Hooker learned to the contrary, he discounted everything negative to his original point of view, ignored what the other side might do and deluded himself that only his original idea could be true. In doing this, Hooker failed to consider or even identify the worst thing that could happen to him. It eventually did!

At any time after Jackson's attack halted, Hooker had the material resources to win the battle. On the 3rd, before the two Confederate corps were rejoined around Chancellorsville, he could have driven between them and eventually defeated each portion. At almost any time, if he had ordered a convergent attack on Lee's portion of the army by Sedgwick and himself, he could have destroyed that force and then dealt with Jackson's corps later. In spite of Lee's and Jackson's brilliant tactics, their victory required an opponent like Hooker, overcome with confusion and timidity, to *lose* the battle. Without Hooker losing his nerve, Jackson would not have had time to devise the counter-stroke; therefore without the time Hooker gave him, Lee would not have *won* the battle.

* * *

There can be no doubt that the Battle of Chancellorsville was a clear victory for Lee and the Confederacy. Lee's problem was that from a strategic standpoint he was right back where he was before the battle had occurred: defending along the Rappahannock River line. Also strategically, the Army of Northern Virginia had lost 12,821 men (22% of the army); these losses raised the question of whether the Confederacy could continue to survive such victories. While the Army of the Potomac lost

17,273 men, this was only 13% of the army, and the North was in a better long-run position to sustain such horrible losses.[18]

If Jackson had remained in the field and accomplished his objectives, Chancellorsville might have brought a far different result. The Union losses would have been much higher. Perhaps enough of the Army of the Potomac would have been destroyed so as to eliminate it for a time as an effective fighting force, and Confederate losses should have been lower. In the short-run, Jackson's mortal wounding may have cost the Confederacy a devastating victory that might have been war-ending.

In the long-run, Jackson's loss cost Lee his most effective subordinate. A massive victory at Chancellorsville would have so enhanced Jackson's stature that his strategic ideas could no longer have been ignored, even by Davis and Lee. If a disastrous loss at Chancellorsville had not brought down the Union, it would have destroyed the confidence the Army of the Potomac had in its leaders and itself. Union politicians would have lost confidence that the Army of the Potomac could continue to protect them. In all likelihood, Jackson and Lee could have devised a campaign against such a weakened Union army that might have ended the war. The fact that Lee trusted and depended on no other subordinate as he had Jackson made continued effective action by Lee unlikely.

Essentially, Jackson was a defensive general. He believed in setting ambushes, counter-attacking a weakened foe, making turning movements against the enemy's flanks or attacking a foe who lacked confidence or was over-confident. He had supreme confidence in his ability to dominate all the Union generals he had so far faced on an intellectual level. He believed in setting up a secure defense as he had at Manassas II and forcing the enemy to attack him under circumstances favorable to Jackson. After Chancellorsville, with Jackson gone, Lee reverted to what he wanted most to do—make brutal, frontal attacks. After Jackson's loss, no one had a strong enough influence over Lee to counter

this tendency in him, and it eventually brought defeat to the
Confederacy.

CHAPTER XI

Both Sides Had to Change the Prevailing Military Doctrine; Was Lee's Best Performance Against Poor Union Commanders?

After Chancellorsville, Lee faced many changes. The pre-Civil War military doctrine employed by both sides had failed badly against weapons that had been radically improved technically since 1847. The Union had discarded its first incompetent commanders in the East, McDowell, Pope, Burnside, McClellan, and Hooker. In June 1863, a more efficient general, Major General George G. Meade, became Army of the Potomac commander. Lee had lost forever his best subordinate, Jackson. Lee had performed well against poor Union leadership. Was this low quality of Union leadership the reason Lee had performed as well as he did? Would Lee be able to accommodate well to the forthcoming changes?

In war, certain objectives or actions come up repeatedly. The prevailing military doctrine is defined as a catalog of standardized best methods whereby an army can overcome these repetitive problems. These objectives occur in all wars although the methods and weapons used to achieve them change from one war to another. These are a few examples of many such frequently repeated objectives:

- Attack a stronger enemy with infantry and artillery.
- Cross a river under fire and establish a sustainable bridgehead.
- Defend against an infantry attack.
- Attack or defend a fort.
- Attack or defend a strongly fortified defensive line.
- Fight successfully in the woods.
- Delay an attacking force until a sustainable defense can be established or reinforcements arrive.

The reason an army develops and promulgates doctrine is to avoid the necessity of each unit having to "invent" methods to meet repetitive situations over and over again. Hopefully, determining in advance how best to meet such situations will avoid many failures and reduce loss of life.

The United States appears to have repeatedly entered its major wars with an out-dated military doctrine designed to face the technical circumstances of and to win its previous war. This is particularly noticeable when the country had failed to maintain a significant peace-time military force between its wars. In World War I, pre-war military doctrine failed all participants, and that war degenerated into the stalemate of trench warfare neither side could win without changes in generalship, weapons, doctrine and tactics. New doctrine that brought the effective use of strafing airplanes and armored vehicles into front line action led to the breaking of the stalemate. Because the Allies adapted new doctrine sooner and better than the enemy, they were victorious. Before they entered World War I, American soldiers were not prepared for these new doctrinal changes, and they had to learn them in action which led to the waste of many lives.

When American troops landed in Europe in World War II, they

were ill-prepared for fighting in Normandy hedge rows, fighting in cities or villages, crossing rivers, attacking forts and deeply fortified defense lines.[1] The pre-World War II doctrine as promulgated in U.S. army protocols did not work well for any of these actions, and if the army was to be successful, the doctrine had to be changed radically and quickly.

The fact that the campaign to defeat Nazism was under way with an old, failed doctrine forced American troops to devise new ideas quickly and well, and new doctrines were forged as they fought their way across Europe.

Before World War II, the combined use of infantry, armor, tactical air strikes and artillery was not proposed in U.S. doctrine or practiced except in the single area of break-through tactics. The key to the development of an effective doctrine was the use of these combined forces in most repetitive combat situations. In 1944, doctrinal changes usually worked best when developed from the bottom up. The time it took for this new doctrine to be formulated and promulgated to all the units of the army that had to use it cost many lives while the army followed the development process while under the fire of a skilled enemy.[2]

Preparations for the Civil War were no exception to the "American rule" of being poorly prepared for war. The promulgated doctrine with which both sides began the war would have been good preparation for the Mexican War, but it did not work well against the *Minie* rifled musket or rifled artillery. The central idea of pre-Civil War doctrine was the use of large close order formations facing one another about 100 yards apart. First, artillery would blast holes in the opposing infantry line with canister, and then infantrymen would charge into the breaches and dispatch the enemy with the bayonet. Against the short-range, inaccurate fire from smooth-bore muskets, this doctrine might have been relatively effective. In 1861, these tactics did not work because the rifled musket was effective at 300 yards, and at 100 yards cannoneers were picked off before the remaining steps of the old doctrine could be implemented. Without effective artillery preparation, very few infantrymen had the nerve to sustain a 300-yard charge against the new weapons even if they survived among their many falling comrades.

Jackson had proposed changes in doctrine and used them in the battles he fought independently. Manassas II was such an example where he set up a strong defensive position, induced Pope to wear his army out in futile attacks following the normal, "old," doctrine, and then, he offered Lee and Longstreet an opportunity to crush Pope with an attack on his open flank. Chancellorsville gave another example where a frontal assault was rejected, but a wide turning movement led to an assault on Hooker's open flank.

In most wars, one important dilemma faced by every commander is whether to make it his main aim to destroy the enemy army or to gain territory. Capturing territory is usually easier and less costly in lives in the short-run than trying to destroy the enemy army. Over the centuries it appears it often takes most of a war for a general to learn that if the enemy army is destroyed or rendered ineffective, territory will fall without much further effort. As a corollary it may take most of a war to find a general who thinks in this way. In attempting to destroy the enemy, one key is to avoid costly frontal assaults as Jackson did at Chancellorsville, Manassas II and in his Shenandoah Valley campaigns.

In the Civil War in mid-1863, it seems clear that both sides in the East were about equal in raw power. Lee's victories against poor Union generals had been Pyrrhic and he still held the same territory. Up to that time, neither side had shown the ability to dominate the other. It appears likely the side that did the better job of improving its doctrine would win the war, but first a commander with substantial authority would have to understand the need for changes in doctrine. Before Union generalship began to show marked improvement in mid-1863, Lee had this opportunity; therefore, one of the measures to be applied to the quality of his generalship is how energetically and creatively he approached doctrinal problems.

CHAPTER XI

*   *   *

When the Confederacy lost Jackson, it lost many values that could not be replaced. Besides being a great leader and fighter, Jackson was an intellectual general who quickly saw the deficiencies in the prevailing military doctrine. He also saw that the South could not win a war where their losses were equal to their enemies, a war of attrition. Based on their actions, Davis and Lee had not realized Jackson's ideas were valid, but he continued to try to influence them by offering sound alternatives to their tendencies to make direct attacks. His death meant they would likely continue to expend Confederate lives too liberally. Generals like Longstreet, who shared Jackson's opinions, did not have the prestige, charisma, or influence to alter matters.

Jackson had also made a compromise with the choice of destroying the enemy or gaining territory. He believed opportunities would arise when the South could destroy or disable the Army of the Potomac if he could develop certain strategies to take advantage of Union over-aggressiveness or exhaustion or if the Union commander made a mistake. Repeats of his strategy at Manassas II would be an example of taking advantage of Federal over-aggressiveness. Finding a way to counter attack after a Union assault would take advantage of his enemy's exhaustion. Chancellorsville offers an example of taking advantage of the enemy commander's mistakes and overconfidence.

A variation he frequently proposed that could draw an attack by Union forces would be the capture of a Northern city that was too important for the Federal Army to ignore. As long as the quality of Union commanders did not improve radically, it was a reasonable expectation that many such opportunities would continue to arise.

The loss of Jackson eliminated many opportunities for the South since they had no replacement for him tactically, strategically or intellectually. The question that remains is whether Union generals could improve in quality quickly enough to defeat

Lee and the generals remaining in the field before the North's war effort collapsed politically.

*   *   *

From the start of the Civil War through May 1863, the Union army in the East, the Army of the Potomac, had been commanded by generals McDowell, McClellan, Burnside and Hooker, and Pope had commanded another Union army in Virginia. All these generals proved to be inefficient and incomplete commanders who failed in at least one of the many qualifications a commander needed to be successful: skill in organization, strategic planning in his overall command area, battle planning, tactics, charisma, keeping his army supplied and providing leadership that generated loyalty on the part of his soldiers.

McDowell had little chance to show whatever skills he had; he commanded an army that was quickly thrown together and poorly trained; and at the same time, it had unreal expectations of easy and quick victory. The force that later became the Army of the Potomac lost the First Battle of Manassas under McDowell. Both sides were unprepared and therefore fought poorly. His defeat was more by chance than by lack of skill. Nevertheless, the defeat ended McDowell's career as an important Union army commander, and he did not command the Army of the Potomac against Lee later in the war.

Major General George B. McClellan, the "young Napoleon," showed great skill at organizing the huge army that eventually became the Army of the Potomac. There is no doubt that McClellan was essential to the eventual success of the Federal Army since his organization of it was skillfully and well done. His strategic ideas were usually sound, and when he landed on the Virginia Peninsula in force in 1862, he gained a strategic position of strength that the Federal armies were not able to duplicate until mid-1864.

Expert in organization, logistics, and wide-ranging strategy,

McClellan failed in fighting battles. He was neither aggressive nor opportunistic, and he had little imagination in devising a way to *win* a battle. He seemed to be so closely attached to his men that he could not bear to place them at risk. He seemed able to plan well but showed little aptitude or appetite in executing his plans. McClellan obtained great loyalty from his enlisted soldiers, but he ran his officer corps as a gentlemen's club rather than as a disciplined organization. He used the misleading intelligence he received from Pinkerton as an excuse to delay action, and he never tried to verify it. This inability to execute plans efficiently was a hopelessly fatal flaw in McClellan as an army commander.

For a short time John Pope commanded the Union Army of Virginia, an army put together to protect Washington while McClellan was far away on the Peninsula. Pope showed few redeeming qualities as a commander and failed in many aspects of command. It is hard to believe that Lincoln could choose a general who proved less adept to lead the Army of the Potomac than McClellan, but he accomplished this in choosing Burnside. In one of the greatest failings of the Federal Army's seniority system, Burnside gained promotion to major general after a small victory early in the war at New Bern, North Carolina. This action enhanced his reputation far beyond its merit, but his early promotion made him senior to many other more able Union generals. Burnside himself said he was unfit for major command.

Under prodding from Lincoln, Burnside decided to move around Lee's right flank at Fredericksburg where he planned to cross the Rappahannock River. In spite of the fact that his ponderous movements allowed Lee to win the race to Fredericksburg thus preventing a flanking movement, Burnside chose to fight Lee there, and Lee accepted his challenge. Rapid movement was the only tactic that had any chance of giving the Union success at Fredericksburg. They had to accomplish the crossing of the Rappahannock before the Confederates could occupy, reinforce and strengthen the imposing defensive positions on Marye's Heights above the town. Burnside's inefficient movements gave Lee almost a month to occupy and strengthen these positions.

The indecisive Burnside could not settle on a plan; he considered one to move between Lee's two corps and another to move around Lee's right flank. Either plan had an outside chance of success, but Burnside's mediocrity gained control; and he abandoned both better plans for an impossible frontal assault up a strongly defended hill. After his defeat at Fredericksburg, Burnside further showed his lack of capability by attempting to flank the left of Lee's position in impossible weather conditions. This failed when the army bogged down in the notorious "mud march."[3]

Immediately after this, Burnside was relieved and replaced by his personal enemy, Joseph Hooker. Almost anyone would have been superior to Burnside as a commander, and Hooker was. He showed skill as a strategist; his plan to attack Lee in April 1863 was excellent; and he had a good tactical plan to execute his strategy.

His organization failings included his army headquarters becoming known as "Hooker's bar and brothel." It is hard to gain the respect of lower echelon officers and men when the army headquarters gains such a reputation, but Hooker had no sensitivity to this since he thought only his own ego and generalship were important. More consequential, Hooker's most important failings as an army commander were his inability to see and act clearly over a wide field such as Chancellorsville and his unwillingness to consider other possibilities than his own, prejudiced, original viewpoint concerning the situation he faced. This narrow view of things, perhaps a lack of respect for the skill of his enemy and an unwillingness to identify and consider the worst thing that could go wrong proved to be a fatal combination for his command.

These generals' failings are well documented by many original sources and they are described earlier in this volume. These generals entered into battle with Lee with a numerical advantage in almost all cases, and they lost or drew their battles with him. This raises obvious questions which seem to have been ignored by many historians. Did Lee win against them because of their failures rather than as a result of his own skills? Would more competent Union generals have avoided their mistakes and defeated Lee? Did the loss of Jackson and all that he offered so seriously disable Lee's overall generalship that he was unable to replace the loss with his own skills? Was it impossible to replace Jackson's contributions even when all the skills of his major subordinates were added to Lee's?

Lee's actions during the remainder of the war may help to answer these questions.

CHAPTER XII

Lee Invades the North

By May of 1863, the Confederacy was in crisis in the West. Poorly led Southern armies were crumbling as they faced superior Union leaders, Grant and Rosecrans, and the loss of both the Mississippi River and all of middle Tennessee seemed imminent. Lee was holding his own in the East where he had won battles but continued to hold the same strategic position for over a year. If Lee continued to maintain his position in the East, the South could still win a victory, militarily or politically, if it could hold the Mississippi or turn Rosecrans back. At this time, Lee made the decision to strike into the North. Was this decision fatal to the Confederacy?

*A*fter a victory at Manassas II, Lee's performance included a defensive draw at Antietam and defensive victories at Fredericksburg and Chancellorsville against the substantial numerical superiority of his enemy in all cases. The down-side for the Confederacy in these battles was its high casualties. If captured or missing soldiers are ignored since most were returned and an estimate for death from disease is added, real casualties for both armies can be determined. On this basis, Confederate losses were 53,521 and Union losses were 61,953.[1] Since losses tended to be understated more by the South than by the North, these numbers are even closer than they appear. If we add losses from the Peninsula fighting, losses for both sides through May 1863 in the East were almost equal.

Besides these losses which approximate the loss of a substantial army in just nine months, the Army of Northern Virginia lost many high quality officers and men. This approximated losing about a fifth of Lee's army in each major battle. Because the Army of the Potomac was larger, percentage losses for them were about half as much, so proportionally more of their higher quality men survived.

Since the North had a much larger pool of available manpower than the South had, the Confederacy would have extreme difficulty in sustaining its armies as long as it suffered equal real losses. Obviously, if one country could draw on a million men to fuel its army and another could only draw on half a million, it would not take many years of equal losses of soldiers to put the larger country at enormous advantage. Almost by definition, the South could not win an extended war of attrition by any military means.

A number of Southern politicians were promoting the ideas that the Army of Northern Virginia should go over to the defensive in the East; reinforcements should be sent west to save Vicksburg; and new leadership should be sent west to replace Bragg and Pemberton. The principal replacement discussed for Bragg and his superior, J.E. Johnston, was Lee. Davis disliked and did not trust J.E. Johnston, but stood behind Bragg in the face of wide-ranging criticism and a near-mutiny on the part of Bragg's subordinate generals.[2] Aside from the political situation and disagreements between Southern generals, the situation in the West was deteriorating on a day-by-day basis against the superior Union leadership of Grant on the Mississippi and Rosecrans in middle Tennessee.

There was much to be said in argument for the movement of Lee to command in the West, and there were at least three very important reasons against the move. It may have already been too late to save the situation in the West. It might be argued that there was no high-quality replacement for Lee in the East. Moreover, the Army of Northern Virginia had just undergone a substantial reorganization due to its heavy loss of officers and men, and only Lee could hold that army together. No one in the Confederate government was willing to state the first argument, although it was probably valid. The second and third arguments may well have also been valid, but some in the Davis administration forwarded the idea of such a move anyway. Their feelings and political strength appeared not to have been strong enough to cause Davis to issue a direct order to Lee to make the move. Lee spent May 14-17, 1863 with President Davis and his Cabinet where he protested against the move of any part of his army to the West.[3] In hindsight, several personal reasons seem valid from Lee's point of view that would have mitigated against such a move. In a personal paper written to Davis in August, Lee refers to a health [heart] problem that occurred in the spring of 1863.[4] The timing of this incident was close to Chancellorsville and when the decision about Lee moving West was being considered. Being in bad health, with little time to recover from the incident, Lee and Davis, who must have been aware of the details, could reasonably have concluded that moving to a new arena and organizing a new command that was in crisis would be too much of an added strain on Lee's health. If the conclusion were made on this basis, it may have been that they also concluded that the health problem was too serious to expect that a move by Lee to the West could possibly prove successful.

A second personal reason for Lee to be against such a change involves his personal loyalties. Only the secession of his home state, Virginia, produced sufficient Southern loyalty for Lee to leave the Federal Army. Only thirty days before leaving the army, Lee repeated the Oath of Allegiance to the United States, and in those thirty days, discussed the possibility of assuming overall command of the Federal Army with General-in-Chief Winfield Scott.[5]

When he was an officer in the Federal service, Lee gave all the appearances of loyalty to the Union. His separation from the army was very painful to him after 36 years of service from the time he entered West Point. Lee stayed in the U.S. Army as state after state seceded from the Union without giving any sign of leaving. In early 1861, few could clearly predict that Virginia would actually secede, but when it did by close vote in April 1861, Lee decided that his primary loyalty was to his home state, Virginia.

Based on his actions in April 1861, it must be concluded that Lee's loyalties were primarily to his state of Virginia and only remotely to the Confederacy as a whole. If his actions truly reflect Lee's feelings of loyalty, it may be that Lee was unwilling to move to the defense of the Western Confederate states, leaving his home state to another commanding general.

Lee's loyalty to his officers and men may also have played a part in his decision. With Jackson dead, there was no outstanding subordinate general in the army. Outside of the Army of Northern Virginia, generals Beauregard and J.E. Johnston might have been candidates to assume command, and there seemed to be no other possibilities. Beauregard had shown an undependable temperament in other commands,[6] and Lee would probably not have supported such a move. Neither Beauregard nor J.E. Johnston had the confidence and respect of President Davis.[7]

One must conclude that any or all of these factors in combination may have contributed to the decision that left Lee and all of his army in the East in the spring and early summer of 1863. The overriding reasons for his staying were the likelihood of the Union making an offensive move in the East and the lack of strong subordinate generals in the Confederate Army. By the end of the war, 55% of all Southern generals would become casualties (killed or wounded), and some were wounded many times.[8] These losses plus the fact that the South had no selection system for finding high quality generals, as the North did, led to a bankruptcy in their supply.

It would probably have been too much to ask for the Army of

Northern Virginia to send enough of its strength West to affect both situations, along the Mississippi and in middle Tennessee. However, the addition of one of its corps to Bragg's army contributed greatly to the defeat of Rosecrans at the Battle of Chickamauga in September 1863.[9] The movement of one corps to join Bragg in May might have had a similar effect: the defeat of Rosecrans north of the Tennessee River. Additionally, the replacement of Bragg with Lee would have added enormously to the leadership in the West.

*   *   *

Of all people, Bragg proposed a search to replace those generals immediately subordinate to him whom he blamed unfairly for all his failures. Besides Lee, the Confederacy's full generals and lieutenant generals had shown little expertise in terms of strategy, tactics and winning. Even Lee, without Jackson, offered little promise for future victories. In view of the fact that the Army of the Potomac was in great disarray after Chancellorsville, May 1863 was probably *the time* for the Army of Northern Virginia to go on the defensive and send a corps to the West.

Who was the central strategic mind of the Confederacy? Who decided the overall military strategy for the country? It was certainly not Lee. It seems that there was no such mind besides that of Davis for the whole length of the Civil War. A few people, Lee and others, had a minor influence on Davis's decisions and ideas, and he did not draw others, no matter how competent they might be, into important, even critical nation-wide considerations.

For whatever reason, Lee showed his Virginia parochialism and disdain for the most appropriate national strategy by pre-empting all strategies but his own. After obtaining reluctant approval from Davis, Lee launched his ill-advised invasion into Pennsylvania. For this invasion, Lee had no plan, only a vague strategic notion. He spoke to Longstreet of fighting only on the defensive against the Union forces.[10] He hoped to live off the country, making the Northerners suffer as Southerners had after Union invasions of their country, and to cut the Union railroad bridges over the Susquehanna River near Harrisburg. While these long, steel bridges would be hard to replace, the Union had alternative rail routes along the shores of the Great Lakes.

While it is likely that Lee made no firm commitment to Longstreet, there is little doubt that Lee spoke to him at some length about forcing the Army of the Potomac to attack against a position he would choose as being favorable to his army. These words were reminiscent of Jackson's theories. What Lee appears not to have done was to propose a specific objective and plan that would have allowed his strategy to succeed. This difference between specific plans and objectives and a general, loose idea of what should be done seems to define the difference in strategic and tactical thinking between Lee and the late Jackson.

Once his invasion started, Lee wandered around Pennsylvania, and in the following action, Lee did not pursue the Susquehanna objectives strongly. He saw a strong defensive position near Cashtown and prepared to fight a defensive battle against the advancing Army of the Potomac which was obliged to drive the Confederates from their territory, but he was drawn accidentally into an offensive battle at Gettysburg. Instead of ordering his troops to return to the Cashtown position after a successful first day of fighting at Gettysburg, he chose to fight offensively, apparently to make up for a vague, lost strategic advantage of some kind once again.

It is difficult to define a logical combination of strategy and objectives that Lee hoped to achieve when he crossed the Pennsylvania state line. He had no idea of capturing and keeping Northern territory on any long-term basis. If his goal was to destroy or disable the Army of the Potomac, all the data available from the war's actions up to June 1863 clearly indicated that attackers lost many more men than defenders in the same battle. Why, then, did he decide to attack a very strong position at Gettysburg?

CHAPTER XIII

Before Their Greatest Battle Both Sides Undergo a Crisis in Command

After Jackson's death, Lee divided the Army of Northern Virginia into three corps. A.P. Hill and Richard Ewell joined Longstreet as corps commanders. Once this plan was in place, it remained Lee's tendency to allow each corps commander to manage his part of a battle without interference. Did this tendency prove to be a detriment under the new command structure? On the Union side, Lincoln had lost all trust in Hooker so he was replaced with Meade just four days before the Battle of Gettysburg. How did these tremendous changes on both sides affect the outcome of the battle and the war?

The Battle of Chancellorsville radically affected the command structure and internal confidence of both the Union and Confederate armies in the East. Jackson's loss was devastating to Southern hopes. Hooker's actions had convinced Lincoln, Stanton and Halleck that he did not have the skills and qualifications to again be an independent commander of a major Union army.

Both sides were desperately short of well-qualified general officers who knew how to fight and win. The Army of the Potomac had serious problems with their many politically-minded generals, most of whom hated one another, and their inability to set these problems aside for the good of their cause. The President and his subordinates concentrated their efforts on finding a replacement for Hooker. They were forced to leave the rest of the army's shaky command structure alone since trying to solve all these problems at once would almost certainly have brought about a paralysis in command and would have led to disaster. Timing for a command change was bad since the campaign season had begun, and a battle could erupt at any time. They concluded that searching for a commander outside of the Army of the Potomac was also an alternative that might present more problems than solutions.

The administration waited until after Lee had invaded Pennsylvania before they replaced Hooker; this was only a few days before the major Battle of Gettysburg.[1] Their choice of Major General George G. Meade was made over his own protests because he despised the army's politics; besides, he felt Major General John Reynolds was better qualified for the job than he. Meade was well respected in the Army of the Potomac as a soldier and was largely outside of its political hassles. He was not considered to be a brilliant leader, tactician or strategist, and he was feared for his violent temper and generally poor disposition. Having command of a 90,000-man army thrust upon him in the heat of a campaign and under circumstances where the very existence of the Union was threatened did little to improve his disposition. With Lee and his full army nearby, there was nothing Meade could do to improve the organization of the army in spite of his recognition of its many needs for changes. He had no choice but to fight Lee with his army as it was. Meade's knowledge of Lee and his aggressive tendencies made him realize that a battle could occur very soon.

*   *   *

The command problems of the Army of Northern Virginia were more in number and much more severe than those Meade faced.

Jackson's loss required replacement, but Lee had no man with close to the same qualities of Jackson. At this time, Lee chose to reorganize the army into three infantry corps and a cavalry corps. He kept Lieutenant General James Longstreet in command of I Corps and assigned newly promoted lieutenant generals Richard S. Ewell and A.P. Hill to command II and III Corps, respectively.

Trying to understand Longstreet has presented a complex problem to all Civil War historians. His war record is full of contradictions, some real and some constructed in hindsight by his Confederate enemies and biased historians. His memoirs, which cover almost the entire war, are rich in historical facts, but they also contain attacks on other Confederate generals and much self-justification. After the wounded J.E. Johnston was replaced by Lee, Longstreet stated his dislike for Lee and a preference that Johnston return to command. Longstreet was a known sulker who pouted for days after a decision went against his wishes. This tendency to sulk was described by both his friends and enemies.

During the war, Longstreet made numerous enemies usually by placing blame upon them for an incident for which he might better have accepted blame. He seemed to revel in controversy, and as a result, Longstreet became hated by most Southerners. Many felt his memoirs were self-serving and mean-spirited and some reached an empirical conclusion from them: "If Longstreet says [it is] so, it is most likely not true."

During Lee's lifetime, Lee was criticized very little by Longstreet, but such criticism increased and became personal as Longstreet became older and began to suffer from senility. Up until he died, Lee refused to believe Longstreet had said the few negative remarks others reported. The fact that Lee kept him throughout the war as his principal subordinate after Jackson died and always spoke highly of him until his death offsets much of the negative thoughts about Longstreet.[2]

Based on experience with new weaponry, Longstreet believed, like Jackson, in the superior strength of the defense over the offense if all other things were equal. In almost all cases,

Longstreet proposed that the army choose a defensive position and force the other side to attack it. Without Jackson joining with Longstreet in support of this position, Lee's tendencies to fight offensive battles were very difficult for Longstreet to counter. There were times when offensive tactics were correct and times when maintaining a defensive position was best. Jackson was expert at determining which was the correct tactic in different situations.

As the Battle of Gettysburg unfolds hindsight shows that Lee's offensive posture was correct until the late morning of July 2nd (the second day of the battle) after which time the Union troops moved to occupy and later successfully defend the Round Tops. In all likelihood, seizure of the Round Tops by the Confederates would have forced Meade to evacuate his strong Cemetery Ridge positions. After failing in this attempt, Longstreet's idea of moving around the Union's left flank to a defensive position of Lee's choosing was probably the most promising tactic for the Confederates to follow. By noon of July 2nd, most of Meade's troops were in place, and his defenses along Cemetery Ridge had become very strong.

At Gettysburg, one of Lee's command problems was that he and Longstreet remained in their fixed opposing mental positions throughout the battle. While Longstreet believed Lee's orders for the attacks on the afternoons of July 2nd and 3rd would not succeed, he carried them out to the best of his ability. There is no doubt this was done somewhat grudgingly since he believed his proposed alternative was better; however, his duty as a soldier to his commander proved to be controlling. While others criticized Longstreet for his actions at Gettysburg, Lee never did. Was this because in hindsight, Lee agreed that Longstreet's proposal would have proved to be a better course of action?

New corps commander A.P. Hill had made one severe mistake in his lifetime that influenced almost everything he did afterward. In the 1840s, he had contracted gonorrhea in New York City while on leave from the Military Academy.[3] The medicines of the time were relatively ineffective, and he began to suffer from bouts of severe prostatitis in his mid-30s. This painful disability continued throughout his life, and he had relief from the depression and pain for only very short intervals throughout his later life. These symptoms added fuel to an already quarrelsome disposition.

A.P. Hill had quarreled frequently with both Longstreet and Jackson; and while he was often an effective leader and fought well, he had a reputation for being restless, over-aggressive and impetuous in action. His timely and aggressive action at Antietam probably saved the Confederate cause that day. At Gettysburg, A.P. Hill was very ill but appointed no replacement so he played little part in the battle, and his actions were dull and unresponsive to what was going on around him.[4]

After the war, the question of a lack of support for Pickett's Charge once he reached the stone wall atop Cemetery Ridge was raised. As army commander, Lee was responsible for all such plans, but can any blame be placed against any of the corps commanders? Ewell was too far away to give immediate support, and Longstreet had committed all of his troops that were rested and in good condition. This leaves A.P. Hill who had a large force nearby that remained largely unengaged.

Ewell was used to working under Jackson who had always given him precise and specific orders, leaving him with few decisions to make. Ewell had a reputation as a hard fighter, but he had lost a leg in earlier fighting, married while on sick-leave, and just before the battle, had returned to the army a changed man.[5] He was still courageous but was far from the fighter he had been previously. Lee soon discovered that giving Ewell discretionary orders just did not work: given the choice of two alternatives he tended toward mental paralysis and chose neither. Lee had had little direct experience with Ewell so he learned of this deficiency after the battle, but Ewell's several periods of indecisiveness proved costly at Gettysburg.[6]

Unfortunately for Lee, both A.P. Hill and Ewell had been

promoted beyond their capabilities. Keeping in mind that there were no alternative candidates available showed just how bankrupt the Confederate general officer corps really was at that time.

His other corps commander was Stuart, who led the army's cavalry. Soon after a cavalry parade reviewed by Lee, Union Brigadier General Alfred Pleasonton attacked Stuart with the goal of penetrating Stuart's screen to determine if Lee's army was moving north in force. Although Stuart held the field, the Battle of Brandy Station was a mutually costly draw. Pleasonton had accomplished his main objective by determining that Lee's army was in fact moving north from Fredericksburg. More important, for the first time the Federal cavalry performed very well against the Southern horsemen, and Stuart was humiliated by his lack of success in the action.[7] This humiliation may have influenced his and Lee's later decision to ride around Hooker's army since he may have wished to make up for his earlier failure and show Lee something spectacular.

Lee's four corps commanders were all showing signs that each might be expected to give him some form of unsatisfactory performance; however, the greatest problem in the command crisis was probably Lee himself. In his letter of resignation to Davis written after the battle on August 8th, Lee stated that nothing had been amiss with his army or his subordinates; then he wrote: "I have not yet recovered from the attack [probably, problems from high blood pressure, a heart attack or congestive heart failure] I experienced last spring. I am becoming more and more incapable of exertion and am thus prevented from the personal examinations and giving the personal supervision to the operations in the field which I feel to be necessary. I am so dull that in making use of the eyes of others I am frequently misled."[8]

In his previous battles, Lee had shown great ability to foresee the movements and plans of his adversaries. Some of this skill arose from Lee's ability to place himself in his enemy's mental position, but much of this advantage arose from intelligence he was able to obtain from local Southerners, spies and Stuart's cavalry scouts. In Pennsylvania, these advantages had now turned against him where his spy system had broken down since he was in Union territory. His cavalry leader was not with him, leaving an adequate force of cavalry behind but under a poor leader. Lee was not physically able to do his own reconnaissance as he had frequently done earlier in the war. He had two untried infantry corps commanders and a third who was at odds with him on tactics; due to his physical limitations, he could no longer personally supervise operations. The Northern newspapers were not as fully informed by Union generals as they had been in the past, and he was no longer in Virginia where he had a detailed knowledge of the terrain. In Meade, he faced a new enemy commander on very short notice, and this change came as a surprise to him.

*   *   *

Major General George G. Meade faced another set of problems internal to his army. He had been one of its several corps commanders, now he was the commander of these men who had previously been his equals. The Army of the Potomac's chief-of-staff, Major General Daniel Butterfield, had been Hooker's choice, but Meade, who despised him, was forced by time and circumstances to keep him.[9]

It was generally thought that Major General John Reynolds was the army's most highly qualified general, and Meade shared this high opinion. Meade expected to depend on Reynolds as his most trusted and principal subordinate, and it was unfortunate for the Union cause that Reynolds was killed in the first few hours of the battle.

The generals of the Army of the Potomac operated in the strange combination of a "club" atmosphere and strong personal hostility between them. The politics of the army were complex and very important to the generals of the Army of the Potomac. All of this interest in army politics developed opposing factions among the generals that led to blame-placing from one to another;

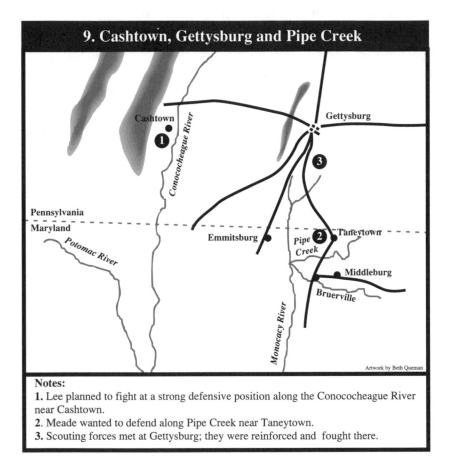

9. Cashtown, Gettysburg and Pipe Creek

Artwork by Beth Queman

Notes:
1. Lee planned to fight at a strong defensive position along the Conococheague River near Cashtown.
2. Meade wanted to defend along Pipe Creek near Taneytown.
3. Scouting forces met at Gettysburg; they were reinforced and fought there.

such disputes and combinations did not work well together for a common effort. Meade had stayed apart from the politics of the army and disliked them, but there was no opportunity for him to deal with any of these problems when he took command.

*   *   *

"Bob" (Lee) and "George" (Meade) were old friends from the Engineer Corps of the Old Army. Now they commanded the armies facing one another as enemies. Both of their commands had many problems; but neither commander had any time to make improvements even if he wished to do so.

In June of 1863, a major battle was destined to occur soon; Lee had to fight or retreat to friendly territory and retreating was far from his liking. The politics of the Union and the demands of the administration and the Northern population forced Meade to fight to defend a Northern state regardless of other considerations; he also had no real choice in the matter. In the event, neither Lee nor Meade had much influence on when and where the battle was to be fought.

Meade had identified a strong defensive position along Little Pipe Creek in northern Maryland where he wished to fortify the position and wait until Lee attacked him. Lee had found a similarly strong defensive position near Cashtown and wanted to wait there for Meade's army to approach, hoping to defeat each Union corps separately as it arrived.

The Battle occurred at Gettysburg because Confederate Major General Henry Heth asked his corps commander, A.P. Hill, if he could go into Gettysburg to find shoes. Lee had ordered that no general action should be precipitated without his prior approval. Getting shoes may have been an excuse fabricated later by Heth and Hill to justify an action Lee did not approve and which proved inappropriate in hindsight. Gettysburg was a shoe production center, and the army was very short of footwear, but Early had previously taken what shoes the town had. Hill gave his permission but did not think it was an important enough decision for him to obtain Lee's approval.[10]

On June 1st, Union Brigadier General John Buford commanded a cavalry outpost at Gettysburg, and he was impressed with the defensive possibilities of the area. He successfully fought a delaying action against Heth until Reynold's I and Howard's XI corps arrived. When Lee ordered Ewell to rejoin the army at either Cashtown or Gettysburg, Ewell tried to avoid making a decision by returning to Cashtown by way of

Gettysburg, and the fight was on. Ewell's corps fell on the north flank of the Union force which led to the defeat of these two Union corps, and it seemed like Lee's plan to defeat the Army of the Potomac in detail was working, so he made the decision to move up the rest of the army to the Gettysburg area. After an auspicious beginning, things began to go very badly for Lee starting at noon of the first day when his command structure showed the first signs of its ultimate failure.

Gettysburg: For the Confederacy, a Great Disaster, a Dark Comedy of Confederate Errors on the Way to Defeat

In December 1862, only six months before Gettysburg, Lee had stood atop a hill at Fredericksburg. He saw Burnside throw away 8,000 men who charged uphill against impregnable Confederate defenses. When the Battle of Gettysburg reached its climax, Lee threw away 6,500 of about 10,500 men who charged uphill against a seemingly impregnable Union position. Burnside had great numerical advantage; Lee had slightly inferior numbers so this proved unimportant in either case. Something besides his high intellect caused Lee to make the decisions behind Pickett's Charge. What could it have been?

The Battle of Gettysburg is described in numerous volumes.[1] These are the key actions that occurred on each day: *THE FIRST DAY,* July 1, 1863: The Army of Northern Virginia defeated two Union corps west of Gettysburg. Later in the afternoon, the Army of the Potomac fell back to and began to occupy Cemetery Ridge. Ewell's corps failed to follow Lee's orders to attack Cemetery Ridge and Culp's Hill in order to dislodge the Union forces from the dominating heights to the southeast of Gettysburg. *THE SECOND DAY*, July 2, 1863: Longstreet's corps attacked the Union left. Earlier, Union Major General Daniel Sickles disobeyed orders and blundered by laying out his defenses very poorly which allowed Longstreet's attack to come near to success; this was the closest that Lee came to victory at Gettysburg. In the afternoon, the two sides raced for the almost undefended Round Tops, and after heavy fighting, the Union forces secured them. Late in the day, Ewell's corps tried to take Culp's Hill and almost succeeded, but when Early's unsupported division was driven off, the attack failed. By nightfall, Meade's army had fully occupied the heights from Culp's Hill to the Round Tops. *THE THIRD DAY*, July 3, 1863: In the morning, there was little activity by either side as Lee's army sluggishly prepared to attack. At 1:00 P.M., Pickett's charge was launched, and by 3:00 it was clear it had failed with heavy losses. No Union counter attack was made. Stuart's late arriving cavalry tried to move around the Union right flank and cut off the army from its trains and destroy them, but after three hours of heavy fighting east of Gettysburg, Union cavalry repulsed Stuart's attack. At nightfall, the battle ended with both armies in the places they had occupied at the end of the first day. In the three days 41,367 Americans had been killed or wounded!

* * *

The list of Confederate errors in tactics and battle management made before and during the Battle of Gettysburg is long, and they were very devastating to the Confederate cause. As commander-in-chief, Lee was ultimately responsible for all errors. In the long list, five errors stand out as being the most critical. *First*, Lee was blinded to the movements of the enemy since his best cavalry leaders, Stuart, Hampton and Fitzhugh Lee, had been sent by him on a diversionary raid around Hooker's army. Following several meetings among Lee, Longstreet and Stuart, a series of orders went to Stuart from Lee to move around Hooker's army, the idea being that this would divert attention away from Lee's main body, gather supplies and damage the enemy. It appears that these three officers simply underestimated the time and difficulty Stuart would face before he could rejoin the Army of Northern Virginia, and they failed to see the value that a Hampton or Fitzhugh Lee would have given Lee in providing him with good scouting information. These mistakes led to the fact that until June 29th Lee received no useful details of Union positions, route of movement and intentions once Stuart had reported the Army of the Potomac was crossing the Potomac. Ultimately, this proved fatal to Confederate efforts in Pennsylvania. The officer Stuart left to provide Lee with screening and scouting support, Brigadier General Beverly Robertson, proved ineffective. Robertson and Lee had never worked together, and Stuart had little confidence in him. He had not adequately trained him in what was now required: working closely with Lee, acting as his eyes. Stuart's orders to Robertson were clear. He may have been bound by the Confederate Army's rigid time-in-rank seniority policy to appoint Robertson, but as cavalry commander, Stuart should have recognized Robertson's failings. Not leaving Hampton or Fitzhugh Lee with Lee was close to criminal. In any event, Robertson was not qualified for his assignment. The diversion failed to accomplish more than a few days of confusion for the Union so Stuart's ride made good headlines and glory but served no meaningful purpose. That Lee recognized Stuart had some part in this failing is shown by the fact that he never promoted him to lieutenant general, a rank that would have been appropriate for a veteran corps commander.[2] *Second,* when leading Union and Confederate elements stumbled into one another west of Gettysburg, Lee was ill with diarrhea and a possible recurrence of malaria[3] and far from the scene of action, but he should have decided whether to withdraw to his previously chosen good defensive position at Cashtown or to advance. Instead, he made no decision and his subordinates, Ewell and Early, committed him to the advance. The Confederates won the battle's first day but were too timid and indecisive to occupy Cemetery Ridge immediately when they could have done so with little effort. Lee's orders to occupy the Ridge were thought to be discretionary so they were ignored. When Lee finally arrived and saw the missed opportunity, it was too late. This placed Meade's army in a very strong defensive position *if* the battle continued beyond the first day.[4] *Third*, there was no reason for Lee to fight an offensive battle against the Union position at Gettysburg once it had obviously become very strong. Longstreet's untimely sulk prevented the assault of the 2nd from taking place as early as 10:00 A.M. when it might well have led to Confederate occupation of Little Round Top and the turning of the Union position. If the Round Tops were not taken successfully by noon, making the assault on the afternoon of the 2nd should have been avoided; and, at any time during the night of the second day, the Confederates could have filed around the Union left flank. The occupation of a strong defensive position between Meade's army and Washington would have forced the Army of the Potomac to attack them on ground of Lee's choosing. Meade showed substantial skill as a defensive general but never demonstrated much skill on the offensive so Lee, would have been at a distinct advantage in these circumstances. *Fourth*, early in the battle, both sides failed to see the tactical importance of the Round Tops, particularly Little Round Top which was close enough to the Union's left flank to bombard most of the line with artillery. High above the left flank of the Union army, the Round Tops dominated the whole Union position. They were not strongly defended since Meade feared the Cemetery Ridge position could be more easily turned on its northeast at Culp's Hill.[5] In the early afternoon of July 2nd, just as the Confederates finally saw the opportunity, Brigadier General Gouverneur K. Warren, the chief engineer of the Army of the Potomac, saw Hood's division advancing toward them. He hurried troops to the Round Tops and organized a last-minute defense that succeeded. The Round Tops were open for easy capture until about noon on July 2nd, and until 3:00 P.M., Hood had a good

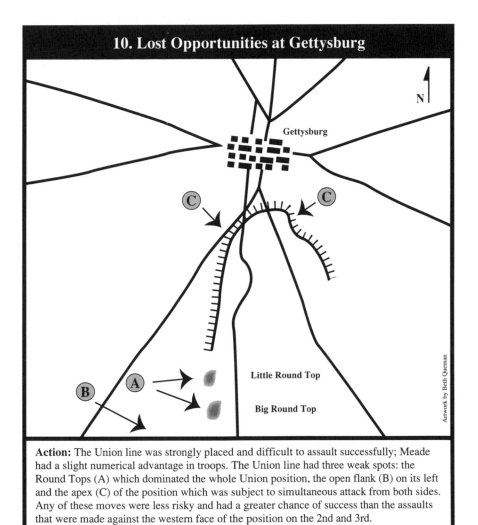

10. Lost Opportunities at Gettysburg

Gettysburg

N

Little Round Top

Big Round Top

Artwork by Beth Quernan

Action: The Union line was strongly placed and difficult to assault successfully; Meade had a slight numerical advantage in troops. The Union line had three weak spots: the Round Tops (A) which dominated the whole Union position, the open flank (B) on its left and the apex (C) of the position which was subject to simultaneous attack from both sides. Any of these moves were less risky and had a greater chance of success than the assaults that were made against the western face of the position on the 2nd and 3rd.

fighting chance to take them. Capture of the Round Tops would have ended the battle quickly since Confederate artillery located there would have driven the Union troops from all of their defensive positions. *Fifth*, the assault on the third day, known as Pickett's Charge, was another example of Lee's tendency to make an impossible attack in order to recover from a lost strategic situation. With no other supporting Confederate troops within a mile of the Union lines, even when the charge made a small breakthrough, Meade's army was under no threat. It was easy for uninvolved Union units to surround and counter-attack the few soldiers who had broken through and force them to retreat, die, be wounded or surrender. The costly assault was strategic disaster to the South, as was the entire battle. A general observation of all of Lee's attacks at Gettysburg is that they were poorly coordinated. The hook-shaped Union defenses gave Meade the advantage of shorter interior lines whereby he could move troops easily to a point of danger. This shape made it difficult for Lee to move his troops from point to point along his line. The disadvantage of Meade's position was that its flanks were poorly protected. Lee failed to develop a mobile reserve to follow up success if any of his four major attacks had shown promise of success. Thus, when Confederates captured a foothold atop Culp's Hill, they could not hold it. Their success against Sickles's blunder could not be made decisive. They fought near the summit of Little Round Top but had no reserves available to capture it. When Pickett's men breached the stone wall atop Cemetery Ridge, his force was too used up, and no support was available to try to secure the fruits of the attack.

Lee's last offensive order at Gettysburg, Pickett's Charge, was one of the most controversial actions of the Civil War. At the time, Lee took full responsibility for its failure.[6] After the war, Lee's nephew, Major General Fitzhugh Lee, wrote a biography of his famous uncle. He wrote this concerning Pickett's Charge:

> "A consummate master of war such as Lee was would not drive *en masse* a column of fourteen thousand across an open terrene thirteen or fourteen hundred yards, nearly every foot of it under a concentrated and converging fire of artillery, to attack an army, on fortified heights, of one hundred thousand, less its two days' losses, and give his entering wedge no support. Why, if every man in that assault had been bullet proof, and if the

whole of those fourteen thousand splendid troops had arrived unharmed on Cemetery Ridge, what could have been accomplished? Not being able to kill them, there would have been time for the Federals to have seized, tied, and taken them off in wagons, before their supports could have reached them. Amid the fire and smoke of this false move these troops did not know 'some one had blundered.'"[7]

While meant to exonerate Lee from responsibility for the errors of Pickett's Charge this quote is unconsciously both critical and condemning of his generalship since the major blunder was Lee's judgment in deciding to make the charge. As to the matter of support, if the assault was to be made, it was Lee's responsibility to order any support required and to detail a specific staff officer to see that it moved off on time. Such support would have to come from another corps besides Longstreet's so it is difficult to blame that subordinate for this failing. Such decisions should be made by the commander-in-chief before the assault. Lee either thought the attack would prove successful without support being needed, or he simply failed to provide for it. Neither of these premises shows consummate skill in generalship.

This whole question of support for Pickett's Charge was raised by Fitzhugh Lee as a cure for Lee's failure at Gettysburg, and it has been carried as a banner by some biased historians since then. While it is speculation since the support was not forthcoming, the whole idea is probably of no consequence. We have Grady McWhiney's excellent statistical analysis of the Civil War which proves that an assaulting force against a strong position held by determined defenders had to have an advantage approaching three to one. Meade had upwards of 70,000 determined defenders, and Lee did not have an army approaching 200,000 men. If support had been sent, the battle would only have been more difficult and casualties much higher for both sides; the outcome would almost certainly have been the same. This consideration gives emphasis to the fact that the weaknesses of the Cemetery Ridge position were its flanks, not within the bounds of the Union army's fortified positions.

The best record that support was considered is Brigadier General Edward Porter Alexander's discussion of the matter.[8] Porter says support was not available from Law's and Hood's brigades of Longstreet's corps because they had been so damaged in the fighting of July 2nd. Porter, who commanded the artillery at the charge, believed Lee did want Wilcox's brigade and Anderson's division, 8,000 men in all, to provide the support needed. He believed they were detailed by Lee to step off toward the heights 300 to 400 yards behind Pickett's 10,500 men. Alexander's belief is that Lee's staff, who had worked on the attack all morning, simply failed to follow Lee's order to be sure the support would move off in time to be useful. Lee's staff was very weak, but he must have been aware of its short-comings so the blunder must be attributed finally to Lee and no one else.

Pickett wrote a report describing the charge from his vantage point. Because many, perhaps including himself, thought Pickett should have been left on the field with his dead followers, his report was probably somewhat defensive. Based on comments from those who saw it, the report was highly critical of those who did not supply support, A.P. Hill and Wilcox, as well as Pettigrew, Trimble and even Lee. Lee suppressed the report, returned it and asked Pickett to rewrite it covering only information on casualties. Lee stated that the original report was too critical, and that the army must guard against dissensions at that critical time.[9]

That Pickett blamed Lee for the disastrous charge is further substantiated by John S. Mosby when he and Pickett visited Lee after the war. When Pickett tried to discuss the charge, Lee refused, and the visit turned cold. As the two left, Mosby reported that Pickett mumbled about "that old man," and said: "He had my division massacred at Gettysburg."[10]

If Pickett's Charge is compared with Longstreet's charge at the Battle of Chickamauga, a great difference in strength may be seen between two assaults each involving about the same number of

11. Pickett's Charge

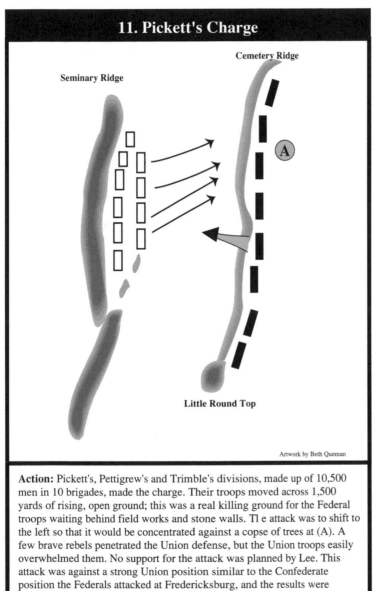

Seminary Ridge

Cemetery Ridge

A

Little Round Top

Artwork by Beth Queman

Action: Pickett's, Pettigrew's and Trimble's divisions, made up of 10,500 men in 10 brigades, made the charge. Their troops moved across 1,500 yards of rising, open ground; this was a real killing ground for the Federal troops waiting behind field works and stone walls. Tl e attack was to shift to the left so that it would be concentrated against a copse of trees at (A). A few brave rebels penetrated the Union defense, but the Union troops easily overwhelmed them. No support for the attack was planned by Lee. This attack was against a strong Union position similar to the Confederate position the Federals attacked at Fredericksburg, and the results were similarly disastrous to the attacking side.

troops. The charge at Chickamauga was two brigades wide with six more following to exploit success so the attack was much more self-supporting. Pickett's Charge was six brigades wide with five supporting brigades following closely. The supporting brigades attempted to move laterally toward the planned point of breakthrough, but this proved too cumbersome to give effective self-support.

The column formation at Chickamauga was much stronger. In all likelihood, Longstreet had learned of this need as a lesson from the failure of the wider, weaker formation used at Gettysburg. As in most successful frontal assaults in the Civil War, there was another reason that the charge at Chickamauga succeeded. By chance the Union line was in total disarray at the point where Longstreet struck it. Because of a Union command error, one division had moved out of the line, leaving a gap, and two other divisions were not deployed, but were marching in column on a road parallel to the front and behind the gap.[11] Whether or not Longstreet's charge at Chickamauga would have been successful if these three divisions had been in the line opposite his assault, is open to question. Regardless of this lucky situation, Longstreet's Chickamauga charge had a much greater chance of success than Pickett's did.

From Lee's point of view, it was not difficult for him to understand Stuart's absence from the army. Lee knew Stuart was following his orders to gather supplies, ride around the Army of the Potomac as a diversion and do whatever damage he could. Lee, Longstreet and Stuart had agreed to Stuart taking these actions.[12] There is no doubt of Lee's wish that Robertson, in Stuart's absence, should keep him informed of enemy movements on a daily basis. Lee apparently expected Stuart to report to him by courier within three days and expressed concern as to why he had not heard from Stuart day after day, but this was probably more a concern for Stuart's personal well-being than anything else.[13]

Stuart had left more than half of his cavalry force at Lee's disposal for scouting and screening so the problem was not that Lee was without an adequate number of cavalrymen. Stuart gave Robertson clear orders to move north and maintain a position south and east of the Confederate army as soon as Hooker crossed the Potomac. After occupying this position Robertson was ordered to report to Lee and Longstreet and follow their orders.[14] The timing of events meant that Robertson should have started north on June 25th, but inexplicably, he remained guarding the passes in the Blue Ridge Mountains south of the Potomac until June 29th. There is no doubt this was the reason for Lee's blindness, not Stuart's absence. At this trying time, a more efficient and dependable cavalry general was most critical to Lee's needs.

That Lee was a competent administrator who kept on top of things is beyond doubt; nevertheless the record of what actually happened is confusing, as it appears in the *Official Records*. One possible explanation that has been stated involves his aide, Colonel Marshall. It was Lee's general practice to dictate his orders to Marshall, and he always read and corrected them before he allowed orders to be released. In this rare, exceptional case, Lee ordered Marshall to repeat (copy) his order to Stuart of June 22nd and send it again on the 23rd, fearing that the first copy might have been lost. Comparing the two orders shows that Marshall's copy was made carelessly and was so different from the original that it appears to be a new and different order.[15] Further, Stuart's adjutant, Major H.B. McClellan, reported that a more lengthy letter from Lee accompanied the second order which expanded upon it, but this letter has been lost.[16]

From all the information that is available, one must conclude that Stuart's raid around the Army of the Potomac was well-considered by Lee, Longstreet and Stuart, and plenty of cavalry was left with Lee, although it was poorly led. That Stuart correctly followed Lee's orders in conducting the raid is also clear. Robertson had not been a well reputed officer for some time, and he had been disciplined for inefficiency several times. For Stuart to leave Robertson as Lee's "eyes" and for Lee and Longstreet to accept this situation, is almost impossible to understand. If it was an oversight, it was a costly one, and the final responsibility for this disastrous choice of personnel must rest with Lee.

*   *   *

Neither the Gettysburg campaign nor Pickett's Charge merited the description "high tide of the Confederacy." From its inception, the Gettysburg campaign promised to be and then became the first great failure, and the first step toward defeat for the Army of Northern Virginia. If there was a "high tide of the Confederacy," it occurred at Chancellorsville where the Army of Northern Virginia came within a few hours of defeating the Army of the Potomac so thoroughly that Washington and the rest of the eastern Union states would have been almost defenseless against it. Another better candidate for "high tide" besides Gettysburg would be Bragg's defeat at Perryville, Kentucky where a serious threat against the Union mid-west was turned back. With the huge defeats in the West at Vicksburg and in the Tullahoma Campaign on the same day, indeed, July 3, 1863 was a very low point in the history of the Confederacy.

Despite his many statements that casualties had thankfully been light after many battles, Lee also showed a lack of knowledge of, or concern about, the manpower cost of a direct assault and its almost certain failure. The question is whether his mind was unhinged by responsibility, poor health, and horror by the evening of July 3, 1863, or perhaps Lee was in a state of denial about all the lives his decisions had cost, or he may have reached a state where he just could not care any more.

*   *   *

The disagreement between Lee and Longstreet was one of the keys to the South's defeat at Gettysburg. Lee's idea of an offense was sound enough that it could have succeeded before noon of the second day. Up to that time, Cemetery Ridge was weakly held, defensive positions were poorly prepared, the defensive line was too long to be well-defended everywhere, and the Confederates outnumbered the Union forces on the scene.

An opportunity existed for Lee to defeat parts of Meade's army, one at a time, as he had done successfully on the first day.[17] If the offense could have been pressed before noon of July 2nd, Lee might have captured the Round Tops, allowing him to drive Meade's army from Cemetery Ridge.[18] Then in subsequent action, he would have had a good chance to defeat the rest of Meade's army. Lee's command problems prevented this from occurring. If his health had been good, he would have seen the opportunity to take the Round Tops early, and perhaps, he would have acted upon this intelligence. He could not see the opportunity, himself, and Longstreet chose not to tell him about it.[19] Instead, Longstreet chose to follow Lee's attack orders implicitly on the afternoon of the 2nd.[20]

By noon on the second day, the offensive opportunity was lost. Now, it was Lee's turn to be obstinate and ignore the merit of Longstreet's proposal to march around the Union left flank. Meade was concerned about such a move and had placed part of Sedgwick's VI Corps (the remainder had been used as a manpower pool as VI units replaced units that suffered losses in the rest of the army) in a withdrawn line facing south as a defense against a flank attack. Longstreet's scouts had not discovered this move.[21] Nevertheless, an opportunity existed for a wide turning movement, say, 2-5 miles to the south, throughout the night of the 2nd.

Many Southern historians have been strongly anti-Longstreet, in part because they had to find someone other than Lee to blame for mistakes. They found Longstreet at fault many times during and after the war. It did not help him that after the war he renewed his friendship with his in-law, Grant, became one of his political supporters and a Republican. Some thought Longstreet deviated from their picture of how a Confederate ex-general should perform and talk. They used these perceived faults to discredit his ideas, his performance and everything he proposed or said, during or after the war. They used this rationale to support positions against all of Longstreet's actions, recommendations and opinions. They imagined Lee would have taken positions contrary to Longstreet, whether or not he actually did. That such "logic" was unlikely to be valid is shown by Lee's behavior toward Longstreet during and after the war.

One major element in the "dispute" between Longstreet and Lee is whether Lee promised him, in advance of the invasion, that he, Lee, would maintain a tactical defense while in enemy territory. Lee later denied this promise, but several things indicate that some assurance of this sort was made by Lee. Besides Longstreet's mention of it after the war,[22] two things stand out. Lee's stated purposes for the invasion were: to interfere with Union campaign plans for the summer, replenish his army's supplies from Union sources, impact the politics of the Union states unfavorably and to draw Union troops from the West to face his threat. Never did he mention in advance that he wished to attack and destroy the Army of the Potomac. Lee did not appear to have a specific objective on the ground; the closest thing to this that he mentioned was when he told Stuart "to capture Harrisburg [and destroy the bridges there] if this proved practical."[23] Note that this was an assignment suitable for a cavalry raid, probably not for an army.

It is clear that Longstreet did propose the idea to Lee that the Army of Northern Virginia should move around the Union army's left flank at the end of the second day, perhaps late on the first. Longstreet's many enemies sought to discredit his idea and support Lee by discrediting Longstreet, the general and man. This is a frequent tactic used by critics of all ages; attack a man's personal habits, morals, politics, or other things, thus discrediting his ideas; and it is patently unfair. While not justifying his sulking posture after Lee rejected his ideas, the fact remains that the idea was sound and was presented in good faith and for the good of the Confederacy.

In Pickett's assault, Lee ordered two brigades to follow the leading left-most one in column; but this order was not followed.[24] This would have markedly increased the strength of the formation at the planned point of breakthrough and might have changed the outcome. A.P. Hill's corps remained inactive observers as the disastrous charge rushed on to failure. Lee was too infirm and did not have a staff strong enough to bring together the disparate elements of his army. Without a commander who could do this, and Lee did not do it, the Confederates were doomed to failure at Gettysburg.

Meade had no confidence in his army's ability to hold against a charge by the Confederates on the third day.[25] Only after a formal conference the night before did he decide to stand and fight. He guessed correctly that Lee would attack his center since he had previously attacked each flank. After losses (killed and wounded only) of 17,684 Federal and 22,638 Confederate troops,[26] both sides did nothing on July 4th when drenching rains began. In three days, 41,367 were killed and wounded on both sides out of 158,343 American effective troops engaged (75,054 Confederates, 83,289 Federals); this proved to be enough bloodshed to satisfy the generals on both sides for the time being.

Lee stated his position about Gettysburg in two letters to Davis. The first of July 31st said, in part:

"...No blame can be attached to the army for its failure to accomplish what was projected by me, nor should it be censured for the unreasonable expectations of the public. I am alone to blame, in perhaps expecting too much of its prowess & valour. It however in my opinion achieved under the guidance of the Most High a general success, though it did not win a victory. I thought at the time the latter was practicable. I still think if all things could have worked together it would have been accomplished. But with the knowledge I then had, & in the circumstances I was then placed, I do not know what better

course I could have pursued. With my present knowledge &
could I have foreseen that the attack on the last day would have
failed to drive the enemy from his position, I would certainly
have tried some other course. What the ultimate result would
have been is not so clear to me...."[27]

This may indicate that Lee still disagreed with Longstreet's idea
of a movement around Meade's left flank, but if he had known
in advance that Pickett's Charge would fail, he would have tried
some other alternative. It is also possible to take Lee's words as
an admission that something went awry with his plans: possibly
he and his staff had failed to be sure Wilcox's brigade and
Anderson's division from A.P. Hill's corps were prepared to step
off 300 yards behind Pickett in support.

In the next week, Southern newspapers printed numerous
critical articles about Lee, the army, and most of his generals. After
more reflection, Lee again wrote Davis on August 8th offering his
resignation and stating that he was no longer fit for command.
In part, he said:

"[Speaking of the people of the Confederacy]...Nothing is
wanted but that their fortitude should equal their [this army's]
bravery to insure the success of our cause. We must expect reverses,
even defeats...

I know how prone we are to censure and how ready to blame
others for the non-fulfillment of our expectations. This is
unbecoming in a generous people, and I grieve to see its expression.
The general remedy for want of success in a military commander
is his removal...

I have been prompted by these reflections more than once since
my return from Pennsylvania to propose to Your Excellency the
propriety of selection [of] another commander for this army. I
have seen and heard of expression of discontent in the public
journals at the result of the expedition. I do not know how far
this feeling extends in the army. My brother officers have been
too kind to report it...It is fair, however, to suppose that it does
exist, and success is so necessary to us that nothing should be
risked to secure it. I, therefore, in all sincerity, request Your
Excellency to take measures to supply my place [assign another

general to replace me]. I do this with more earnestness because no one is more aware than myself of my inability for the duties of my position. I cannot even accomplish what I want. How can I fulfill the expectations of others? In addition I sensibly feel the growing failure of my bodily strength...not yet recovered from the attack of past spring... incapable of any exertion, making personal examinations, doing the personal supervision which I feel necessary...dull in making use of the eyes of others and frequently misled. Everything, therefore, points to the advantages to be derived from a new commander, and I the more anxiously urge the matter upon YourExcellency from my belief that a younger and abler man readily be attained...he will have as gallant and brave an army as ever existed to second his efforts...I hope Your Excellency will attribute my request to the true reason, the desire to serve my country...

I have no complaints to make of any one but myself. I have received nothing but kindness from those above me, and the most considerate attention from my comrades and companions in arms..."[28]

Again, this document supports the idea that only Lee (and his staff which must be considered only as an extension of himself) were solely responsible for whatever errors had been made at Gettysburg. It is most interesting to note that Lee made no mention of any possible candidate to succeed him. These are the words of an honest man who fully recognized his own limitations and the ill-effect of them on their cause.

President Davis replied, rejecting Lee's offer of resignation and assuring Lee that he had done the best any man could have done. The problem Davis faced was the complete bankruptcy of quality high commanders in the South, and Lee, in spite of his limitations, was the best he had.

Lee was right about criticism occurring about him in and out of the army. Somehow this reached him and hurt him. A few examples included: A diary entry of Randolf H. McKim said he "went into the last battle feeling victory must be ours...now I feel that unless He sees fit to bless our arms, our valor will not avail."[29] General Wade Hampton wrote J.E. Johnston: "To fight an enemy superior in numbers at such a terrible disadvantage of position in the heart of his own territory, when freedom of movement gave him [Lee] the advantage of accepting his own time and place for accepting battle, seems to have been a great military blunder...the position of the Yankees there was the strongest I ever saw...we let Meade choose the position and then we attacked.[30] Longstreet wrote his uncle right after the battle: "[the] battle was not made as I would have made it."[31] Robert Garland Hill Kean of the War Department wrote in July that: "Gettysburg has shaken my faith in Lee as a general."

President Davis continued to support Lee in spite of his view that the scope of Lee's invasion of the North was greater than his more conservative concept of what the campaign was to be and a more limited set of objectives than he expected it to accomplish.[32] In his memoirs, Davis defended Lee against charges made by others concerning Gettysburg, but he did concede: "that it would have been better to withdraw than to renew the attack of the third day."[33] In 1863, Davis probably saw no reason to cry over "spilled milk" since it was too late to change things, and Lee was the best general he had. Did the quote in his memoirs represent his thinking in 1863? In most probability, it did.

In 1866, Edwin A. Pollard, the staunchly pro-Southern editor of the *Richmond Examiner*, summed up Southern feelings when he wrote about Gettysburg: "a persistent popular opinion in the South [is] that Gen. Lee having failed to improve the advantage of the first [day], did wrong thereafter to fight at Gettysburg."[34]

In a strange reversal, written in typical media double-talk, Pollard went on to justify the attack on Meade. Only after Lee's death did these negative interpretations of his performance at Gettysburg begin to disappear from the press and private communications and turn to more favorable comment and excuses.

For those who believe all this discussion of Gettysburg and Pickett's Charge is only hindsight, Lee's personal experience and observations before Gettysburg deserve consideration. Lee had *no positive precedents to his decision* to order the charge; he had three negative ones: his own failed and costly assault at Malvern Hill, Pope's near disastrous attack on Jackson's line at Manassas II and Burnside's charge against Lee's Marye's Heights position. Lee had overall responsibility for his own and the actions of all his subordinates, and this made for an overwhelming burden of responsibility. Many of his subordinates did let him down in one way or another. Some of the support Lee received after his death was from these same officers who failed him and who were attempting to cover up their own deficiencies. This kind of support would not have been considered honorable by Lee when their support included criticism of other officers whom he had not criticized himself. In repetition, Lee never publicly, or otherwise as far as we know, criticized Longstreet. He kept him in high command through the end of the war and held him in high esteem until Lee died. This indicates Lee did not blame Longstreet. The fact remains that Lee gave up a substantial advantage when he assumed an offensive strategy against Meade who would have been at similar disadvantage if his army had been allowed to attack Lee as it eventually would have been forced to do. If anyone was at fault for the disaster who could it have been but Lee?

CHAPTER XV

Meade Allows Lee to Escape a Further Disaster Against the Flooded Potomac River

On July 4, 1863, Lee and his army dug into defensive positions on Seminary Ridge which were almost as strong as Meade's had been the day before. Meade had learned from Fredericksburg and from Pickett's Charge that to attack uphill against such a position would be unsuccessful and overly costly. Lee began his retreat to Virginia on the 5th. Meade saw no good opportunity to attack Lee under favorable circumstances, and he lacked the imagination to develop a battle plan based on pursuit. After many difficulties, outstanding efforts by his engineers enabled Lee and the Army of Northern Virginia to escape final disaster and cross the Potomac.

After both sides spent July 4th collecting their many wounded and while surgeons treated them, Lee began his retreat during the night of the 4th. Having 18,735 wounded Confederate soldiers stressed the hospital facilities, and many were untreated as the hospital wagons and walking-wounded moved off toward the Williamsport crossing on the Potomac on the afternoon of the 4th. These men suffered one of the most horrible trips humanity has ever experienced before they arrived in Williamsport during the afternoon of the 5th. Among other things, they were attacked by Union cavalry and were short of food, water and medical help.

Besides losing 28% of his army, Meade had lost three corps commanders, his chief of staff and numerous other generals and colonels to death, wounds or capture. The rains and mud made pursuit difficult so the Army of the Potomac was in poor condition for more fighting, and Meade had no mind for it. Overwhelmed by his own army's problems, Meade failed to recognize the opportunity Lee's impetuous attacks had given him. He should have been able to conclude that the Confederates could not have fought effectively much more because of their losses and a shortage of artillery ammunition![1]

The retreating Confederates reached Williamsport, Maryland on July 6th, but their advance elements found the Potomac River flooded so the army could not use the fords, and Union cavalry had destroyed the pontoon bridge they had used on their move north. They set up defenses that covered the fords at Williamsport and Falling Waters while they tore down nearby houses and used the lumber to construct a new pontoon bridge. During the week it took to build the bridge, a small rope-drawn ferry was used to move many of the most seriously wounded across the river. This rickety but useful pontoon bridge was one of the more remarkable engineering feats of the war.[2]

Cavalry from both sides fought each other as the main force of Lee's army retreated toward Williamsport, but the main Union body followed too slowly to become part of the action. Unable to cross the river, Lee set up a defensive line just west of Hagerstown which enclosed Williamsport, Falling Waters and space for the army to wait until the bridge was finished. These defenses were very strong; the southern flank was against a loop of the Potomac; and the north flank was on the Conococheague Creek.

By July 11th, the Army of the Potomac arrived; it had received some reinforcements after Gettysburg. Meade, his Chief Engineer

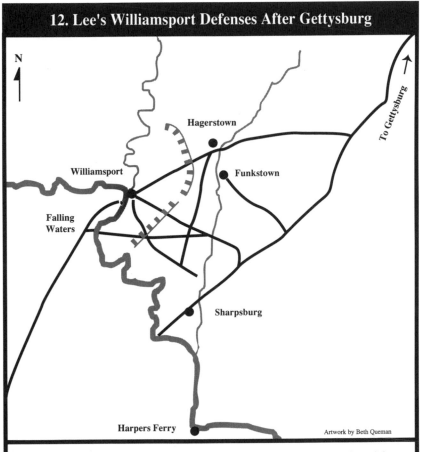

12. Lee's Williamsport Defenses After Gettysburg

N

Hagerstown

Williamsport

Funkstown

Falling
Waters

To Gettysburg

Sharpsburg

Harpers Ferry

Artwork by Beth Queman

Both Union and Confederate armies had lost almost a third of their strength, and the survivors were emotionally drained. The Army of the Potomac had lost three corps commanders including their two best. An aggressive commander like Grant or Sheridan would have cast aside the difficulty, seen the opportunity to end the war and acted. Meade was not this kind of general; he wanted to preserve his victory and not risk a reversal. Lee's army was so spent that the chances of such a reversal were slight. The Army of Northern Virginia used great skill to escape across the flooded Potomac River, but good luck was also an essential contributor.

Warren and his new Chief of Staff, Major General A.A. Humphreys, made an examination of Lee's lines. "Wherever seen, the position was naturally strong, and was strongly in trenched [sic]; it presented no vulnerable points, but much of it was concealed from view. ...its flanks were secure and could not be turned."[2]

On the 13th, Meade ordered a reconnaissance in force to be made on the 14th. This would probably have led to an allout assault on the Confederate positions. It was too late. As the troops moved forward, it became obvious that most of Lee's army had escaped over the river into Virginia. In spite of the criticism he received, Meade always stated that the Confederate fortifications at Williamsport, in Lee's capable defensive hands, were far too strong to be taken by assault.[3]

Finally, on July 14th, Lee's rear guard crossed the river. Meade was hailed for his great victory at Gettysburg, receiving the "Thanks of Congress." In spite of his great victory, he was severely criticized for "letting Lee escape."

*   *   *

Excluding his thoughts leading to his surrender, the time between sundown on July 3rd, when the battle ended, through the 14th, when the rear guards of his army crossed the Potomac to safety, was the period of highest stress for Lee throughout the war. After a disastrous defeat that followed a poor decision to fight under unfavorable circumstances, huge losses and deciding not to fight any more on the ground at Gettysburg, Lee showed his great strength of will in those eleven very long days. He put all these concerns and failures aside and concentrated on the sole objective of extricating his army from its terrible predicament. His first thoughts were for his wounded, and he spent the night of July 3rd and most of the 4th planning their withdrawal first and then that of his army.

Lee must have been exhausted, and this man suffered from

severe physical problems; nevertheless, he did the planning of the complicated retreat by himself. This situation is illustrative of a severe weakness in the command system of the Army of Northern Virginia in particular and the Confederate Army in general. Lee's staff was made up of young Virginia aristocrats who had little military experience, although they were all bright young men. While the army was in camp, they were reasonably good administrators. In the field, they performed as secretaries, record-keepers, couriers, personnel managers and comprehensive aides. All of them were far from qualified as military advisors; therefore they could not contribute to Lee in making military plans, criticizing his military ideas, judging the qualifications of Lee's subordinate generals or making battle decisions. This weak form of staff was typical of all military staffs from Davis's to those of other Confederate armies.

Most Union army commanders approached their army staff organization very differently. They usually appointed a chief-of-staff who had substantial military experience. Examples in the Army of the Potomac were major generals Daniel Butterfield, Andrew A. Humphreys and Seth Williams who sequentially held the position as chief-of-staff from early in 1863 through the end of the war. All had commanded corps or divisions in major battles; they acted more as advisors, planners or logistical managers for the commander rather than as mere secretaries or aides. These men also managed a staff of other officers who were expert in such things as logistics and intelligence.

As the size of armies radically increased during the Civil War, the demands on the time and effort of army commanders multiplied. The Union Army reacted to these demands by giving the commander a high quality, militarily experienced general as his chief-of-staff. This proved a better solution to the staff and command problem than that of the Confederate armies which continued to add "smart young men" to the staffs of commanders. These were relatively safe assignments for "favorite sons," so keeping such assignments open may have helped relations between Davis and leading Southern families.

Lee understood the issues that his own health problems were causing, yet he failed to take the step of adding a qualified chief-of-staff even though this might have mitigated some of his personal concerns. Instead, he chose to push himself to the edge, and beyond. Lee had the influence with the Davis Administration to get such an appointment approved, but he made no attempts to gain such approval. Generals like Pender or Pettigrew would appear to have been excellent candidates for such an appointment. Why did Lee not take such a step? Possibly the Confederacy felt no good general could be spared for such staff duty because they were so short of good generals. Perhaps, no well-thought-of general would consider such an appointment, thinking it was demeaning. It may be that Lee was satisfied with things as they were. Or, he may have felt he could not deal with a close and competent associate at such a high level all day, every day.

There was such a clear distinction between the Union and Confederate armies on this point that it may have been Davis's influence that settled the matter. This makes one question whether Lee's generalship was at fault, either by his accepting Davis's view, or by his not giving consideration to this possible solution for his problems, both military and personal.

CHAPTER XVI

Lee Thinks It Is Time for Him to Be Replaced; Longstreet Moves West; the Armies Return to the Rapidan Line

Lee suffered from heart trouble. Jackson was sorely missed and no substitute was available. By his own admission, Lee could no longer do what he thought a commander should do.[1] He had won or drawn many battles with numerical odds substantially against him, facing poor Union leadership. Many of his best officers were gone, others had lost faith in him after his Gettysburg fiasco. If Appomattox is discounted as being inevitable by that time, the summer and fall of 1863 had to be the worst of times for Lee. Union leadership was greatly improving. Only the Confederacy's extreme lack of qualified commanders prevented the acceptance of Lee's offered resignation.

*A*fter Gettysburg in the summer of 1863, Lee must have reflected on what he had accomplished since the beginning of the year, what had gone against him and what he could expect in the future. From a positive viewpoint, Lee had scored a great victory at Chancellorsville where he had succeeded in disrupting the summer campaign of the Army of the Potomac. He had moved the line of conflict from the Rapidan to the Potomac. He had gained supplies from Pennsylvania and given the farmers of Virginia a chance to plant their crops and to harvest them out from under the feet of two huge opposing armies that would have taken their harvest.

On the negative side, his greatest loss was Jackson. To that date in 1863, he had lost in killed and wounded about 45,000 men, and his remaining strength after Gettysburg was only about 46,000.[2] He had lost many of his best generals, commissioned and non-commissioned officers, including many of his best, experienced veteran soldiers. The manpower pool of the Confederacy had about run dry where the number of "hot-bloods" who really wished to fight and risk dying had become negligible. Lax draft laws made it possible for many able-bodied, white men to remain outside of the war's manpower pool.

These battle losses had caused the desertion rate to increase alarmingly, and Lee saw great difficulty in keeping an effective army in the field.[3] He also recognized that the quality of replacements could not come close to equalling the quality of the veterans he had lost.

The offsetting losses to the Union of about 30,000 that far into the year did not have such a devastating affect on the manpower pool of the North. Replacements for Union army losses were more plentiful even though they, too, were of lower quality. Union leadership was improving, whereas that of the Confederacy was declining due to losses. Thus, Lee faced a situation of diminishing strength of his own making whereas relatively, the Union Army was increasing in strength. The situation with respect to Lee's enlisted men was bad, indeed, but that of his officer corps was far worse.

Reading Lee's report to President Davis of August 8, 1863,[4] in the context of the happenings that year through that date explains why Lee questioned if someone else could do a better job than he could of leading the Army of Northern Virginia. One must accept the reality of his illness. Lee also believed he could not perform up to his own standards so he, as an honest man, could only conclude that another commander could do the job better. The foremost question for the Confederacy at that time was: who could qualify as such a replacement? The reality of the times was that the Confederacy had no general of quality who could come close to replacing Lee, no matter how serious his shortcomings were!

*   *   *

To make matters worse for Lee and his weakened army, the Confederate Administration chose September as the time when Longstreet's corps should be sent to the West to reinforce Bragg's army. This markedly improved the situation in the West. Two divisions and a brigade, about 12,000 men, were moved west. This left Lee with only about 45,000 men, some of whom were very raw replacements. With Jackson dead and Longstreet in the West, A.P. Hill and Richard Ewell were his only remaining corps commanders. Lee recognized that these generals were of a far lower level of quality than either Jackson or Longstreet.

Longstreet's reinforcement of Bragg led to the defeat of Rosecrans and his Army of the Cumberland at the bloody Battle of Chickamauga.[5] This enormous Union defeat in the West led to great changes in the organization of the Union armies in the West. Rosecrans was replaced by Major General George Thomas,the only Union general who had really performed well at Chickamauga. In addition, Major General Ulysses S. Grant was appointed as overall Union commander in the West. The move of Grant proved to be a harbinger of things to come for this superior general. An army under Major General W.T. Sherman and two corps from the Army of the Potomac, under Hooker, were sent to join Grant's force in Chattanooga and a small army, under Burnside, occupied Knoxville.

After Chickamauga, Longstreet joined the conspiracy of generals in the Army of Tennessee against its commander, General

Braxton Bragg. Longstreet became the spokesman of the group to the Davis Administration, but his political strength was not strong enough to gain Bragg's removal. Although Longstreet and Bragg hated one another, Longstreet was too well thought of for Bragg to cause him to be relieved. This hateful stand-off led the incompetent Bragg to make a disastrous decision that contributed heavily to the doom of the Confederacy.

In mid-October, the unhappy Longstreet and his corps were sent to drive Burnside from Knoxville. This move, the poor design of the Missionary Ridge fortifications and an unreal and wishful Confederate evaluation of the strength of the positions opposite Grant's forces, led to another Confederate disaster at Chattanooga. Although it seemed inconceivable, this debacle proved even worse than that at Gettysburg. By October 30th, the Confederate siege of Union-held Chattanooga was lifted when a short and secure supply line, the "cracker-line," was opened from the main Union supply depot at Bridgeport, Alabama to Chattanooga. On November 23rd, Union forces captured Orchard Knob, and on the 24th, Hooker's two corps scaled the 1,100-foot heights of Lookout Mountain and captured it. The main Confederate positions were on Missionary Ridge which was a commanding position about six hundred feet high above Chattanooga. These defensive positions appeared to be very strong.

On the 25th, Grant ordered Hooker to assault the west end of Missionary Ridge while Sherman was ordered to continue the attack he had begun the previous day on the east end. These assaults failed, and at about 3:00 P.M., Grant ordered divisions of Thomas's Army of the Cumberland to drive forward and capture the Confederate rifle-pits at the base of the ridge. To his surprise, these troops did not halt at the base as ordered, but instead continued up its steep face and captured it.[6]

The defenses atop Missionary Ridge were poorly engineered and were not nearly so strong as they appeared; nevertheless, it was in this charge that Grant noticed the efficiency, aggressiveness and fearlessness of Sheridan. When his troops began their charge up the ridge, this major general went up with them, and only his division maintained sufficient cohesion to continue a chase of the Confederates down the south face of the ridge.[7] It was in those few hours that Sheridan earned the position of strong favor with Grant that he never lost.

*   *   *

Because the North began the war in a more desperate need for able commanders than the South then perceived, the Union Administration followed a trial-and-error selection process which resulted in the elimination of a large number of inefficient general officers and army commanders. After the Battle of Chattanooga, it was clear to the powers that be in the North that Grant was by far the best general in the Federal Army, and Sherman and Meade were also more efficient than any previous Union army commanders.

After his victories at Chattanooga and Vicksburg, Grant began to receive substantial support to become general-in-chief of the Union Army. From Lee's point-of-view, this likely change marked the beginning of his demise. Provided Grant, Meade and a reorganized general officer corps actually proved to be great improvements for the Army of the Potomac, Lee would no longer face Union leadership of the quality of McClellan, Pope, Burnside and Hooker. Would this improved leadership prove to be the difference between Lee being a dominating general and a charismatic leader or an ineffective commander-in-chief? Could Lee continue to perform well against the new Union leadership? Would Lee continue to fight Pyrrhic offensive battles, or would he finally be forced to fight on the defensive by more skillful opponents and by his own self-inflicted losses?

If Lee were forced to fight defensively, a situation in which he had shown great skill, would he be able to wear down the Union army? If Lee inflicted additional heavy losses on the Army of the Potomac, would this make it appear to the political hierarchy of the Union that Grant was accomplishing little and was only a butcher? Would frustration among the Northern populace lead to political collapse of Northern support for the Civil War and a Confederate victory by default? There were two mile-posts that could be early predicted to occur in 1864 that would do much to define the outcome of the war: (1) Grant would surely invade Virginia in the spring; and (2) the presidential election process would occur in the fall. These two things played on each other. How successful would Grant be? If Lincoln were not re-nominated and re-elected, it was highly questionable if another president would continue to lead a strong and aggressive war effort.

CHAPTER XVII

Mine Run: An Aborted Union Opportunity

In the little-remembered Mine Run Campaign, Lee was outnumbered 48,500 to 69,600 effectives; nevertheless he showed great defensive skill. Twice the Army of the Potomac successfully maneuvered the Army of Northern Virginia into a position where it could be out-fllanked and surrounded; twice the Union leadership moved sluggishly, failing to follow up its hard-won advantage. Lee reacted very well defensively. This was the last campaign before Grant's entrance on the scene. The Mine Run Campaign was the last one from which the Army of the Potomac left the field to move back to its comfortable camps north of the Rapidan River after a defeat or failure to reach its objectives.

With the exception of Meade and Grant, the Union high command believed they were in a strategic position nationwide from which they could quickly end the war. They thought they had a great advantage against Lee because they rated Longstreet as the most effective of Lee's corps commanders, and he, with 12,000 of his men, was in Tennessee. They reasoned that a campaign in the fall of 1863 would either allow them to defeat a weakened Army of Northern Virginia, or if Longstreet and his men rushed back to Virginia, Grant and his armies could decisively defeat Bragg and perhaps drive him as far south as Atlanta.

Meade was not enthusiastic about such a campaign because he thought his army needed more time to restore itself after the hard fighting and huge casualties at Gettysburg.[1] The experienced Meade may have also recognized that a seven to five advantage 'for his army in an attack against a skilled defender was not really as strong an advantage as it may have appeared to his superiors. In spite of his doubts, Meade was a soldier of duty; consequently he and his staff began to plan for such a thrust against Lee's army.

On October 9th, the Union Signal Corps intercepted a dispatch from Stuart to Fitzhugh Lee ordering him to prepare to move. Recognizing that this was a preparation for the cavalry to move against his right, Meade moved his main body toward Centerville and the old Manassas battlefield. This movement led to a week of heavy skirmishing with the loss of over a thousand men by both sides. The result of these actions was that Lee withdrew to the Rappahannock River line.[2]

Meade had recommended that the Army of the Potomac cross the Rappahannock near Fredericksburg so as to avoid fighting in the Wilderness. Then, the army would move around Lee's right flank and try to gain a position between his army and Richmond. Because of a concern that this move might leave Washington unprotected as it had been in 1862, Meade's recommendation was denied by Halleck who ordered Meade to develop a new strategy against Lee.

The plan Meade and his staff developed was to cross the Rappahannock and Rapidan rivers quickly, move rapidly through the Wilderness and place themselves between Lee's troops, who were centered around Gordonsville, and Richmond to the south. If this strategy were successful, it would place the Army of Northern Virginia in danger of being surrounded which would force them to attack in order to escape.

13. The Mine Run Campaign

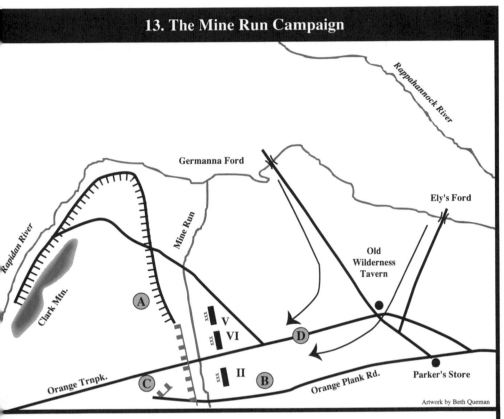

Artwork by Beth Queman

A. Original Confederate prepared defenses.
B. On November 29th, Warren and II Corps outflanked Lee's old lines, but was too slow in preparing to attack.
C. On the night of the 30th, Lee reinforced his lines to the south which made Warren abandon the idea of attacking.
D. Lee was exposed to being flanked, but Meade moved too slowly to take this advantage. When the Army of the Potomac retreated, Lee did not change his position and remained exposed.

Through most of the forgotten Mine Run Campaign, Lee performed poorly both tactically and strategically, but his last, strong tactical maneuver was good enough to save his army. Lee had decided to defend the line of the Rappahannock River; however, Meade's successful night crossings of the river at Kelly's

Ford and Rappahannock Station on November 7, 1863 surprised him. The Army of the Potomac lost several opportunities to fight on favorable ground of Meade's choosing because their movements were too lethargic. When the two sides fought at Payne's Farm on November 27th, there were no decisive results. Lee recognized that this position was too weak defensively so he fell back to the high ground west of Mine Run that night.[3]

On the 28th, Meade had a great opportunity to move around Lee's right and surround him, but he respected Lee too much. He delayed too long while he over-examined Lee's positions. Lee began to fortify the high ground on the 28th and resisted all weak Union attempts to cross Mine Run that day. On the 29th, Warren, by then a major general temporarily commanding II Corps on the left of Meade's army, discovered that his corps overlapped Lee's open right flank. Lee's great tactical and engineering error was barely offset by Warren's timid approach to making an attack on the 29th. After preparing all day, Warren finally attacked too late, and nightfall forced him to give up the attack. The failed attack fully exposed to the observant Lee that Warren intended to repeat the effort the next day. Lee's tactical response was excellent when he reinforced and extended his right. The next morning the obvious strength of the improved defenses persuaded Warren that an attack was impossible, in spite of the fact that Meade had shifted more than half of his army to II Corps.[4]

When Meade could not develop an alternative attack mode and retreated to the north of the Rappahannock, it revealed the strong mental advantage Lee had over Union generals. They over-rated Lee's tactical and strategic skills and were simply afraid of him. This fear had partially defined the outcome of every battle the Army of the Potomac had fought with the Army of Northern Virginia through 1863. This changed, finally and for all, when Grant took command nation-wide and stationed himself next to Meade's headquarters in order to guide strategy and movement personally.

CHAPTER XVII

*   *   *

The Mine Run Campaign proved very important to the Union cause because it made a great contribution to solving the command problems in the Army of the Potomac and the rest of the Union Army. It showed Lincoln, Stanton and Halleck that Meade would not stand up to the needs of handling an offensive campaign efficiently. At almost the same time, Grant won a great offensive victory at Chattanooga. The winter suspension of active campaigning also gave the Administration time to make carefully considered changes.

Lincoln and his Administration also saw the need for a generalissimo, an officer who was expert in developing and executing a nationwide strategy, in choosing good tactics and, most important, in winning battles. The failure of the Mine Run Campaign also demonstrated to Meade and his superiors that the Army of the Potomac needed to be seriously reorganized. Inefficient and mostly politically-minded generals had to be replaced with militarily competent officers. These considerations led to the appointment of Ulysses S. Grant as lieutenant general, ranking above everybody in the Union war effort except Lincoln who said he would allow Grant to win or lose the war without his personal interference. He even made it clear that this prohibition of interference also applied to his Secretary of War, Stanton. Lincoln told Stanton that they had been trying to win the war for some years and had done poorly, so now they should allow someone else to do it, and that man was Grant.[5]

The Army of the Potomac was streamlined into three corps, II was under Hancock, V under Warren and VI under Sedgwick. Major generals "Tardy George" Sykes and William "Whiskey Barrel Bill" Franklin were reassigned to other less critical duties, and their corps were consolidated into the other three. Major General Daniel Sickles, the consummate politician, was not asked to return to the field after losing a leg at Gettysburg. Major General Daniel Butterfield, Chief-of-Staff under Hooker at

Chancellorsville and Meade at Gettysburg where he was wounded, was replaced. He was sent to the West with Hooker who was by then a corps commander under Sherman. Butterfield was not well liked by many, but his replacement as chief of staff, Major General Andrew A. Humphreys, was well regarded by all. Humphreys had shown great skill earlier in combat as a division and corps commander, and he was one of the most talented army chiefs-of-staff developed during the war. All these changes were made before Grant arrived, and they were made politely, with no one being publicly criticized, in keeping with the "gentlemen's club" atmosphere of the Army of the Potomac's officer corps.

As a result of these changes, the Army of the Potomac took on a more professional, less political, aspect. The army still had several incompetents and political officers in lower commands, but all that could practically be done in the time available was done. With Meade in administrative control and Grant in command of all its strategic actions, the army was like nothing Lee had faced before. After Grant's reorganization, a command conflict between Grant and Meade constantly simmered, but both men were excellent professional soldiers. They worked together reasonably well and resisted conflict between them, maintaining good cooperation until after the war. Then, various biographers of each pointed out the several times the conflict approached an acute level. It should be pointed out that Meade was acting as "assistant commander" of the Army of the Potomac under Grant as commander. Ironically, this was the same position Grant had held under Halleck after Shiloh which Grant found to be intolerable.

Lee had defeated all commanders of the Army of the Potomac prior to Meade's taking its command in spite of the fact that they often had substantial numerical advantage. Meade had performed well against Lee as long as he remained in a defensive position. In the following spring, Lee would have to face a combination of Meade and Grant. It would soon become clear whether or not the new Union command would prove more effective than had those of the first three years of the war. How would Lee perform against Grant? Did he have adequate high-quality subordinate generals to give him the support he required? Could Lee continue to hold his army together and have it continue to be effective in the face of more desertion and his high rate of casualties? How would Lee's declining health affect the 1864 fighting?

CHAPTER XVIII

Grant: A New and Different Challenge for Lee

Until the spring of 1864, Lee successfully turned back each commander of the Army of the Potomac in five major Union efforts to invade Virginia. Four of these times, the Union army left after only one battle. Longstreet, a pre-war friend and in-law of Grant, warned Lee of Grant's skills. "He will doggedly keep up the fight until one of you is dead or beaten. He will never turn back from his goal after a defeat or a victory!"[1] This prophecy proved true. Lee was now in a war of attrition he could not have wanted, and he was soon forced by Grant to maintain a defensive posture and finally to abandon all offensive movements.

Grant was appointed Lieutenant General of the United States Army on March 9, 1864 and General-in-Chief of the Armies of the United States on March 12, 1864. It had been widely known for several months that his promotion to overall command would be forthcoming soon.[2]

After modest performance at West Point where he graduated 21st of 39 in the Class of 1843, Grant performed well in the Mexican War. He found army garrison life on the frontier monotonous, and he missed his family too much to continue the necessary sacrifices. Frustrated and depressed, he turned to drinking and resigned from the army as a captain rather than face a court martial for drunkenness in 1854. Unsuccessful in all the pursuits he attempted in civilian life, Grant applied to join McClellan's staff but was rejected. Later that year when Lincoln called for volunteers in 1861, Grant joined the volunteer army as a colonel and was soon promoted to brigadier general. Fortunately for the Union war effort, this gained Grant relatively high seniority early in the war.

In his first command effort, Grant's small army fought at the Battle of Belmont on November 7, 1861. He made an ill-conceived attack and then managed the battle poorly although it ended in a draw. In the West, Grant's seniority allowed him to keep his command. His strategy was to gain naval control of the major rivers of the South to enable Union ground troops to penetrate comparatively easily into the heartlands of the western Confederate states. In February 1862 in cooperation with the U.S. Navy, Grant's forces captured Fort Henry on the Tennessee River and Fort Donelson on the Cumberland River. The removal of these strong Confederate defensive barriers allowed Union gunboats to move up these rivers deep into Tennessee bringing with them large numbers of troops and tons of supplies.

The first major test for Grant as an army commander occurred at the Battle of Shiloh.[3] Grant's army of 41,682 effectives was camped near Pittsburg Landing on the Tennessee River just north of the Mississippi border while Grant was at a meeting nine miles away. Sherman was left in command, and both Grant and Sherman believed that the army under General Albert Sidney Johnston was not strong enough to make an attack against them. Because of this over-confidence, the Union army had not fortified its camp and was ill-prepared to meet an enemy attack. Major General Don Carlos Buell's army of about 20,000 was en route to join Grant and was expected to arrive on April 7, 1862, and

Grant's plan was to attack the army of A.S. Johnston as soon as Buell's force joined his.

One of the five originally appointed Confederate full generals, A.S. Johnston, with a force of about 40,000, planned to advance north from Corinth and attack Grant before Buell could join him. Johnston's attack was delayed for several days, but he finally made his assault on April 6th. Surprise was complete, and by the end of the first day, the Union army had been driven back almost to the Tennessee River where Sherman, Grant and other officers rallied the troops along a new and strong defensive line. In one of the major disasters of the war for the Confederacy, about 2:00 P.M. on the 6th, A.S. Johnston was struck by spent bullets, one of which damaged an artery. No one recognized the severity of his wound, and in a half-hour Johnston died while surrounded by his staff. Contrary to the opinion of many previous historians, Dr. Jack D. Welsh believes the wound was not serious enough for Johnston to have bled to death under the conditions. In his book on the medical conditions of Confederate generals, Welsh concludes that it was likely that Johnston, a man of 59, died of a heart attack brought on by the heavy action and the minor wounds.[4] His successor, General P.G.T. Beauregard, called off the attack in mid-afternoon even though many thought there was still a great chance of overwhelming the Union forces.

The Second Day at Shiloh was Grant's day; the combined forces of Grant and Buell drove Beauregard and his army from the field. With Union losses of 10,162 (16.4% of the combined force, killed and wounded) and Confederate losses of 9,735 (21.6% of the force, killed and wounded),[5] this was the first of many very bloody battles of the Civil War. This first truly horrible battle of the Civil War shocked the civilian population on both sides. Grant was blamed in many quarters for Shiloh being such a bloody battle. Major General Henry W. Halleck, Grant's immediate superior, was particularly miffed by the huge casualties which he believed negated Grant's ability and his success of which he was very jealous. Halleck replaced Grant in command of the army and set him aside as an assistant commander with little or nothing to do. After this slight, Grant wished to resign, but Sherman persuaded him to stay.

When Halleck was ordered to move to Washington to become General-in-Chief of the Federal Army, Grant succeeded him as overall commander in the West. In the summer of 1862 widespread diseases like measles, malaria, yellow fever, tuberculosis, typhoid fever, several forms of dysentery and small pox reduced the strength of the armies to a point where neither side could fight effectively. A stalemate resulted around Corinth, Mississippi where General Braxton Bragg replaced General Beauregard who showed the classic symptoms of battle fatigue and stress. Electing to assume the offensive and leave swampy northern Mississippi, Bragg shifted most of his army to Chattanooga from where he began a move north into Kentucky. Buell was sent in pursuit of Bragg leaving Grant with about half of his previous force, about 50,000 men. Ordered to pursue Bragg, Buell was removed from Grant's command and was ordered to report directly to Halleck.[6] In Mississippi under Grant's overall command, the Union fought and won battles at Iuka and Corinth. His subordinate, Major General Rosecrans, was in independent command at the Battle of Corinth on October 3 and 4, 1862.

When Bragg invaded Kentucky, Buell raced him to Louisville, and with great difficulty, Buell won the race. Bragg's hopes of raising 25,000 Confederate recruits in Kentucky and establishing a stable and secure Confederate state there failed. The two sides fought at Perryville, Kentucky on October 8, 1862. After being defeated, Bragg was threatened with being surrounded so he hastily retreated into Tennessee. Buell failed to mount an effective pursuit of Bragg so both generals were severely criticized for their failures. The Federal Administration demonstrated greater toughness of mind when an army commander disappointed them; Buell was replaced by Rosecrans. In spite of his failure, Bragg remained in command of the Confederate Army of Tennessee.

Grant's primary Western strategy was to sever the Confederacy by capturing the Mississippi River and splitting the Confederate States into two less powerful segments. By October 1862, the Union controlled the Mississippi except for the stretch from just north of Baton Rouge to just south of Memphis. The key position defending this stretch of the river was the bastion of Vicksburg, Mississippi. In December 1862, Grant began to mount a series of attempts to capture Vicksburg.

His first attempt was to send 40,000 troops south from Memphis along the railroad toward Vicksburg while Sherman took 32,000 men by river to Chickasaw Bluffs north of the city. This attempt failed when the overland advance was stopped at Holly Springs and Sherman's men failed to capture the Bluffs. Four unsuccessful Bayou expeditions were made in February, March and April 1863.

On March 29, 1863, Grant began his final and ultimately successful attempt to capture Vicksburg when he ordered a road to be built on the west side of the river to a point south of the city. From April 11th through the 18th, the Navy ran by the Vicksburg batteries at night and successfully joined the army south of the city. Having exposed his planned line of attack to the south, Grant ordered two diversions: Sherman was sent to attack Haines's Bluff north of the city and Colonel R.H. Grierson was ordered to raid the rear areas of Mississippi east of Vicksburg.

Grant wished to cross to the east side of the Mississippi River and land at Grand Gulf, but after the Navy bombarded that Confederate strong point for six hours without neutralizing it on April 29th, he elected to land at Bruinsburg, which he did unopposed on the 30th. Having successfully moved his army across the broad river, Grant first moved east to Jackson where he attacked a force commanded by General J.E. Johnston. Grant did not want Johnston to be able to attack his rear as he moved west toward Vicksburg. After defeating Johnston at Jackson on May 14th, Grant turned toward Vicksburg. Pemberton's main army of defense for Vicksburg came out of its fortifications to meet him at Champion's Hill. In near-fought battles on May 16th at

Champion's Hill and at the Big Black River on the 17th, Pemberton's force was driven back into the fortifications of the city.

On May 19th, the first Union assaults against the very strong Vicksburg defenses failed with heavy losses, and the battle for Vicksburg became a siege. After six weeks of hard fighting while the soldiers and civilians in the city approached starvation, Vicksburg capitulated on July 4, 1863.[7] The Vicksburg Campaign demonstrated the strong character and great and diverse skills of Grant. He showed a stubborn tendency to continue the battle until he succeeded, regardless of many more timid recommendations from his own generals. At Vicksburg, Grant showed great flexibility in changing his plans: he tried assaulting the heights north of the city; he tried an overland movement from the north; he tried amphibious assaults; finally he outflanked Vicksburg by landing to the south. He assumed the center position between two enemy forces, first neutralizing the weaker and then turning on the stronger in a classic maneuver favored by Napoleon. He maneuvered to destroy Pemberton in the open, and only after trying all these things, the stubborn Grant resorted to a siege.

The campaign defined the determination and bull-dog tenacity of Grant. This was the kind of man and general Lee would have to face in 1864.

*　　*　　*

After the Union disaster at Chickamauga in September 1863, the Army of the Cumberland was besieged by Confederate troops which occupied the heights of Lookout Mountain and Missionary Ridge above Chattanooga. Their direct and easy routes of supply were cut off leaving a rough, muddy mountain road as the sole way to bring in supplies. Adequate amounts of food and fodder to feed Union soldiers and horses could not be brought in by this route. Most of the army's horses died or were eaten by the soldiers.

Grant was appointed overall commander, assigned to relieve the siege of Chattanooga and to resume the offensive against Bragg. One of his first acts was to relieve his personal enemy, Rosecrans, whom he replaced with Major General George Thomas, "the Rock of Chickamauga," one of that battle's few heros.

Two corps under Hooker and Sherman's Army of the Tennessee were ordered to move to join Grant's command. With Hooker attacking from the west and troops attacking from Chattanooga, the "cracker line," a direct route from the army's main supply depots at Bridgeport, Alabama to Chattanooga, was opened by October 30th. This coup successfully lifted the siege and allowed the armies of Grant to be well supplied.[8]

Grant elected to perform a double-envelopment strategy against Bragg. Hooker was ordered to move to a position from which he could capture Lookout Mountain and then to prepare to move against the west end of Missionary Ridge. He also ordered Sherman to move his army behind the hills on the north side of the Tennessee River and prepare to cross the river and subsequently attack the east end of Missionary Ridge.

On November 23rd the Army of the Cumberland captured Orchard Knob and Indian Hill. After this, Grant's strategy moved quickly: on the 24th, Lookout Mountain was assaulted and captured by Hooker's forces. Also on the 24th, Sherman crossed the Tennessee River and assaulted the east end of Missionary Ridge but his attack fell short. Finally, on the afternoon of the 25th, Grant ordered the Army of the Cumberland to assault and capture the rifle-pits at the base of Missionary Ridge.

Unexpectedly, three divisions continued their assault up the 600-foot high ridge without higher authority. Because the Confederate defenses at the top of the ridge were poorly designed, the seemingly strong position was taken with unexpected ease.[9]

At Chattanooga, Grant had faced and solved a long series of very complex problems that most other commanders in the Civil War would have not even tried to tackle. Again, his determination just would not allow for failure, and he was able to bring together a number of different-thinking subordinates who were willing to follow his resolve to victory without any lack of willingness or reservations. This ability in a man who was not fundamentally a charismatic leader was probably Grant's greatest asset. Soldiers followed him not because of charisma, but because they recognized his determination and ability to win.

*   *   *

After the Battle of Chattanooga, Grant's reputation was so enhanced that it was widely believed only he could solve the military impasse in the East. Lieutenant General Ulysses S. Grant assumed overall command of the Federal Army with excellent credentials for the highest military command. In the years of 1862 and 1863, he had successfully commanded these types of military operations:

- The planning and accomplishment of a very complex regional strategy against the Confederacy
- Performing two difficult but successful sieges of the enemy, at Ft. Donelson and Vicksburg
- The rescue of the Army of the Cumberland after it was besieged at Chattanooga
- Turning defeat into victory at Shiloh
- Successfully performing the maneuver of attaining a center position east of Vicksburg from which he could attack both forces of the enemy in detail
- Successful integration of his armies with the U.S. Navy in his attacks and using the navy to deliver supplies efficiently
- The successful use of a wide range of complicated battle tactics in the combination of all of his battles
- Successful command of a group of several armies in very complicated and widely spread operations

The common positive threads in Grant's performance were

intelligence, strategic insight, good logistics, flexibility in approaching a military problem or objective, great determination and the ability to select and develop superior subordinates. As of the beginning of 1864, no Civil War general on either side could show such a rich, successful and varied *Curriculum Vitae* in the field of military expertise. In the coming fifteen months Grant would have to show by performance that his previous successes were not the result of fighting second rate Confederate generals. Would he prove as successful against the South's best general, Robert E. Lee?

While Grant was a good organizer, he was not interested in performing the administrative details required for running an army, so he needed a man like Brigadier General John A. Rawlins who acted as Grant's principal staff officer from late 1861 through the end of the war. Grant was able to become fully occupied, involved and interested whenever action was imminent or while he was in battle. At other times, he became bored easily and Rawlins and Mrs. Grant did what they could to keep him from drinking; usually, they were successful. There was no doubt that Grant would be a far more skilled foe than any other commander Lee had faced. Only time would tell whether this formidable foe would prove more effective against Lee than his earlier enemies had been.

CHAPTER XIX

The Battle of the Wilderness: The Beginning of the End for Lee

In the burning woods of the Wilderness, everything changed forever for Lee. In perhaps the ghastliest battle of this ghastliest of wars, the most important change happened after the battle when Grant turned south and prepared to fight again. After less costly battles against Lee, former Union commanders had turned back, but Grant did not. Lee made his last great offensive move of the war in the Wilderness. He lost his last great corps commander, Longstreet, to wounds and was left with very inadequate replacements. From that battle forward in the war, the initiative remained with Grant.

*A*fter Grant accepted the assignment as Lieutenant General and General-in-Chief of the U.S. Army in March of 1864, he could make any changes in personnel he wished. Of the generals he thought well of in the West, he brought only Major General Philip H. Sheridan with him, as commander of his cavalry corps. With the arrival of Grant and Sheridan, Lee could no longer depend on tardy and inept performance to save the day for him. Nor could he hope that the Union army would retreat to its camps after a hard battle.

Longstreet was a close pre-war friend of Grant's. They were at West Point together for three years. Julia Grant, nee Dent, was a cousin of Longstreet who had introduced her to Grant, and Grant had introduced Longstreet to his future wife and was his best man at his wedding. For many years, the relationship between these two men was close and intimate, but now they were sworn enemies. Being at war did not interfere with their respect and concern for one another. When Longstreet rejoined Lee from the West, he warned him that Grant was skillful, determined and would not give up until he had won or died trying.[1]

As soon as Grant arrived in the East, the destruction of the Army of Northern Virginia became his main strategic objective. To Grant, geographic gains were of minor importance. To him, the only benefit to be gained by taking pieces of enemy territory was that they might help to cause Lee to make ill-advised moves, leading to his own destruction. Grant planned to move against Lee from three directions. The Army of the Potomac would attack Lee directly. Sigel's Department of West Virginia troops would attack Lee's left flank in a drive down the Shenandoah Valley. Butler's Army of the James would attack its right flank by moving up the James River with support by the U.S. Navy. Grant's assignment to Sherman was to disturb the rear areas of the Confederacy in what was equivalent to a gigantic raid. Grant told him that whatever Confederate troops Sherman occupied in local fighting against his Western armies could not be moved north to fight against the Army of the Potomac. Another assignment Grant gave to Sherman was to destroy the Confederacy's arms manufacturing centers, capture their support sources, break down their infrastructure and destroy enemy morale.

Grant's preferred strategic goal was to destroy Lee's army by skillful maneuver in the open field before it retreated to the strong Richmond defenses. However, Grant had enough respect for Lee to think it would be unlikely that Lee would allow him such an opportunity. Therefore, as a second choice, he preferred a war of attrition to a siege, since a siege would allow Lee to defend against him with fewer troops, releasing some Confederate troops to reinforce other armies. Grant knew his battle against Lee would not be short or easy, and he thought siege warfare might well prove to be the only alternative Lee would allow him.

The replacement of Pleasonton with Sheridan to command the cavalry corps eliminated the last strongly politically-minded general in corps level command. Using ties to various Republican politicians, with whom he often communicated directly, Pleasonton gained the rank of major general just prior to Gettysburg. He immediately promoted three of his favorite officers to brigadier general over numerous colonels and majors. The three men promoted were Elon Farnsworth and Wesley Merritt from captain and George Armstrong Custer from first lieutenant. Farnsworth was killed almost immediately; however, the other two officers served with great distinction throughout the rest of the war.

Sheridan had served well as an infantry division commander in the battles of Perryville, Stones River, Tullahoma, Chickamauga and Chattanooga. Earlier in the West, he had commanded a cavalry brigade. He was an intense, demanding man who loved a fight and was fiercely loyal to his superiors, provided they were competent, and he was even more caring for the officers and troops who served under him. He reorganized and rearmed the Cavalry Corps in just a month. He was not a politically-minded officer, his loyalty in the East was to the Union and to Grant whom he greatly admired and respected. Above all, Sheridan would do all in his power and could be depended upon to carry out any assignments given him well and without any reservations. He had expected to be assigned to command an infantry corps under Sherman in the spring of 1864, and he was fully qualified for that post. In his new assignment, he wanted to change the role of the cavalry arm from being messengers and guards to being an offensive weapon fighting beside the infantry. He believed equality for cavalry with the infantry and artillery in main battle would allow the Union armies to use new tactics to their great advantage. This was a radical idea at the time, not shared by any leading general on either side except for Grant and Thomas.

Grant demanded that many changes in the Union command system be made. Grant, acting as the Federal Army's generalissimo, was responsible only to President Lincoln. He was strongly against residing in Washington, where he was sure the politicians would interfere adversely with his doing his duty by demanding explanations and even approval of his plans. He elected to remain with the Army of the Potomac, but, since he wished to avoid all the administrative headaches of commanding an army, he left Meade as its titular commander. Meade would report to Grant as would Burnside with his large IX Corps, and Grant would make all strategic and tactical decisions. He assigned Major General Henry W. Halleck as Chief-of-Staff of the U.S. Army and passed most commands to his far-away army commanders, like Sherman, through Halleck. Sometimes Halleck modified his commands, but most of the time he did not do so, and the system worked well.

Grant instituted an Army Regulation stating that no officers were to communicate about the war except through Army and War Department channels. This was meant to prevent communication of private views, biased opinions or military secrets by officers directly to politicians and newspapers. The regulation stated that any officer disobeying the regulation would be discharged. Up until this time such generals as Sickles, Rosecrans, Pleasonton and many others, along with many lower ranking officers, used newspapermen and congressmen to gain personal advantage, promotion or the elimination of a commander with whom they were in disagreement. Frequently, the War Department or an army commander would learn of a subordinate's complaint or discontent only when he received a critical letter from a congressman or learned of the problem from a newspaper. The problem was widespread and intolerable, and Grant's action and a few examples reduced problem incidents to a trickle.

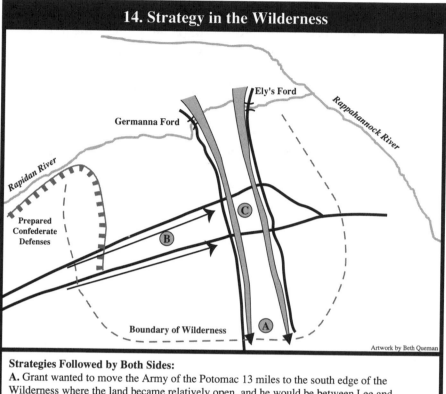

14. Strategy in the Wilderness

Ely's Ford

Germanna Ford

Rappahannock River

Rapidan River

Prepared
Confederate
Defenses

Boundary of Wilderness

Artwork by Beth Queman

Strategies Followed by Both Sides:
A. Grant wanted to move the Army of the Potomac 13 miles to the south edge of the Wilderness where the land became relatively open, and he would be between Lee and Richmond.
B. Lee responded quickly by trying to cut the Army of the Potomac in two and push one column back upon the other, causing confusion.
C. Both strategies failed, and brought on the Battle of the Wilderness with 18,000 Union and 10,500 Confederate casualties.

*   *   *

    To accomplish his strategic aims, Grant decided to try to move around Lee's right flank to gain a strong tactical position between the Army of Northern Virginia and Richmond. Grant rejected making a move around Lee's left because it would be much more difficult to supply his army by overland routes which could be under frequent attack by Confederate cavalry. By the more eastern route, the army could be supplied by ship through Chesapeake Bay. Grant's first such move into the Wilderness was similar to Meade's move in the Mine Run Campaign. When this failed, he repeated his plan which led to repeated bloody battles over six weeks, with great losses for both sides. Lee succeeded in keeping Grant from moving between his army and Richmond until he was finally forced to move into the Richmond-Petersburg fortifications on June 18, 1864.

The Union army crossed the Rapidan at Germanna and Ely's fords on May 4, 1864. Contrary to Sheridan's desires, Meade ordered the Cavalry Corps divided into its three individual divisions: the 2nd and 3rd Divisions initiated each crossing and protected the two pontoon bridges they had built across the Rapidan until a sufficient number of infantry had crossed and each bridgehead was secure. The 1st Cavalry Division was assigned to protect the army's huge supply trains. Once the Germanna bridge was secure, Brigadier General James H. Wilson's 3rd Cavalry Division was ordered to penetrate the Wilderness to the Orange Turnpike and then move west on that road until it established contact with any Confederate forces advancing toward them.

Grant and Meade held the opinion that Lee would fall back and occupy the old Mine Run defenses, but Lee knew how closely he had come to being outflanked there in the previous November. Lee knew Grant would move much more quickly than Meade had in attempting the move and this might encircle him. Therefore, he decided his best tactic was to launch an all-out attack on the west flank of the Union army as it was marching in two columns south through the heart of the Wilderness. He wanted to strike Grant's columns before they could march the 13 miles to the south border of the Wilderness where they would enter into open ground and have an advantage over Lee in maneuvering.[2]

Being attacked in the flank while marching in column, four abreast, was the worst nightmare of all Civil War generals. They took elaborate precautions against such occurrences so it

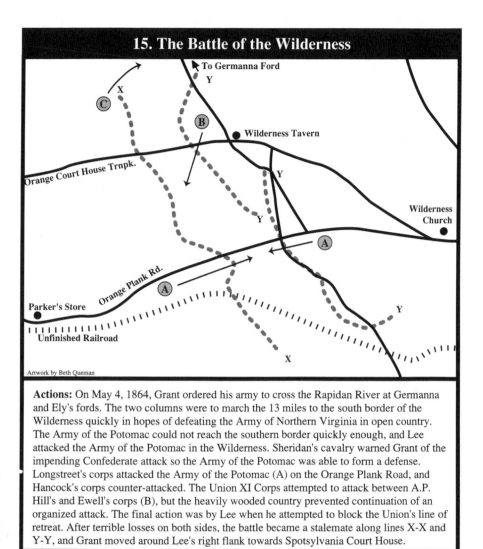

15. The Battle of the Wilderness

To Germanna Ford

Y

X

C

B

Wilderness Tavern

Orange Court House Trnpk.

Y

Y

Wilderness
Church

A

Orange Plank Rd.

A

Parker's Store

Y

Unfinished Railroad

X

Artwork by Beth Queman

Actions: On May 4, 1864, Grant ordered his army to cross the Rapidan River at Germanna and Ely's fords. The two columns were to march the 13 miles to the south border of the Wilderness quickly in hopes of defeating the Army of Northern Virginia in open country. The Army of the Potomac could not reach the southern border quickly enough, and Lee attacked the Army of the Potomac in the Wilderness. Sheridan's cavalry warned Grant of the impending Confederate attack so the Army of the Potomac was able to form a defense. Longstreet's corps attacked the Army of the Potomac (A) on the Orange Plank Road, and Hancock's corps counter-attacked. The Union XI Corps attempted to attack between A.P. Hill's and Ewell's corps (B), but the heavily wooded country prevented continuation of an organized attack. The final action was by Lee when he attempted to block the Union's line of retreat. After terrible losses on both sides, the battle became a stalemate along lines X-X and Y-Y, and Grant moved around Lee's right flank towards Spotsylvania Court House.

happened rarely, but when it did happen as at Chickamauga, the results were devastating. Lee also believed that a fight in the rough ground, dense underbrush and woods of the Wilderness would even the numerical odds between his army and Grant's larger one.

Just east of Mine Run, James H. Wilson's cavalry met advancing

Confederate cavalry followed by their main infantry body, advancing eastward. Wilson was easily forced back, but the noise of the engagement warned Grant that the Confederates were coming, and he was given time to deploy and prepare to receive the Confederate attack. Two days of fighting under the worst imaginable conditions occurred in the Battle of the Wilderness. The woods were on fire, smoke was everywhere, visibility was only a matter of a few yards and it was difficult to tell friend from foe. The rough terrain broke up unit cohesion and did not allow normal formations to be used. Tactical control was lost on both sides, and 190,000 men were reduced to fighting small, bloody, man-to-man engagements where leadership was secondary to individual fighting skill which was the only thing that allowed one to survive. Many helpless wounded died in the flames of the burning woods.

The Union lost 18,000 men and the Confederates 10,800.[3] It was the last time Lee used his full army to make a major assault in the war. Finally he recognized he could no longer afford the casualties that this and many preceding attacks had cost. Grant had suffered a defeat if we judge the outcome based on comparative losses. Lee thought such losses would cause the Army of the Potomac to retreat rapidly to its bases north of the Rapidan as it had done so many times before. Not considering the battle as a defeat, Grant was too tough-minded to even consider a retreat, and he elected to move again around Lee's right flank towards Spotsylvania Court House. When his soldiers realized they were going farther south and were not retreating, they cheered Grant strongly in spite of their heavy losses. Although he hated the war and its deadly risks, the private soldier resented the wasted loss of his comrades' lives that had preceded past retreats. In spite of a doubtful future, the move south offered these soldiers the hope that the end of the horrible Civil War might be coming, at last.

CHAPTER XX

A Bloodbath at Spotsylvania: The Union Army Takes Tentative Steps Toward New Tactics

To win the war, new tactics were needed. At Spotsylvania the bloodbath continued, but Union generals experimented with three new tactical ideas: (1) Sheridan tried a "seize and hold" tactic; (2) Upton tried night infiltration rather than a direct assault on strong defenses; and (3) Hancock attempted other infiltration techniques. These previously untried tactics failed, but even so, they showed great promise. These improved ideas demonstrated the depth and imagination of the improving Union leadership. Supported by the flexible Grant, these new tactics would continue to bring new tests to Lee's abilities.

The conflict between Meade and Sheridan which arose at the battles of the Wilderness and Spotsylvania illustrated the differences between those who recognized a need for change and those who were either satisfied with things as they were or were afraid of change. Only fifty years earlier in Napoleonic times, cavalry had been part of the main effort in battle, sometimes successfully charging against and defeating infantry.

With the improvement of artillery, it was thought that cavalry would no longer be effective as part of the main battle. Before the Civil War, Lieutenant General Winfield Scott, the Federal Army's General-in-Chief, believed artillery would dominate all future wars with infantry being its greatest support. Because of these feelings, Scott de-emphasized the importance of cavalry.[1] Scott's beliefs led to fewer cavalry units being formed. These feelings were wide-spread throughout the army so few officers of quality wished assignment to the cavalry.

In the late 1850s, Scott and others began to have different thoughts about cavalry. Perhaps, they had begun to see the value of cavalry in fighting Indians on the Frontier, and in a war the cavalry could chase defeated troops and conduct raids that might prove useful. As a result, such well-respected officers as Albert Sidney Johnston, Lee and Stuart were assigned to form an elite cavalry regiment that would form the basis of other similar units.[2] This change of emphasis was not in time to influence the actions of cavalry for either side until fairly late in the Civil War. Strength levels of cavalry units, particularly in the North, were less than called for in their tables of organization, usually only about 40%. The combination of de-emphasis and the resulting shortage of well trained cavalrymen made it easy for the officers who were against change to limit the duties of the cavalry to guarding the flanks of the main force, conducting raids and being couriers, guards and generals' aides.

On the Union side, some Western generals like Rosecrans, Thomas and Grant had asked for greater numbers of cavalry. Thomas believed that Buell's failure to trap Bragg's army when it was forced to retreat from Kentucky was due to a lack of cavalry. To Thomas, the idea of infantry chasing and catching fleeing infantry would never work. Chased men have a greater incentive to move fast than those pursuing them on foot. What was needed in such a pursuit was the greater mobility of cavalry which could ride around the head of a fleeing infantry column, set up a road-block and hold it until the pursuing infantry arrived. These cavalry tactics would be adopted before the war ended, but even as late as early 1864, no effective pursuit tactics existed.

In his six-month long preparation for his Tullahoma Campaign in 1863, Rosecrans proposed a substantial increase in the cavalry of the Army of the Cumberland. He wanted to use a large cavalry force to move around Bragg's army, capture the main Confederate supply base at Tullahoma and cut off Bragg's retreat toward Chattanooga.[3] Such tactics should have led to the destruction of Bragg's army, but the War Department did not share his views so it refused to give Rosecrans any additional cavalry. When Rosecrans tried to make the same move using only infantry, foot-troops could not move quickly enough to gain the necessary favorable positions behind Bragg's lines. This slowness of movement allowed Bragg to escape the trap, and Rosecrans only succeeded in driving Bragg across the Tennessee River. This move damaged Bragg's army rather than destroying it. It is interesting to note that Sheridan was close to Rosecrans at the time of Tullahoma and commanded an infantry division in the campaign.

Until this time in the Civil War, "Stonewall" Jackson had been the greatest proponent of "seize and hold" tactics. As described previously, several times Jackson proposed seizing a Northern city and holding a strong defensive position, forcing a costly Union attack against the position. Now Sheridan proposed a slight variation of "seize and hold" tactics: he would use his cavalry to capture Spotsylvania Court House and the bridges leading to it over the Po River. Then he would hold these positions until the Union infantry arrived and strengthened the position. If this move proved successful, it would keep Lee's army west of the Po and give Union forces a route to the flatter lands north of Richmond where maneuvers would be easier and would favor Grant's larger army.

At Todd's Tavern, on the edge of the Wilderness, Sheridan gave Stuart a severe defeat. Then, the aggressive cavalry commander executed his plan to capture Spotsylvania. Sheridan's plan failed due to the mutual inability of two men with vastly different

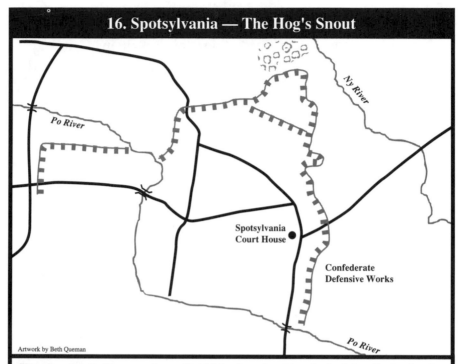

16. Spotsylvania — The Hog's Snout

Ny River

Po River

Spotsylvania
Court House

Confederate
Defensive Works

Po River

Artwork by Beth Queman

Situation: The Po River was deep with high banks and could not be forded easily. Lee barely beat the Army of the Potomac to the bridges and Spotsylvania, establishing a position between Grant and Richmond. Grant chose to fight Lee at Spotsylvania. Lee built a line of field works around Spotsylvania Court House, which was anchored on each end by the Po. The strength of this salient, or hog's snout as it was called, was that its interior lines allowed defenders to move forces about easily while any attacking force on its outside had longer lines and less ability to shift troops quickly. Lee hoped an attack on one side would allow him to hold with few troops and concentrate to attack on the other side of the salient.

military theories, Sheridan and Meade, to understand one another. Sheridan did not tell Meade of his plan in advance because he thought Meade would reject it out of hand. He captured Spotsylvania but failed to hold the town. Still, it was a demonstration of what cavalry might accomplish that was not lost on Grant.

Lee reached Spotsylvania Court House ahead of the Union troops because luck intervened in Lee's favor.[4] Major General

Richard H.Anderson, who had replaced the wounded Longstreet in command of I Corps, was ordered by Lee to march toward Spotsylvania beginning at 3:00 A.M., but his men could not sleep in the burning woods of the Wilderness so they left four hours earlier. Sheridan's cavalry had captured Spotsylvania, but could not hold it against Anderson's infantry which arrived before Sheridan's men could capture the three key bridges over the Po River. This failure led to two weeks of extended fighting and heavy casualties at Spotsylvania.

Since his exhausted troops were no longer capable of offensive tactics, Lee tried a different defensive tactic at Spotsylvania: he set up his lines in a salient or "hog's snout" formation. If Grant tried to apply great force to one side of the salient, Lee could defend against the attack with fewer forces, and after a Union attack was spent he could counter-attack with his reserves. Alternatively, he could shift more force to the weaker Union side and perhaps make an overwhelming assault against it.

The inherent weaknesses of such a salient formation were its two flanks and its apex. In this case the flanks were somewhat protected by the Po River which could not be easily crossed by infantry and artillery where it was not bridged. Grant tried to turn the north flank on May 9th and 10th, sending II Corps, under Hancock, to turn Lee's left while V, VI and IX Corps held the rest of the Confederate defenders in place. This time, Grant's command system failed when Meade ordered Hancock to make a reconnaissance-in-force rather than the all-out attack on the flank Grant wanted. This gave Lee time to shift Early's corps to his left where it counter-attacked Hancock and caused the plan to fail, with heavy casualties to both sides.

Grant never exposed himself to Lee's hoped-for opportunity to counter-attack him, but Lee used the formation skillfully on the defensive. Grant recognized the weakness of the dual command system, and from this point on, he continued to issue his most important orders to Meade, but made sure key corps commanders also received copies of the same orders directly. Meade resented

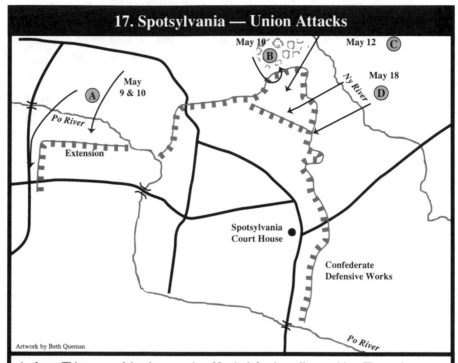

17. Spotsylvania — Union Attacks

May 10

May 12 C

May 18 D

May 9 & 10 A

Po River

Ny River

Extension

Spotsylvania Court House

Confederate Defensive Works

Po River

Artwork by Beth Queman

Actions: This map explains the strengths of Lee's defensive salient position. The weaknesses of the position were its flanks and its apex. On May 9th and 10th, Grant ordered Hancock's II Corps to attack the Army of Northern Virginia's left flank (A). This attack nearly turned the position, but Lee moved two of Early's divisions from his right which successfully repulsed this attack. On May 10th, Colonel Emory Upton led his brigade through woods close to the defenses; and they broke through the lines at dawn (B); but when the assigned support did not come, they were repulsed. Hancock's Corps attacked the apex under cover of band music which allowed his leading elements to reach the defenses undetected; they broke through the apex (C) and threatened the whole position; but John B. Gordon established a new line across the base of the apex and this attack was fought off with great difficulty. Attacks on the right of the new apex (D) were made on the 18th, but these also failed. Grant's losses were 18,000 in these attacks, and Lee lost about 10,000. Grant concluded he could not defeat the position and moved around Lee's right again.

this intrusion on his authority, but for the good of the cause and because he could do nothing about it, he accepted the change.

At dawn on May 10th, Colonel Emory Upton's brigade infiltrated through the woods to within a hundred yards of the

Confederate line on the north side of the salient. In planning for his subsequent attack, Upton ordered his men to load but not cap their rifles before they charged. They were to run the hundred yards all-out to the defensive works and attack with bayonets. Only when they were on the works were they to cap and fire their rifles. He succeeded in making a major penetration of the line but was driven off by Confederate reserves when support that had been arranged for failed to materialize.

On May 12th, Hancock tried another new idea. A Union band began to play loud music before midnight and continued throughout the night. This music covered II Corps' quiet approach to the Confederate lines; the men began quietly crawling toward the enemy lines at 3:00 A.M. Just before dawn, these men rose up directly outside the Confederate works and surprised the defenders; then, II Corps penetrated the apex of the salient with 20,000 men. For a time, the Army of Northern Virginia was in danger of total defeat, but Lee sent Brigadier General John B. Gordon to form a new defensive line across the base of the "bloody angle." This tactic succeeded in stopping II Corps men from dividing Lee's army into two parts. Another Union attack was made on May 18th, but, this and other smaller ones later failed.

In the ten days of fighting around Spotsylvania the Union lost another 18,000 men and the Confederacy 9,500[5]; each side lost about 15% of the forces they had in the field. In the sixteen days since Grant's army crossed the Rapidan, Union corps commander Sedgwick had been killed by a sniper and Confederate corps commander Longstreet had been incapacitated for six months due to serious wounds. The Union lost four other generals, killed or wounded, but the Confederate losses included eleven generals killed, wounded or captured, including Longstreet and Lee's cavalry corps commander, Stuart, at Yellow Tavern. For the Confederate Army, these losses could never be replaced, and they exacerbated the problems of the already over-stressed Confederate command. To make matters worse, another of Lee's corps commanders, Ewell, suffered an ailment "of the nature of scurvy" with severe diarrhea in mid-May.[6] Subsequently, he was found unfit to continue to command in the field on a temporary basis.

In the Wilderness and at Spotsylvania, the Union Army had lost 36,000 men and the Confederate Army almost 20,000 in just two weeks. Except for the Gettysburg campaign, these were the greatest casualties of the war in such a short time, and since Grant again continued his move south, there was little doubt that heavy casualties would continue. If the attrition of his men and especially officers continued at that rate, Lee faced the problem of keeping an effective army in the field.

Grant faced a different set of difficult problems. After three years of war, the recent heavy rate of casualties was far from popular in the North. Would Grant continue to have the support of Northern politicians and the civilian population if such a rate of losses of sons and husbands continued? In past campaigns, the Army of the Potomac had had time between battles to recover and accept the loss of their comrades. Now, Grant seemed to move quickly from battle to battle without giving the survivors any time to recover. In the face of this high level of intensity and aggression with heavy casualties being one result, would Grant's army continue to hold together as an effective fighting force?

Only the development of new tactics offered any hope of change from the previous mode of costly frontal assaults. At this time, the North had an advantage. Grant was flexible, Sheridan was anxious to use his cavalry in new ways and some subordinate infantry generals were attempting to use other tactics than charging defensive works in closed formations. The Confederacy was immersed in the overwhelming problem of finding barely adequate general officers to keep its armies in the field. Southern commanders had little time available to consider new tactics. In any event, neither Lee nor Davis were advocates of change.

CHAPTER XXI

Grant Strikes at Lee's Eyes and Supplies Well Behind His Front Lines

Devoted to all-out war, Grant was not content with fighting only Lee's main army; he sent Sheridan and his 10,000 cavalrymen deep behind Lee's lines. Grant wanted to "blind" Lee to his other movements; Sheridan wanted to destroy Stuart and his force. Lee had two viable responses: (1) send all his cavalry after Sheridan; or (2) send none, have Stuart raid the Union army's trains and warn the rear areas that they would have to take care of themselves. Whether in an act of conceit or lack of consideration, Lee did neither; he split his cavalry, did nothing effective with the portion he kept and doomed Stuart to certain defeat.

A violent argument had occurred between Meade and Sheridan after the failure to capture Spotsylvania Court House before Lee could occupy that key town. Both men were fiery and hot-tempered. Angrily, Meade accused Sheridan of insubordination. Angrily, Sheridan responded that he thought Meade was too cautious, slow and had personally contributed to the failure of his attempt to seize and hold the town. In May of 1864, Meade and the infantry corps commanders considered

Sheridan to be a Western outsider, an upstart ex-infantry division commander who was far below them. They saw him as an undeserving protege of Grant who was wild and reckless, having little skill.

The disagreement between Meade and Sheridan was so severe that Grant was almost faced with choosing whether Meade or Sheridan could continue to serve together in the Army of the Potomac. This was a choice Grant did not wish to make since he valued the abilities of both men. When Meade told Grant of Sheridan's offer to "chase down J.E.B. Stuart and beat him," Grant saw an opportunity to keep both men. Confident in Sheridan's ability, Grant told Meade to order Sheridan to take his corps and do just that.

Sheridan's movement gave Lee a dilemma. He could allow Stuart to take enough cavalry to fight Sheridan effectively; but, if he did so, he would seriously reduce the scouting ability he needed to keep track of Grant's frequent maneuvers. Alternatively, he could let the rear areas take care of themselves as he had when Stoneman had raided the Richmond area at the time of Chancellorsville or in February 1864, when the Union undertook the Kilpatrick-Dahlgren cavalry raid against Richmond. On the occasions of both of these raids, Lee's decision had disturbed the politicians in Richmond who felt personally threatened so Lee knew a similar decision in May 1864 would be equally unpopular. Unable to make a decisive choice, Lee made a weak compromise. By sending only three brigades after Sheridan's seven, Lee gave Stuart no chance to defeat Sheridan's cavalry, and he gave the rear areas inadequate protection.

On May 9th, after slipping around Lee's right flank, Sheridan attacked Beaver Dam Station and destroyed 504,000 rations of bread and 904,000 of meat and most of the Confederate army's medical supplies. In addition, miles of the railroad Lee depended on for supplies were demolished.[1] This loss of more than a week's total food ration for every man in the Army of Northern Virginia was very severe to an army that was already on short rations of food. With continuing battles going on around Spotsylvania, the loss of medical supplies probably cost the lives of wounded from both sides.

Previous Union cavalry raids into Confederate territory were of the "hit and run" variety: move in fast at a gallop, accomplish a limited aim and get out as quickly as possible. Sheridan's plan was very different. Once he was out of reach of Lee's infantry, Sheridan believed there was no other Confederate force in Virginia large and strong enough to defeat his 10,000 men. He ordered his cavalrymen to move at a comfortable trot, save their horses for the coming fight and let Stuart find them.

Convinced that Sheridan's objective was to enter Richmond and wreak havoc there, Stuart drove his horses and men at a break-neck pace to reach Richmond ahead of the Union cavalry. Stuart divided his small force. One brigade was following in Sheridan's tracks while two tried to move around the head of his column and prevent it from reaching Richmond. Sheridan assigned one brigade as a rear guard to prevent the trailing Confederate brigade from interfering with the movements of his main body.

Near an abandoned stage stop called Yellow Tavern just six miles north of central Richmond, Stuart set up a defensive line on a low hill parallel to Sheridan's line of advance. When Sheridan's force of six brigades arrived on the Mountain Road which led into Richmond from the northwest, Stuart, with two brigades of about 2,500 men, was looking down on about 8,000 Union cavalrymen in the process of deploying against him. This numerical inferiority had been thrust upon Stuart by Lee's decision to allow Stuart to take only three brigades with him. Nevertheless, in the numerical superiority ratio of just over 3:1, Sheridan could not be certain of defeating Stuart if he attacked against a strong and well-prepared defensive position.

Stuart could not hope to win by attacking the much stronger force directly so he did not choose to block Sheridan's entry into Richmond or to attack him in his flank. He did send a courier to General Bragg, who commanded the Richmond defenses, suggesting that he send all available troops north to intercept Sheridan's corps. Sheridan mounted a complex double-envelopment attack against Stuart's position on the afternoon of May 12th. He used a combination of mounted and dismounted cavalrymen to move around both flanks and charge the center, all simultaneously. After several hours of fighting at Yellow Tavern, Stuart was taken from the field, mortally wounded.[2] Stuart lived only eight days fighting against Sheridan, a much more skillful and clever cavalryman. Sheridan's losses were 400, 4% of his corps, and it was estimated that the Confederate cavalry lost 1,000, 28% of the force he took with him in actions against Sheridan's Richmond raid.[3]

After Stuart's death, the local Confederate commanders believed Sheridan's corps was trapped and that they would destroy it. On the other hand, Sheridan knew his force was strong enough to take on any available Confederate troops and defeat them. The Cavalry Corps easily fought its way out of the Richmond area, inflicting additional casualties on the Confederate cavalry and local militia troops that opposed it. Killing Stuart, inflicting heavy casualties on the Confederate cavalry, and destroying supplies at Beaver Dam Station were the substantial goals of the operation, and these were accomplished. Also, Sheridan demonstrated to all that the Union cavalry had been developed into a strong force and had gained ascendancy over their Confederate opponents. This success did much to support Sheridan in his proposals that his cavalry take on much more important roles in the coming fighting.

From a personal standpoint, Sheridan had qualified to command an infantry corps in the West, and his ability as a combined-force commander, tactician and strategist, approached that of Jackson. In reorganizing and re-equipping the Cavalry Corps in such a short time, only one month, Sheridan had shown great organizational skills. There was no doubt about Sheridan being a charismatic leader of men. Sheridan had also shown that he could handle the logistics of an independent command well. Grant needed a soldier with these skills, and Sheridan would soon become a great leader in the East.

CHAPTER XXII

Lee Sets a Trap at Ox Ford; Grant Adroitly Avoids it

After Antietam in September 1862, Lee's army consisted of 36,000 officers and men. At Ox Ford in May 1864, he had about 50,000. In the intervening period he had fought six major battles, won two, lost one and drawn three. He had lost about 80,000 men. He had lost his three best subordinate generals, Jackson, Longstreet and Stuart to death and wounds. On May 12th alone, eleven generals had been lost. Were the two bloody wins in this period satisfactory results for the men serving under Lee? Is it any wonder rates of desertion in his army were rising rapidly? Were these deserters voting their lack of confidence in Lee with their feet?

*T*he Mine Run campaign and the maneuvers that culminated along the North Anna River near Ox Ford are largely forgotten episodes of the Civil War. Although small in comparison with the great battles of the Civil War, in the fighting along the North Anna, the two sides lost a combined 5,000 men, and both Lee and Grant showed tactical brilliance.[1] This small campaign was important because it demonstrated that the weakened command structure of the Army of Northern Virginia had collapsed into incompetence. At that time, the question was whether the tired and bloodied Army of the Potomac still retained enough strength to take advantage of the situation.

Having concluded that a stalemate had been reached in the fighting near Spotsylvania, the tenacious Grant decided to move south around Lee's right flank for a third time in a month. This time, he tried a new tactic to draw Lee into a fight in the more open ground north of Richmond: he held most of his forces in their lines around Spotsylvania while he directed Hancock, whose II Corps consisted of 20,000 men, to move widely around Lee's right flank and march as far south toward Richmond as he could until he was stopped. Sheridan with about 10,000 troopers was already in the vicinity of Richmond, and Major General Ben Butler was in the Bermuda Hundred enclave with about 20,000 men. Butler and Sheridan were within 15 miles of Richmond. If one, or both, of these Union forces joined Hancock, they would form a formidable army-sized threat against Richmond.

When Grant crossed the Rapidan on May 4th, his army had 116,000 effective troops. He had lost over 36,000 in battle, Sheridan with 10,000 was on a raid, and Hancock with 20,000 men was detached. Many men were sick and some enlistments had run out. Grant's strength in his main body along the North Anna was down to about 50,000 men while Lee could also put about 50,000 in the field.[2] Seeing a need to strike while the circumstances were numerically as favorable to him as he could ever hope they would be, Lee felt the urge to fight Grant before replacements and detached units could join him.

As had been the case since he lost Stuart and Longstreet, Lee had severe problems with the quality of his subordinate officers which greatly reduced the efficiency of his army. Of the four corps commanders he had at Gettysburg, Stuart was dead, Longstreet was home recovering from wounds, Ewell had been relieved as unfit for service, and A.P. Hill had just returned from extended sick-leave. Hill, Lee's second-in-command, was with him, but he was still ill and not very fit. Lee's other replacement corps

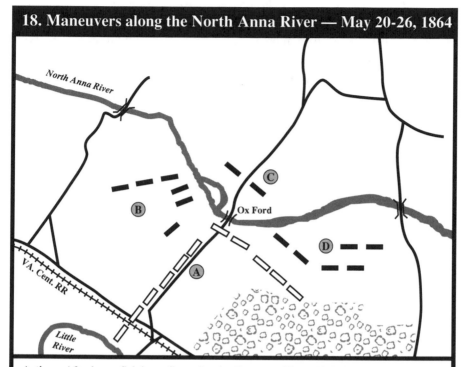

18. Maneuvers along the North Anna River — May 20-26, 1864

Actions: After heavy fighting at Spotsylvania, Grant sent Hancock's II Corps toward Richmond hoping the Army of the Potomac could attack Lee's rear if he moved against Hancock. Lee did not take the bait and retreated to the North Anna River. Without II Corps and Sheridan's cavalry which was on a raid toward Richmond, each side had about 50,000 men after the heavy casualties in the Wilderness and at Spotsylvania. Lee sought to fight on the North Anna while the numbers were so even. The Federals had forced crossings of the river and built bridges. The distance between these bridges by road meant the right (B) part of the Army of the Potomac could not easily support the left (D). Lee set up a defensive salient (A) and blocked Ox Ford. If the Army of the Potomac attacked on both sides of the salient, Lee could defend against one side and attack and hopefuly crush the other. Lee was ill, and his subordinates were unable to take advantage of the situation. Grant elected not to attack the position, and he ordered the Army of the Potomac to move around the right flank of the Army of Northern Virginia again.

commanders were untried and inexperienced at the corps level of command. Similarly, untrained and inexperienced officers had advanced to the command of many of Lee's divisions and regiments; some had advanced beyond their merit.

Once he was convinced that Grant had resumed his move south, Lee decided the next best defensive line was along the North Anna River, and he began a retreat to positions that would block the Union forces from crossing that river. Grant had sent Hancock's corps southward independently as bait to draw Lee into an ill-advised attack. If Lee attacked Hancock's smaller force, then Grant hoped to move with the rest of the Army of the Potomac against Lee's rear. Wisely, Lee resisted the bait and moved directly to the North Anna positions.

As soon as he knew Lee was on the move, Grant ordered his army to follow the Confederates as closely as possible. Under his urging the Army of the Potomac stepped up its speed of pursuit. To Lee's surprise, after he had crossed the North Anna River on May 22nd, he discovered that on the same day Grant had forced two crossings of the river. The Chesterfield Bridge was captured intact, and at Jericho Mill they had forded the river where Union engineers quickly built a pontoon bridge. During the night of the 23rd, the Union army crossed in force at each of these points, about 3 miles apart. However, by the good roads an army required for quick movement, this distance was much greater, 10 to 12 miles.

Lee saw an opportunity to trap the Army of the Potomac and "strike a strong blow against them."[3] He had been dissatisfied with the results of his salient formation at Spotsylvania and had sworn never to use that formation again. However, he now saw such possibilities in the formation that he could not resist using the concept again. He chose to form his lines in an inverted "V" formation with the point of the "V" facing north and strongly blocking Ox Ford, the only good crossing between the two Federal bridgeheads.

Lee was convinced that Grant was a rash and overly aggressive commander, and he hoped he would attack both sides of the salient which the Confederates had strongly entrenched. To avoid the types of attack with which Upton and Hancock had nearly succeeded at Spotsylvania, a deep belt of obstructions was placed in the open ground in front of his trenches. Should Grant attack from both of his bridgeheads at once, Lee could choose which side he wanted to concentrate his force against and perhaps wipe out that part of Grant's army. The numerical strength of the two armies was less a degree of concern to Lee than they had been in any battle since Gettysburg, nor could he expect the odds would ever be as favorable in the near future.

Grant was not as rash as Lee thought, for he ordered Burnside's IX Corps to force a crossing of the North Anna at Ox Ford before he considered ordering a general assault. When Burnside proved unable to cross, this established the fact that Lee was strongly defending the ford for some good reason, and Grant began to suspect the trap. Immediately, Grant ordered more roads and bridges built to better allow quicker movement of troops from one side of the "V" to the other.

Lee still saw an opportunity to attack the weaker of Grant's forces, but before Lee could organize the details of an assault plan, he became ill. As a result, he remained incapacitated in his tent for five days. His idea had a reasonable chance of success, but he was not physically able to organize and lead a battle himself. This situation seemed to be happening more frequently: he had no subordinate strong and trusted enough to plan the details and execute the attack before Grant completed strong defenses against it.

The action along the North Anna promised to turn into trench warfare, which Grant did not want. On May 26th, his army left their trenches and moved around Lee's right flank for a fourth time toward the old Richmond battlefields of 1862. Both sides lost another 4-5% of their strength in the North Anna fighting: the Confederates lost 2,500 and the Federals 2,600. Both commanders had shown tactical brilliance in setting traps but not falling into the other's trap, but Lee was the clear loser since he would never again see an opportunity where his strength in numbers would approach equality with Grant's.

CHAPTER XXIII

A Union Disaster at Cold Harbor; Lee's Last Victory, May 1864

"If I widen my lines, he [Grant] will break me; if I strengthen my lines, he will flank me." With these words,[1] Lee described his situation at Cold Harbor. In what Grant later described as his worst decision of the war, Grant ordered a frontal attack against Lee's lines, certain he could break them. Like Gettysburg and Fredericksburg, the assault was across open ground against a strongly entrenched enemy. Predictably, it failed, presenting Lee with his last major battle victory of the war. Grant's ill-considered charge also extended the war since, for a time, it caused the Army of the Potomac to lose faith in Grant's generalship.

*A*fter neither side accomplished much with their efforts at Ox Ford, Grant turned south around Lee's right flank again. As he moved farther south, Grant was running out of space for maneuver since he would soon reach the deep water of the wide James River. He was also driving Lee closer and closer to the well-prepared fortifications around Richmond so the likelihood of having to mount a siege of the Confederate army, protected by those works, was increasing. This was the last thing Grant wanted because Lee was a leading expert on the construction of defensive works and could be expected to use them very well. The fact that he was running out of room to maneuver drove the usually patient Grant to an unusual state of desperation. This led to his making one of his few great mistakes in the Civil War.

The Cavalry Corps had rejoined Grant's army after its raid to Yellow Tavern, and after a little rest, it was available for more action. Wilson's Third Cavalry Division was assigned to protect the right flank of the Army of the Potomac. Lee made a diversionary thrust in that direction, but it was easily turned back.

In his desperation, Grant decided to follow another of Sheridan's suggested tactics. The cavalry would ride quickly to capture a critical objective, and closely following infantry would consolidate the position. In this case the objective would be the important transportation intersection of (Old) Cold Harbor and some strategic higher ground to the west of the town. Coincidentally, Lee's strategy called for a flanking movement around Grant's left that was designed to roll up the line of his southernmost corps. These two opposing strategies were like two powerful trains running toward each other at great speed.[2]

The two divisions of Union cavalry that Sheridan led fought two divisions of Confederate cavalry led by Major General Wade Hampton at Hawes Shop. The fighting was some of the heaviest by cavalry in the war. The Confederates were driven back, and Sheridan succeeded in capturing Old Cold Harbor and holding it. This was the first time a combined cavalry-infantry attack of this kind was made and the planning was inadequate. The VI Corps commander was not solidly behind the effort, the cavalry leader, who fought in front where he could see what was going on, was subordinate to him, and the infantry commander was nine miles behind the cavalry. Nevertheless, after heavy cavalry fighting until the infantry arrived and fortified itself there, the town was held, but no further movement to the critically strategic higher ground to the west proved possible.

This movement and the results were important for two reasons.

First, since it was Sheridan's first action in which he was part of a combined cavalry-infantry force, this action furthered Sheridan's education in generalship and would pay dividends in later campaigns. Second and most important, the reason Confederate cavalry and Anderson's corps reached Old Cold Harbor in such a timely manner to meet the combined Union force was that these were the lead elements of Lee's planned turning movement. The incidental collision of these two large mixed forces spoiled Lee's flanking strategy.

After these offensive attempts by both sides had failed, the two sides set up defensive lines opposite one another. Lee's line was about six miles long, Grant's almost eight miles long. One of Grant's aides, an engineering officer, Lieutenant Colonel Cyrus B. Comstock, had been insisting for some time that the Union army had enough numerical superiority to break through the Confederate line by direct assault.[3] Lee also considered that this was a distinct possibility because, when asked if he had any reserve in case of a breakthrough, he said: "I do not have even a regiment in reserve. If I shortened my line to develop one, he [Grant] would turn me. If I weakened my front to develop a reserve, he would break me." The number of effectives in Grant's army had been restored to 108,000 with the return of Sheridan's cavalry, the return of II Corps, the transfer of Major General William F. "Baldy" Smith's XVIII Corps from the Army of the James to the Army of the Potomac and from replacements. Many of the latter troops were of poor quality. Lee then had about 59,000 effective troops.[4]

Skirmishing along the long line occurred on June 1st and 2nd to little effect. Bowing to the idea of a direct general assault, Grant, through Meade, ordered over 40,000 men in the II, VI, and XVIII corps to attack the center of the Confederate line, which was its strongest part. No detailed planning went into the assault, and the tactics used were simple: it was purely a "smash 'em up" operation. Starting at 4:30 A.M. on June 3rd, the Union forces lost 7,000 men, killed and wounded, in just 20 minutes.

Probably, Cold Harbor was the greatest blemish on Grant's entire military career. The horrible loss of life left him in his tent in tears.

By noon the fighting was over, but wounded continued to die in the "no man's land" between the lines as Grant and Lee bickered about a truce that would give them relief. Neither general wanted to *ask* the other for a truce since under the military etiquette of the time, this was considered to be an admission of defeat. Neither general showed much humanity in the situation; for, when a truce was finally agreed upon on June 6th, only a few hundreds of the thousands who had been wounded were still left alive.

There was little success or credit to be claimed by Grant or Lee for the bloody results of Cold Harbor. Lee had for the last time won a great battle in the field. Grant wrote in his *Memoirs*: "I have always regretted that the last assault at Cold Harbor was ever made."[5]

After a day of grief following the terrible losses at Cold Harbor, Grant returned his thinking to his main objective: defeat Lee and end the war with victory. He still hoped to avoid a siege, but he knew he had lost his chances north of the James River. He began to plan a move across the James to land where maneuvers might still be possible. What he did not understand at the time was that his troops had lost some of their faith in his mystique.

CHAPTER XXIV

Grant Blinds Lee to His Crossing of the James, Comes Within Hours of Ending the War

After losing Stuart when he chased Sheridan to Yellow Tavern, Lee realized Grant detached his cavalry only with a purpose. As a ruse, Grant sent Sheridan with two cavalry divisions to disrupt the Virginia Central Railroad and join Hunter's Army of the Shenandoah. Then, this conbined cavalry-infantry force would attack Richmond from the west. The real purpose of the raid was to cover his James River crossing. Predictably, Lee sent most of his cavalry after Sheridan, blinding himself to Grant's massive movement. Only the timidity brought on by the exhaustion of the Army of the Potomac's officers and men after a long, bloody campaign prevented that army from gaining victory in June 1864.

*N*apoleon said "strategy does not win battles; tactics do." He meant that good strategy may place an army in a position where it *can* win, but no victory can occur unless the strategy is followed up by good troops who perform well, using effective tactics. On June 6, 1864 following his defeat at Cold Harbor, Grant recognized that further fighting north of the James would only result in Lee retreating into the strong fortifications around Richmond. To avoid undertaking a siege and still in hopes of defeating Lee in battles of maneuver, Grant decided to initiate a new and complex strategy.[1]

This new strategy consisted of two major movements. First, he ordered Major General David Hunter to drive south in the Shenandoah Valley, expecting that Lee would send troops from the Army of Northern Virginia to relieve the Confederate defenders there. Second, the Army of the Potomac would cross the James River. Petersburg was the key railroad junction necessary for materials to move to Lee's army and Richmond from most other parts of the Confederacy; and that June, it lay open for easy capture since it was almost totally undefended.

The James is a tidewater river which was up to 180 feet deep and about 2,100 feet wide at the point where Grant wished to cross. Beside the great engineering difficulty of designing and rapidly building the huge pontoon bridge that an army of about 100,000 men needed for such a crossing, a Confederate attack while the army was part way across would be devastating. Grant was fortunate that Major General Benjamin Butler's Army of the James held the south side of the river so any potential threat would be against the portion of the Army of the Potomac that was still on the north side of the James.

After considering Lee's reaction to Sheridan's raid toward Richmond in May when he sent a weak force after the Union cavalry and lost Stuart as a result, Grant thought it unlikely that Lee would repeat the same action that had proved so disastrous to him in May. This time, Grant's purpose was to blind Lee to the movements he planned toward and then across the James, and he was reasonably certain that if he sent his cavalry on a raid, Lee would send most of his cavalry after it in a chase, leaving Lee with an inadequate force to keep track of Grant's moves. On June 6th, Grant ordered Sheridan to take two divisions of cavalry and move around the left flank of Lee's army. Beside the ruse of the move, Sheridan was ordered to tear up the Virginia Central Railroad and

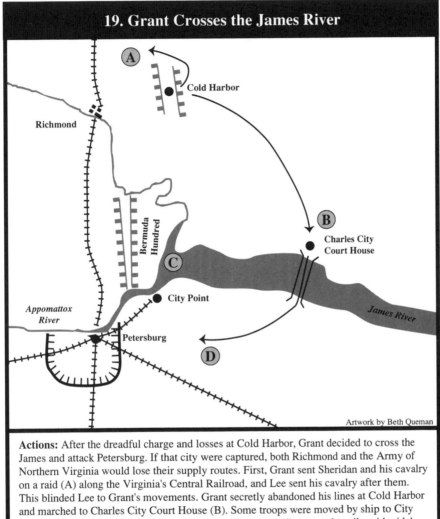

19. Grant Crosses the James River

Richmond

Cold Harbor

Bermuda Hundred

Charles City Court House

City Point

Appomattox River

Petersburg

James River

Artwork by Beth Queman

Actions: After the dreadful charge and losses at Cold Harbor, Grant decided to cross the James and attack Petersburg. If that city were captured, both Richmond and the Army of Northern Virginia would lose their supply routes. First, Grant sent Sheridan and his cavalry on a raid (A) along the Virginia's Central Railroad, and Lee sent his cavalry after them. This blinded Lee to Grant's movements. Grant secretly abandoned his lines at Cold Harbor and marched to Charles City Court House (B). Some troops were moved by ship to City Point and Bermuda Hundred (C), and a large bridge was built across the mile-wide tidal James River. Much of the Army of the Potomac was across the James and attacking the fortifications around Petersburg (D) before Lee was aware Grant had crossed the river.

then to proceed west to join Hunter in the vicinity of Charlottesville. Then, this combined force would advance on Richmond from the west.[1] Wilson's division of cavalry would remain with the Army of the Potomac to help screen its actions from Lee.

Grant's brilliant strategy in moving his huge army across the James River was perfectly conceived and worked well from the beginning. After Sheridan began his move, Lee sent Hampton with two divisions of cavalry after him. Hunter's drive up the Shenandoah Valley to the vicinity of Lynchburg prompted Lee to send Lieutenant General Jubal Early with two divisions to halt Hunter. These two moves did what Grant wanted: Lee's army of Northern Virginia had been weakened and blinded.

*   *   *

When Grant's army crossed the James River, operations moved to a new area. This crossing also marked the end of the bloodiest campaign of the Civil War through that date. Both armies had been battered, and neither was the same army it had been on May 4th when Grant crossed the Rapidan. Lee and his army were still in existence even though he would never launch a full-army offensive again. The Confederate army had become locked with its larger opponent in a war of attrition that it could not hope to win unless some political intervention occurred. Despair in the Northern electorate and political maneuvering by Confederate politicians, supported by their able secret service, were the only hopes for a Confederate victory. In light of all this, was it possible to determine a clear victor in the Virginia Overland Campaign? Was it Lee or Grant, recognizing that any answer would be very close judgment?

The question of whether one general or another won, or lost, a campaign or a battle is complicated. If one wipes out or captures the other's army or receives a surrender, the answer is clear, but what if nothing like this happens? The rule before and during the Civil War was that the side who held the ground on which the fighting took place at battle's end was the winner, but what if both sides were essentially in the same positions that they held when the battle started? Examples of this situation abounded in the spring of 1864: The Wilderness , Spotsylvania and even Cold Harbor. Is it which side suffered the greatest casualties? Probably this is a better argument, but not necessarily, since the one who lost the least may have suffered more percentage-wise, and could he afford his losses? This last argument is too complicated.

Probably the answer to who won lies in the wills of the two commanders who fought one another: the winner was the one who forced his will upon the other. After Gettysburg, Lee held his ground for a full day, then retreated; but clearly, Meade forced his will on Lee by making him abandon his attacks and the invasion of the north; and this made Meade the winner. Similarly, at the Wilderness, Lee attacked and wanted to force Grant to retreat back across the Rapidan. When he failed to accomplish this, Grant moved his army deeper into the South. Grant won the Battle of the Wilderness because Lee had not succeeded in enforcing his will upon him, and Grant did what he wanted to do. Spotsylvania was a similar win for Grant. At Cold Harbor, Grant made a major effort to break Lee's line, and Lee successfully resisted his attempt which forced his will upon Grant so Lee was the winner at Cold Harbor.

The winner of a campaign, like the Virginia Overland Campaign of May and June of 1864, may be pointed out more easily than for a single battle. In the whole campaign, Grant was never stopped and turned back by Lee although Lee made many efforts to make him retreat back to the north. Grant's position in front of Petersburg in mid-June was strategically superior to his position on the Rapidan before May 4th. Lee's army lost more men than the Confederacy could afford. The Army of the Potomac, if given a little rest, would be close to being as strong as ever. Conclusion: Grant won the campaign.

CHAPTER XXV

Beauregard Saves the Confederacy at Petersburg

Unknown to Lee, many of Grant's forces were across the James on June 15, 1864. These cut through the main Petersburg defenses, and nothing was in their way. The usually erratic and unreliable Beauregard made the difficult moves that saved the Confederacy, not Lee or Davis. Unsteady after Cold Harbor, Union corps commanders abandoned the assault when war-ending victory was very close. Lee failed to see the extreme seriousness of the threat until Beauregard pulled all of his troops out of the Bermuda Hundred defenses. Only then did Lee move his army to Petersburg. Twice the Confederacy avoided total defeat by minutes and the siege of Petersburg began.

Not only was Grant's strategy to cross the James River a maneuver against Lee, it was a stroke against the overall military command structure of the Confederate Government. Confederate central military command was made up of President Davis who was aided by two full generals: Bragg, Davis's principal military advisor, and Samuel Cooper, his Adjutant General and Chief-of-Staff. All military department commands throughout the country reported directly to Davis as though he were a spider in the center of an enormous web.

Lee's command in Virginia extended south to the James River although his principle assignment was to resist the incursion of Grant into Confederate territory and fight him and the Army of the Potomac wherever he could. General P.G.T. Beauregard commanded the Military District of Southern Virginia and the Carolinas, and the northern border of his command was the south side of the James. Thus, Grant's move struck simultaneously at all three of these commands. The closest thing to an overall command overlapping those of Lee and Beauregard was Davis's central military command in Richmond. In this situation, the Union actions were all within twenty miles of Richmond so Davis had no excuse that he was uninformed about what was going on as he might have if the problems were a thousand miles away, say, in Mississippi. Nonetheless, the central Confederate command did not recognize the seriousness of the threat in anything like a timely manner. In any event, they were paralyzed by the happenings, were totally indecisive and made little or no contribution to solving the problem.

Lee knew he had been in deadly combat with the Army of the Potomac only a week earlier, but by June 15th, he had completely lost contact with his enemy. He feared that the apparent move by Grant was a ruse designed to make him move his army further south precipitously, leaving Grant a free route into Richmond. If Grant moved only a part of his army south of the James but left two corps on the north side and Lee moved completely to the south side, Richmond would be open to easy Federal capture. Gone were the days when Lee would look for a situation that would allow him to concentrate his army against part of the Union force; now he was just thinking of survival. Lee did not trust or believe Beauregard when that general reported heavy Union crossings of the James and their threat to Petersburg. As a result of this doubt, Lee did nothing until Beauregard took actions that forced Lee to protect Richmond and his own army.

CHAPTER XXV

Of the three commands affected by Grant's crossing of the James, only that of Beauregard acted in a timely and decisive manner, probably because the troops that represented the threat were right in front of it. Both the Confederate central military command and Lee failed to respond in a responsible manner, so only Beauregard's response saved the Confederacy for another nine months. It is remarkable that this general, who had not performed well since the First Battle of Bull Run and who had performed very poorly in many subsequent assignments, found a way by himself to turn Grant's great strategy back on June 15 and 16, 1864.

Most of the Union force was over the James before Lee realized that it was Grant's intent to move the bulk of his army across. Smith's XVIII Corps returned to Bermuda Hundred, from where it crossed the Appomattox River and approached the Petersburg works on June 15th. Hancock's II Corps soon arrived in Smith's support. Beauregard had only 2,200 low-quality militia defending Petersburg on the 15th, and they were faced by about 30,000 men in the two Union corps. June 15, 1864 was a dark day for the Union because it was the day on which Grant failed to take the necessary actions that would, almost certainly, have ended the war that summer.[1] With so much in its favor, how could the attack have failed?

The Dimmock Line, the main defense east of Petersburg, was said by Grant "to be the strongest works he had seen in Virginia."[2] Held by 25,000 men, supported by adequate artillery, this line would have been almost impregnable against a far larger force, but held by only 2,200 militia, it should have presented only a minor obstacle to veteran troops. William F. Smith was in tactical control of the attack Grant designed to take Petersburg, and he let Grant and the entire Union cause down that day. Overly impressed by the strength of the line, Smith failed to recognize the easy opportunity and need for quick movement if he were to take Petersburg before reinforcements arrived. Smith was overly slow in planning his attack of June 15th, but when he finally moved, his troops easily broke through the Dimmock Line, and the way was clear into Petersburg.

Late on the 15th, Hancock came to Smith's support; but Meade had failed to tell him of the importance of the move, and he had not ordered him to strongly support Smith. Neither general was willing to undertake the difficult night attack that would surely have been successful. Smith was too timid to do so even though he knew the ground; Hancock, who did not know the ground, was suffering extremely from his Gettysburg wound which had reopened. Because of his poor physical condition, Hancock waived his seniority rights which put Smith in overall command of the effort. Smith was the wrong man at the wrong time for such a critical action, but he received little support in his efforts from Grant, Meade or Hancock.

During the night of the 15th, Beauregard hastily prepared a second defensive line around Petersburg. In spite of his pleas to Lee and Bragg, no one would come to his aid so Beauregard independently made a powerful desperation move to remedy his highly threatening situation. Since Bragg, Davis's "military advisor," was unwilling to decide whether to defend Bermuda Hundred or Petersburg and since he could not do both, Beauregard chose to evacuate the Bermuda Hundred lines during the night of the 15th moving these troops to Petersburg. Simultaneously with the issuance of the abandonment order, Beauregard notified Lee of his intent and Lee received the message with alarm at 2:00 in the early morning of the 16th. Beauregard told Lee that the Bermuda Hundred defenses were being abandoned and asked if Lee could occupy them. Lee moved within an hour directing his troops to march quickly by the most direct route.[3]

Beauregard's move gave temporary relief to the defenders of Petersburg, but this opened a window of opportunity when there would be no Confederate troops between Richmond and Butler's army in Bermuda Hundred. At dawn on the 16th, Butler's pickets told their commander that the Confederate lines opposite his at

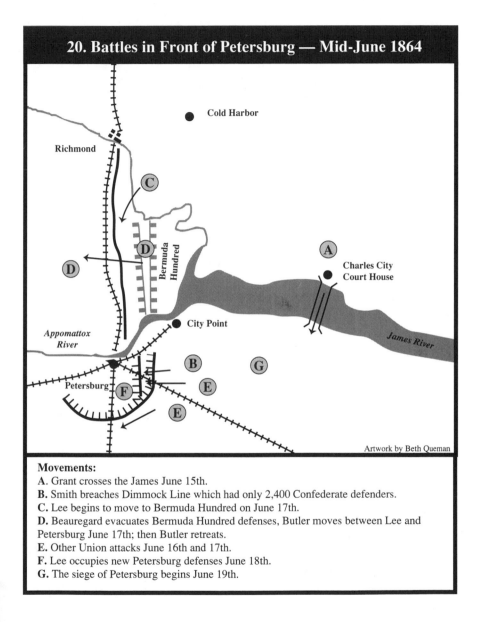

20. Battles in Front of Petersburg — Mid-June 1864

Artwork by Beth Queman

Movements:
A. Grant crosses the James June 15th.
B. Smith breaches Dimmock Line which had only 2,400 Confederate defenders.
C. Lee begins to move to Bermuda Hundred on June 17th.
D. Beauregard evacuates Bermuda Hundred defenses, Butler moves between Lee and Petersburg June 17th; then Butler retreats.
E. Other Union attacks June 16th and 17th.
F. Lee occupies new Petersburg defenses June 18th.
G. The siege of Petersburg begins June 19th.

Bermuda Hundred had been abandoned. During the morning of the 16th, Butler's forces occupied the enemy lines and captured the railroad and turnpike between Richmond and Petersburg.

Effectively, he had placed a strong force between Lee's army and Beauregard's Petersburg defenders and cut a main supply route to Richmond and Lee's army. If this position could have been held and exploited, Petersburg would have fallen, since Lee would have been unable to reinforce its defenses. Petersburg's fall would probably have forced Lee to abandon the Richmond area; otherwise he would be surrounded, starved out and made to surrender.

Butler was one of the worst Federal army commanders. He had been appointed major general early in the war and had high seniority. He was one of many politicians who were thought qualified for high military rank by the Lincoln Administration. Even though he had shown little military skill, he was a leading "war Democrat," and the administration was fearful of losing support from this group if they relieved him as military matters dictated. Grant reluctantly kept Butler in command of the Army of the James. This joint political decision now cost the Union dearly.

About noon, Butler reacted with panic when he learned Lee was crossing the James on his right flank. Fearing a miraculous attack by Lee, Butler ordered his advanced positions to be abandoned without a fight. When Grant had learned of Butler's strong strategic position, he ordered VI Corps to support Butler, but when they arrived, the position had been abandoned, and it was too late. By this time, Lee had about 22,000 men on each side of the James and still did not know if most of Grant's army was south of the James. By late afternoon of the 16th, Lee had driven Butler's forces out of their second defensive line at Bermuda Hundred and was pressing the first, erasing all of the great advantage Butler had gained. The 16th was also a day in which the Union lost a war-ending opportunity.

The morale of the Army of the Potomac and XVIII Corps had degenerated substantially during the Overland Campaign. Captains commanded most regiments, replacing colonels and majors who had been lost. The ill-considered assault at Cold

Harbor had soured all the troops to making attacks on any fortified positions that even appeared to be similar to those at Cold Harbor. These Federal troops believed their leaders had thrown away the lives of many of their comrades foolishly at Cold Harbor, and they no longer trusted the judgment of their generals to decide where they should fight. Most of the men were exhausted by the heavy marching from their positions north of the James, and the generals, including Grant and Meade, were suffering from extreme mental fatigue following the numerous battle actions they had directed since May 4th. These symptoms of emotional fatigue at all levels of the army would pass in time, but in mid-June of 1864, they were very costly to the cause.

In the near approaches to Petersburg, the Army of the Potomac also missed more opportunities on June 17th. Warren's V Corps was ordered to advance to the Jerusalem Pike which would have flanked the Confederate Petersburg positions, but he halted the move when he met only weak Confederate pickets. His abandoned attack was half-hearted at best. He reported that the defenses were too strong to attack, but in fact, his troops did not even try to drive off the Confederate pickets which would have disclosed an open road into Petersburg since there were no Confederate defenders in strength behind the pickets. Another attack broke through the Confederate defense line but no follow-up was made and the successful troops were driven back. On the 18th, Meade organized an all-out attack involving four corps; but by now, the defenses had been strengthened physically and by more of Lee's troops, and it was too late.

In June 1864, the Army of the Potomac failed to take Petersburg due to the physical and mental exhaustion of its officers and men. This failure forced a siege upon them which eventually cost many more than 100,000 casualties. Under the able leadership of the expert on military fortifications, Lee, Confederate soldiers built and continuously improved formidable works in front of Petersburg and Richmond. These works eliminated all opportunities for substantial offensive maneuvers against the

Army of Northern Virginia in that vicinity until operations that would further wear the Confederate armies down by attrition were completed, that is, until April 1865.

Thus, Grant's strategy to take Petersburg in June 1864 failed due to the lack of good tactical follow-up by himself, his subordinates and the men of his army. The rest of his strategy also failed. Hunter was defeated by Early at Lynchburg, and cavalry under Sheridan and Hampton fought to a costly draw at Trevellian Station. These actions prevented Hunter and Sheridan from joining forces, and Sheridan returned to the main army. After June 18th, there seemed nothing that could prevent the contest between the Northern and the Southern armies from becoming a costly and long siege. For the time being, the initiative had moved from Grant to Lee. How long would it take Grant to find new ways to recover the initiative?

CHAPTER XXVI

Safe Behind the Petersburg Works, Lee Sends Early to Threaten Washington and Distract Grant. The Battle of the Crater.

Lee knew he was no longer strong enough to leave the fortifications around Petersburg and challenge the Union army in the open field. He recognized that staying behind fortifications would be fatal; Grant would eventually wear him down and defeat him. He needed to draw Grant away from the siege; therefore, he ordered Early, who was in the Shenandoah Valley, to threaten Maryland and Washington. Lee expected that the Union politicians would order Grant north to defend them as they had McClellan in 1862. What were the chances that this strategy would work against Grant in 1864? In July, the North fought the disastrous Battle of the Crater.

Once he was secure behind the strong Petersburg-Richmond fortifications, Lee recognized three strategic facts. First, he knew he could resist the attacks of the stronger Union armies for six months, or more, and would inflict great casualties on any attackers. Second and inevitably, the Army of Northern Virginia would be worn down physically and emotionally by a siege, and he would lose the war unless he could affect the progress of the war elsewhere. Third, he needed to retain the Shenandoah Valley as a source of food for his army and the people of Richmond. Davis would not allow Lee to abandon Richmond, no matter how strategically unimportant holding it was and how desirable from a pure military standpoint might have been to abandon it. Therefore, Lee became fixated with protecting Richmond at any cost, and this dominated his thinking until the end of the war. Most of Lee's subsequent strategic errors resulted from the faulty concept that Richmond must be held.

Lee remembered 1862 when two threats against the North helped him turn McClellan away from his strategically strong position on the Virginia Peninsula. First, Jackson's victories in the Shenandoah Valley prevented McDowell's corps from joining the Union army on the Peninsula east of Richmond. Second, Lee's and Jackson's move against Pope caused political upheaval in Washington which resulted in the withdrawal of McClellan and his army from the Peninsula. He also remembered Jackson's strategic suggestions that an interruption in supplies reaching Washington would greatly interfere with the organization of the on-going Union war effort.

Even before Grant crossed the James, Lee had decided he could spare a corps under Lieutenant General Jubal A. Early. He chose to send Early to recapture the Shenandoah Valley from the poorly led and weak Union forces then occupying it. Early's force and those Confederates already in the Valley would total about 20,000 men. From a strategic viewpoint, this was a large enough force to capture, occupy and hold the Valley, but it had no chance to capture and hold Washington although it could do considerable damage there. Nevertheless, it could mount the appearance of a meaningful threat against the Union capital. Lee elected to send Early, who was his least regarded corps commander to lead this effort, so it was clear that he considered the Valley effort to be secondary, not of critical importance.[1] Early had a good reputation as a fighter but a very poor one as a tactician or strategist. Knowing this, Lee made a bad decision to send too few troops to do the assigned job under a poor commander. It was almost a decision to throw 20,000 much needed men away. This was another example that illustrated the extreme bankruptcy of the Confederacy as far as its supply of well-qualified general officers was concerned.

In June and July of 1864, Early recaptured the Valley and moved against Washington. He did not recognize the essence of time so he foolishly wasted some while raising ransoms against the destruction of some Northern towns along the way. These delays, together with a heroic rear-guard action by greatly out-numbered Federals at Monocacy, Maryland, allowed relief to reach Washington just as Early arrived. The threat had frightened Lincoln, the War Department and Northern politicians. They demanded strong help from Grant, and he sent his army's VI Corps to their defense. Grant resisted their demands that he come to command the defense himself, and he refused to send more than one corps of the army to Washington from the Petersburg lines. Part of XIX Corps, which was on its way from New Orleans to Petersburg was diverted to Washington, and all available Union troops in West Virginia were sent to defend the Shenandoah Valley.

Early succeeded in bringing a number of Confederate regimental flags to within sight of Washington, but when he saw he was confronted by the veteran VI Corps, he retreated to the Valley. Early's threat proved to be an important Confederate failure in that it weakened the Army of the Potomac very little, and it elicited an unexpected response from Grant which led to more disasters for the Confederacy. He made one of his great decisions of the war when he appointed an independent army commander to drive Early from the Valley, end sources of Confederate food in the Valley and remove the threat from Washington, once and for all.

At first, Grant and the War Department considered appointing old warhorses to command in the Valley, generals like William B. Franklin and Meade, the latter because Grant was losing faith in his abilities. When Grant considered how useful large bodies of cavalry could be in the Shenandoah Valley in support of infantry because of its unique topography, he realized he had a general who had extensive experience commanding both cavalry and infantry in many battles. This man was Major General Philip H. Sheridan, and his choice proved to be brilliant.[2] Stanton, the War Department and most politicians thought Sheridan was too young and inexperienced for assignment as an independent commander of a full army, but Grant was for him, and Lincoln backed Grant so the appointment was made.[3]

*　　*　　*

The Petersburg Mine Assault which led to the Battle of the Crater was an example of a great military idea that was far ahead of the capabilities of the staff and command skills of Civil War officers. The idea was proposed by Lt. Colonel Henry Pleasants, who was a Pennsylvania underground coal miner. He commanded the 48th Pennsylvania Regiment which was mostly made up of coal miners.

Pleasants's plan was to dig an adit from a low portion of the Union lines to a point under a Confederate fortification, Elliott's Salient, and then a large gallery would be formed under the fort. The gallery would be filled with powder, and a breach would be blown in the Petersburg defenses. The idea was sold to Burnside, IX Corps commander, who controlled the area, and Grant approved it. The digging began on June 25th and was completed, with the powder in place, on July 27th. Having approved the idea, higher command gave Pleasants and his men little support, and once 8,000 pounds of powder were in place twenty feet under the Confederate fort ready to explode, no commander seemed to have a clear idea of what to do. Meade and the Chief Engineer of the

Army of the Potomac, a Major Duane, thought the project was useless and would accomplish no military purpose.

Grant's determination to give Lee some problem that would prevent him from detaching troops to Georgia or elsewhere forced Meade to use the mine. Burnside had been training Major General Edward Ferrero's 4th Division of his IX Corps for two weeks to make a breakthrough after the mine was blown. This division was mostly made up of colored troops who were fresh but untried in battle. At the last minute, with the mine in place and ready, Meade changed his tune and considered this attack to be critical, and he believed the untried colored troops would fail. Meade forced Burnside to replace the specially trained colored troops with untrained white troops. Unfortunately, Grant agreed. One of the reasons Meade advanced for replacing the colored troops as later reported by Grant to a Congressional Committee was: "[if] it should prove a failure, it would then be said, and very properly, that we were shoving these people ahead to get killed because we did not care anything about them. But that could not be said if we put white troops in front."[4] While this may have been a consideration made after the fact, it showed Grant's and Meade's fundamental lack of confidence in the project.

The plan of attack for which the colored troops had trained was sound. First, one brigade was to advance to the defensive lines on each side of the crater, and taking advantage of the shock of the explosion, would roll up the Confederate defenses on each side to widen the gap. They had specific orders not to enter the crater itself, and once the gap was widened, a third brigade was to pass through the gap and capture Cemetery Hill behind it. Another corps was detailed to follow them through the gap, and this would have placed a substantial number of Union troops behind the last defensive lines of Petersburg. If Lee weakened his lines elsewhere to meet the breakthrough, a general assault all along the lines was to be made. Overall success using this plan was possible, perhaps even probable.

The explosion and the start of the attack was scheduled for

3:30 A.M. on July 30, 1964. Everything possible went wrong, but problems had begun late the previous afternoon when Meade, with Grant's approval, ordered Burnside to designate another attack force to replace the colored troops. Burnside did not select his best division commander to lead the assault; instead, he had his three division commanders draw lots. Of course, the worst possible commander, Brigadier General James Ledlie, drew the assignment. At the last minute, Meade changed the attack plan. He ordered all troops to drive through the gap and capture Cemetery Hill and to ignore the lines on each side of the crater. A faulty fuse delayed the explosion until 4:45 A.M. which greatly disturbed the men detailed to make the attack.

The explosion produced a crater 30-feet deep, 60-feet wide and 170-feet long. It killed about 300 Confederate defenders and destroyed all their ordnance. The attack was made in disorder, and about 2,000 Union soldiers immediately entered the crater and became trapped. Too late, others tried to widen the gap which they did to about 500 yards, but they were not able to reach the artillery batteries on each side that were firing effectively against the Union troops in the gap. Once they were committed, the colored troops were especially effective and performed well. Despite about 5,000 casualties, the last minute changes, the use of troops not specially trained for the task, only the futile movement of Union troops into the crater allowed the Confederates time to mount fierce resistance once they recovered from the shock of the explosion. This loss of time brought failure to this imaginative effort. Afterwards Grant said: "Such an opportunity to carry a fortified line I have never seen and never expect to see again."[5] He blamed the lack of success on corps and division commanders who stayed in safe bunkers behind the Union line and did not lead their men from the front where they could know what was going on.

Neither the Confederate nor the Union armies were prepared for such a different style of attack. Even though Union soldiers were digging for a month only twenty feet below them, and this could not have been done silently, no serious warning of the threat was given to Confederate commanders. Rumors were frequently received that the Union army was mining the Confederate lines, but this did not bring any action either. Only the inefficiency of the Federal generals brought the scheme to failure; otherwise, the effort would have hastened the defeat of the Confederacy by months.

From the Federal standpoint, failure resulted from many sources and could be blamed on commanders of all levels. For such an important effort, Grant should have assigned a high-ranking staff officer to get the miners what they wanted, to help them and to be sure the planning for the attack was well-founded and the troops were specially trained and fully supported by Meade and his staff. Once the mine was in place, it was only a matter of time before the Confederates found it and took action against it so there was reason to use it before this could happen. Still, this was no excuse for the foolish changes that were made at the last minute which doomed the effort and uselessly cost so many lives. This careless inattention to detail cost the Union dearly since it extended the war into the following spring.

CHAPTER XXVII

Summer and Fall 1864; The South Is Near Political Victory. Farragut's and Sherman's Victories and Lee's Gifts of Union Victories in the Shenandoah Valley Elect Lincoln

In July 1864, the Northern populace was ready to quit the war and give the South anything in exchange for peace. There was little chance Lincoln could be nominated, much less elected. All the South needed to do to win the Civil War was to keep the Union from gaining victories. At Mobile and Atlanta, Farragut and Sherman scored great victories. In Virginia, Lee made the fatal mistake of sending an insufficient force under an inadequate general to the Shenandoah Valley. Early could not cope with the energetic Sheridan, a rising star, who used new tactics. Grant and these Union officers gave the Union the victories it needed to save its war effort.

Mid-summer of 1864 was a time of despair for both the Union and the Confederacy. Huge Union losses in May and June more than counterbalanced Grant's great strategic success in reaching the gates of Richmond, something McClellan had accomplished in 1862. Sherman had started his drive toward Atlanta on May 7th, and by July 4th, he had reached the Chatahoochie River in sight of Atlanta, but there he appeared stalled.

Compared to Grant's, Sherman's losses were light since he made a series of turning maneuvers as he moved from Chattanooga south toward Atlanta. Sherman's total casualties through July 4th were 11,300 (about 11% of his force), while his opponent, J.E. Johnston's losses were 7,400 (about 10%). Union losses in Virginia and Georgia amounted to almost 80,000 in May-June 1864[1] which were enormous by any measure and devastating to Northern civilian morale. Richmond, Atlanta and several major seaports were still in Confederate hands; therefore, there was a general feeling in the North that little had been accomplished with all the loss of their sons' and husbands' blood. Copperheads, numerous other pro-Southern organizations and "peace" Democrats in the North harped on the idea that the war was a total failure.

In the South, their total casualties in the same period reached about 40,000. While Southern losses were fewer, their losses could not be replaced as easily as the North could replace theirs. Confederate armies had been driven back on all fronts. Lee ceased to be the aggressive attacker after the Wilderness, and J.E. Johnston was conducting a withdrawal in strength to conserve his army in Georgia. Lost battles and non-aggressive style of fighting had sapped Southern morale. Both sides were in deep depression, and neither side could see any clear road to victory, nor was it yet clear to either side that defeat was inevitable.

Exacerbating the morale problems of both sides were two main factors. First, death and incapacitation from diseases like malaria, smallpox, measles, yellow fever, tuberculosis, typhoid fever, pneumonia, infections and dysentery resulted in close to twice the number of deaths that were caused in battle.[2] Second, until 1864, most prisoners were exchanged and went back to the war, but at the beginning of 1864, Grant made a difficult decision. He had experienced capturing 14,000 men at Ft. Donelson and

28,000 at Vicksburg who returned to fight after exchange. He concluded that the Confederacy gained more from even prisoner exchanges than did the Union so he stopped most prisoner exchanges. This doomed many men on both sides to rot in the terrible conditions of prisoner of war camps. Grant knew that he was sentencing good men, even old personal friends on both sides, to die at places like Andersonville, but he put winning the war ahead of sentiment.

The siege of Petersburg limited strategy and tactics in Virginia. Lee held his position in the strong defensive lines around Richmond and Petersburg, and he was a master of the defense although he did not prefer it to attacking. Nevertheless, his position was difficult if not impossible in the long run. A siege was something he knew he would eventually lose unless he could find a way to delay the end of the war so as to cause the North to lose heart. He believed he could resist the siege only through the coming winter, at best.

Lee's main strategic move, Early's occupation of the Shenandoah Valley and the threat against Washington, might cause a significant number of troops to be sent from Grant's army to defend against Early, and this might allow Lee to increase the time his own army could continue its resistance. Any delay of a Union victory would improve the chances of a political settlement in favor of the Confederacy. Although he never stated so publicly, Lee agreed with most of his generals that the war could no longer be won by military means alone. These feelings at the highest levels had a strong negative effect on the army's morale.

Grant's position was hardly better. His popularity with the public and politicians was at a low ebb as a result of having had such huge casualties in the Virginia Overland Campaign. Offensive siege operations were slow, methodical, arduous and costly in lives; moreover, Grant had no expectation of ending siege operations against Lee quickly. Farther south, Sherman was slogging his way toward Atlanta; there seemed to be little hope for the quick capture of that city.

Early's threat against Washington had all the politicians in panic, and they were pressuring Grant to return to Washington and lead its defense personally. This would so divert his attention that the efforts against Lee would lose their strength. Neither Butler, the senior general remaining if Grant moved, nor Meade had shown in earlier operations that they were capable of leading an aggressive siege against Lee. By making an error, they might even give Lee the chance he wanted to take the offensive and perhaps gain a victory. Faced with all these problems, only a man with the utmost determination and skill could plan strategies to meet all of them; Grant was this kind of man.

The greatest single problem facing Grant, his generals and the Union was the November 1864 presidential election. Without some positive actions, victories, the possibility that Lincoln would be re-elected was poor. Without Lincoln's support in the office of the presidency, Grant would never have the opportunity to try to win the war, no matter how great a general he might be.

Beginning in late June 1864, Grant became very concerned that Lee would send reinforcements to J.E. Johnston which might allow him to halt Sherman's drive toward Atlanta. Grant was fortunate that Lee had no nation-wide responsibilities and was limited to being the commander of the Army of Northern Virginia; otherwise Lee might have made sending reinforcements to J.E. Johnston of higher priority. Lee's limited responsibility allowed him to do what he thought was best for Virginia so he sent Early and his corps to the Shenandoah Valley. The man who was directing the nation-wide strategy of the Confederacy, Davis, chose to allow this movement, not seeing the opportunity to send reinforcements against Sherman and the sterile possibilities of Early's operations in the Valley. Lee did not consider strategy outside of his district, and in particular, he did not choose to act on his own to try to avoid the likelihood that in six months Sherman and his huge force would become an imminent threat to his own southern flank.

To remove their despair, the North needed several victories;

otherwise, the chance of the North losing the Civil War politically was excellent. Few major Republican politicians believed Lincoln had any chance to be nominated; most advised him not to seek the 1864 Republican nomination. Many agents of the Confederate Secret Service were active in attempting to influence Copperheads and the "peace branch" of the Democratic Party. They were able to have a plank included in the 1864 Democratic Party platform calling for an immediate armistice after a Democratic president's inauguration, followed by a negotiated peace. This would be tantamount to allowing the Confederacy to win the war by default. To maintain and improve their position and allow time for the political discontent in the North to further develop, the South had to deny the North opportunities for victories. Their best way to do this was to stop Sherman, hold Grant before Petersburg and Richmond and put no other minor armies in the field that would be exposed to possible defeat.

*   *   *

When Sherman began his move toward Atlanta, it was on May 7th, three days after Grant's move across the Rapidan. Sherman's three armies totaled about 100,000 men against J. E. Johnston's 64,000. Since Sherman had to attack defended positions with a numerical advantage of less than 3:1, that is 1.56:1, the Confederates had a definite battle advantage. Also, they had a better knowledge of the rough country over which Sherman had to cross. Only Sherman's skill in generalship kept the Confederate army from stopping him several times. Sherman showed his superiority in a series of turning movements that forced J.E. Johnston to retreat from one position to another until he reached Kennesaw Mountain.

Sherman commanded three armies: the Army of the Cumberland under Major General George H. Thomas, the Army of the Tennessee under Major General James B. McPherson and the smaller Army of the Ohio under Major General John M.

21. Sherman's Atlanta Campaign

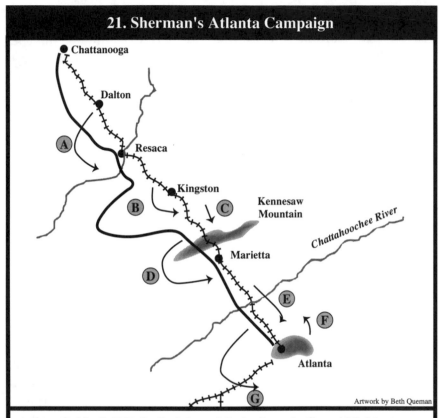

Chattanooga

Dalton

(A)

Resaca

Kingston

(B) (C)

Kennesaw
Mountain

Chattahoochee River

(D)

Marietta

(E)

(F)

Atlanta

(G)

Artwork by Beth Queman

Actions: On May 7, 1864, the Confederate defensive line under General J.E. Johnston was at Dalton. Sherman ordered McPherson to lead his army through the hills west of the railroad and take Resaca in Johnston's rear (A). This move failed, and Johnston counter-attacked, almost successfully, but Union artillery repulsed his attack. Sherman successfully flanked the Confederates out of several positions (B), until the Confederates were able to establish a strong defense at Kennesaw Mountain. Sherman made a costly direct assault on the Kennesaw position (C) which failed, but he ordered a movement around the left of the position (D) which threatened Johnston's line of retreat, causing him to fall back. The Confederates retreated to prepared defenses along the Chattahoochee River. Hood replaced Johnston as Sherman crossed the river (E). Hood made two strong counter-attacks against Sherman's left (F) which were very costly but were almost successful. Sherman had tried to move his cavalry to the left of Atlanta, but this move failed. In late August, Sherman moved a large infantry force to his right (G), and this cut the railroads leading into Atlanta and forced Hood to evacuate the city.

Schofield. At the start of the campaign to capture Atlanta, manpower strengths were: Cumberland—60,700, Tennessee—24,500 and Ohio—13,600.[3] Sherman's total force was at the end of a more than 400 mile rail supply line from Louisville through Nashville and Chattanooga to an advancing depot immediately behind his armies. He had another 30,000 to 40,000 men guarding this tenuous supply line. Since the supply line was about at its limit for security and its ability to move quantities of supply, it was not a viable strategy for Grant to send additional fighting forces to Sherman. As it was, Sherman had to obtain a large portion of his food and fodder locally. In support of Sherman, the best strategy Grant could follow was to prevent Lee from sending J.E. Johnston any reinforcements.

The Confederate Army of Tennessee was in a low state of morale following its disastrous defeat at Chattanooga which was felt to have been disgraceful. J.E. Johnston had replaced Bragg in command, Lieutenant General James Bell Hood replaced Breckinridge in command of a corps and the Episcopal bishop, Lieutenant General Leonidas K. Polk, brought a corps from Mississippi. After Chattanooga, J.E. Johnston had retreated to defensive positions north and west of Dalton, Georgia. On May 7th, Sherman ordered Schofield to press the Confederate lines strongly while McPherson's army secretly moved 15 miles south through Snake Creek Gap to seize the railroad near Resaca, Georgia. Sherman ordered McPherson to "fall on the enemy's flank when he retreated." McPherson failed to capture the railroad by brushing aside the few Confederate brigades defending Resaca; and, as a result, Sherman lost his best chance to surround or seriously damage J.E. Johnson's army which retreated to Resaca.

On May 14th and 15th, the armies fought near Resaca where a Confederate counter-attack against the left of the Union army nearly succeeded in defeating Sherman, but when Union artillery gained some key heights, they could direct heavy fire on Johnston's supply lines. This threat plus that of a Union division that had crossed the Dostanaula River downstream at Lay's Ferry threatened to outflank the Confederate army and forced a series of retreats to three successive lines of defense at Adairsville, Cassville and Allatoona. Sherman successfully flanked Johnston out of each of these positions and forced his retreat to strong positions along a line through Dallas, Pickett's Mill and New Hope Church.

After heavy fighting along this line, Federal cavalry occupied Allatoona Pass and forced the abandonment of these strong Confederate positions, and subsequently, Johnston fell back to the Kenesaw Mountain line. There, Sherman's costly frontal attack failed, but Schofield moved around the Confederate left and entrenched. This prompted Sherman to move McPherson around Schofield's rear which seriously threatened Johnston's line of retreat. By July 2nd, the Confederates had retreated to an already fortified bridgehead west of the Chattahoochee River. When Sherman moved to front these defenses, he could clearly see his objective, Atlanta, from the hills behind his positions.

Following Bragg's relief from command in the West, Davis made him his chief military advisor. In a peculiar move, Davis authorized Bragg to go to Atlanta, interview Johnston, his successor, and decide whether another officer should replace him. Since neither Davis nor Bragg liked Johnston or respected his cautious, defensive style of generalship, his replacement was probably foreordained. On July 18th, Johnston was replaced by Hood as commander of the Army of Tennessee, and Hood was promoted to the temporary rank of full general.

*   *   *

On August 5, 1864, the first high profile victory of the year decisively in the Union's favor occurred when Rear Admiral David G. Farragut forced a passage between defending Confederate forts and ships and entered Mobile Bay. There he captured the C.S.S. *Tennessee,* an ironclad ram considered to be the strongest naval vessel in the world, and closed this major port to Confederate blockade-runners. A few days later, cooperating with troops of Major General Gordon Granger's XIII Corps and using the captured *Tennessee* as a battery, Farragut reduced and captured the Confederate forts guarding entry to the bay. This was a heavy blow to the Confederate cause since it left only the east coast ports of Savannah, Wilmington and Charleston available for Southern blockade-runners to bring in arms and goods from overseas.

*   *   *

In front of the Petersburg lines following the disaster of the crater, Grant attempted tactics to accomplish two aims: to hold Lee's forces in place and to cut the Weldon Railroad which fed supplies into Richmond and Petersburg from the Carolinas. Assaults were made toward Globe Tavern on the Weldon Railroad and the tracks were cut. Although a less efficient route, Lee made arrangements to move supplies by wagon from the end of the Weldon Railroad to Petersburg.

Grant countered this by having II Corps tear up the tracks all the way to Reams Station, and the limited road network forced Lee's wagons to take a long round-about route through Dinwiddie Court House to get to Petersburg. Grant ordered several assaults north of the James River using II Corps and Sheridan's cavalry corps, but Lee outmaneuvered him and prevented any substantial gains. These widely spread attempts served good purpose by forcing Lee to keep all of his troops in place along the whole defensive line which eliminated the possibility of his sending troops as reinforcements against Sherman.

*   *   *

Several sound strategies were open to Lee to thwart Grant's efforts to capture Petersburg. The Union forces had two fundamental weaknesses that were open to Confederate attack: their supply depot at City Point and their open left flank to the

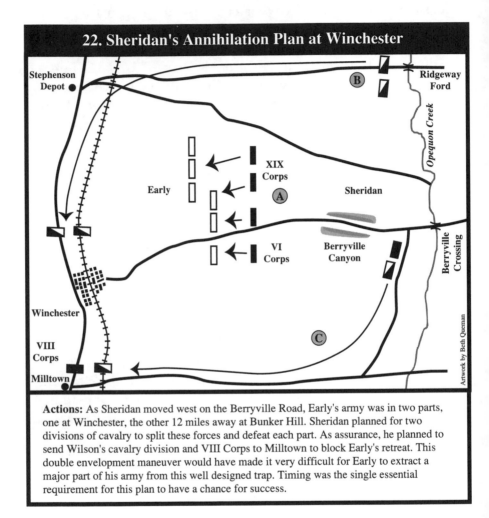

22. Sheridan's Annihilation Plan at Winchester

Stephenson Depot

Ridgeway Ford

B

Opequon Creek

XIX Corps

Early

A

Sheridan

VI Corps

Berryville Canyon

Berryville Crossing

Winchester

VIII Corps

Milltown

C

Artwork by Beth Queman

Actions: As Sheridan moved west on the Berryville Road, Early's army was in two parts, one at Winchester, the other 12 miles away at Bunker Hill. Sheridan planned for two divisions of cavalry to split these forces and defeat each part. As assurance, he planned to send Wilson's cavalry division and VIII Corps to Milltown to block Early's retreat. This double envelopment maneuver would have made it very difficult for Early to extract a major part of his army from this well designed trap. Timing was the single essential requirement for this plan to have a chance for success.

south. City Point, the port for Petersburg on the tidal James River, was one of the ten largest deep-water ports in the world in the summer of 1864. The Union army's huge supply dumps were served by dozens of wharves that were all concentrated in a very small area; all ammunition, arms and other military needs went to the Army of the Potomac through the huge port. Also in this tight area were facilities for baking bread, butchering cattle,

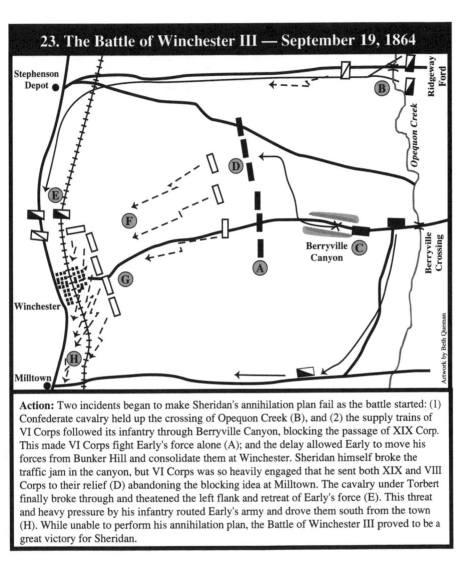

23. The Battle of Winchester III — September 19, 1864

Stephenson
Depot

Ridgeway
Ford

Opequon Creek

B

D

E

F

Berryville
Canyon

C

Berryville
Crossing

A

G

Winchester

H

Milltown

Artwork by Beth Queman

Action: Two incidents began to make Sheridan's annihilation plan fail as the battle started: (1) Confederate cavalry held up the crossing of Opequon Creek (B), and (2) the supply trains of VI Corps followed its infantry through Berryville Canyon, blocking the passage of XIX Corp. This made VI Corps fight Early's force alone (A); and the delay allowed Early to move his forces from Bunker Hill and consolidate them at Winchester. Sheridan himself broke the traffic jam in the canyon, but VI Corps was so heavily engaged that he sent both XIX and VIII Corps to their relief (D) abandoning the blocking idea at Milltown. The cavalry under Torbert finally broke through and theatened the left flank and retreat of Early's force (E). This threat and heavy pressure by his infantry routed Early's army and drove them south from the town (H). While unable to perform his annihilation plan, the Battle of Winchester III proved to be a great victory for Sheridan.

processing mail and other needs for an army of over 100,000. Large herds of cattle were fed nearby. The U.S. Military Railroad laid tracks from the port toward Petersburg and then moved through the rear areas of the army all the way to the Weldon Railroad, delivering supplies along the way.

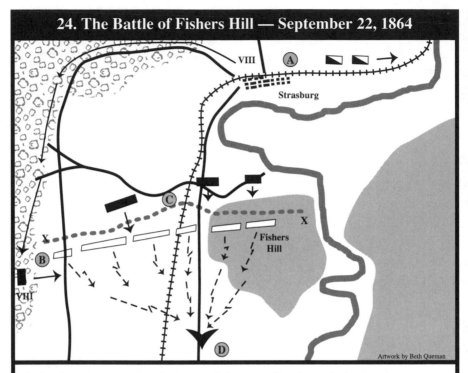

24. The Battle of Fishers Hill — September 22, 1864

Artwork by Beth Queman

Action: Just three days after his victory at Winchester, Sheridan again developed an annihilation plan against Early. He planned to move his cavalry under Torbert (A) up the Luray Valley to the east, around Massanutten Mountain and to a position to attack Early as he retreated. At the same time, he planned to move VIII Corps secretly through the woods to Little North Mountain (B) where it would gain a position behind Early's left flank. Again, the annihilation plan failed, this time because the cavalry was unable to penetrate a Confederate cavalry screen and enter the Luray Valley. The rest of Sheridan's plan worked perfectly; VIII Corps crushed the Confederate left; and this made it impossible for the rest of Early's line to hold against the attacks of VI and XIX corps. Again, this was a great victory for Sheridan. The fact that his annihilation plan failed was secondary to his victory, and it must be remembered that very few Civil War generals on either side considered such plans, much less came very close to executing them.

Lee responded by ordering Hampton's cavalry to raid the cattle herd, and it successfully drove off 2,000 head to feed the Confederate army. He also ordered Confederate spies to set a bomb on an ammunition lighter in the port of City Point. The resulting explosion killed many, destroyed some ammunition and supplies and personally endangered Grant who was at his headquarters nearby. Lee was unable to develop a way to attack City Point, largely because the building of a strike force would require overly weakening the Richmond defenses. Davis and Lee would not consider any action that might allow a threat against Richmond.

Grant was concerned that Lee would mount an offensive south of the James. City Point was a possible target, but he thought a move against the army's open left flank was more likely. Again, Lee was unwilling to concentrate enough force for such an action since Richmond might be exposed. While Richmond was the capital of the Confederacy, its importance to the Confederacy was over-rated. Lee's feelings in the matter were probably parochial.

The action around Petersburg in the summer and fall of 1864 along with Early's actions in the Shenandoah Valley exhausted the last of Lee's reserves and made possible the defeat of his army in the spring of 1865. Lee had two better strategies: maintain only defensive actions and send reserves to Johnston; or if he had to move offensively, mount a major offensive against either City Point or the Union left flank. This consideration of defending Richmond should not have prevented following any strategy that may well have changed the course of the war even though such a strategy might have placed the city at risk.

* * *

By the end of August 1864, Sheridan had organized and was in full command of the Army of the Shenandoah. Sheridan moved his new army into the Valley, and for six weeks, he sparred with Early. Early was a conceited man, and Sheridan's delay in bringing on a fight convinced Early that Sheridan was timid and afraid of him. While Grant was anxious for Sheridan to go over to the offensive, his messages to Sheridan were subtly changed by Halleck and the War Department so that they counseled more caution than Grant really wanted.

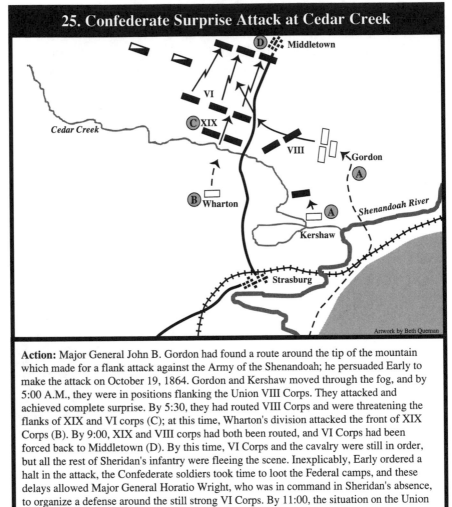

25. Confederate Surprise Attack at Cedar Creek

Artwork by Beth Queman

Action: Major General John B. Gordon had found a route around the tip of the mountain which made for a flank attack against the Army of the Shenandoah; he persuaded Early to make the attack on October 19, 1864. Gordon and Kershaw moved through the fog, and by 5:00 A.M., they were in positions flanking the Union VIII Corps. They attacked and achieved complete surprise. By 5:30, they had routed VIII Corps and were threatening the flanks of XIX and VI corps (C); at this time, Wharton's division attacked the front of XIX Corps (B). By 9:00, XIX and VIII corps had both been routed, and VI Corps had been forced back to Middletown (D). By this time, VI Corps and the cavalry were still in order, but all the rest of Sheridan's infantry were fleeing the scene. Inexplicably, Early ordered a halt in the attack, the Confederate soldiers took time to loot the Federal camps, and these delays allowed Major General Horatio Wright, who was in command in Sheridan's absence, to organize a defense around the still strong VI Corps. By 11:00, the situation on the Union side had stabilized, and Sheridan had returned to resume command of his army.

While there was some merit in allowing Sheridan time to train his staff and army, he believed he had been ready for weeks and was much frustrated by the delay. When he finally went on the offensive on September 19th, it was only after a personal visit from Grant who made his views and concerns clear. Grant was

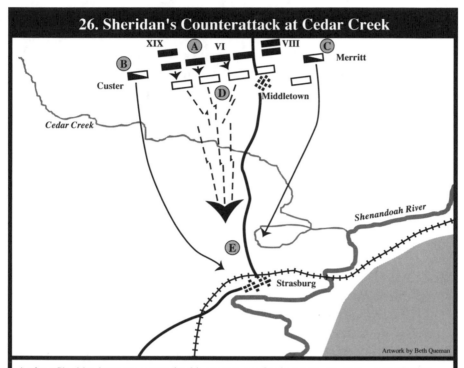

26. Sheridan's Counterattack at Cedar Creek

Action: Sheridan began to reorganize his army soon after he returned to it about 10:30 A.M. Before considering a counterattack, he made certain there was no threat against his rear by Confederate forces coming through the Blue Ridge Mountain passes behind him. By 4:00, he was ready to attack. VI Corps was the least affected by the morning's actions so he placed them in the center; XIX and VIII corps had been beaten up but had reached some level of organization so he placed them on the flanks of his infantry (A). Custer's division (B) and Merritt's division (C) of cavalry were further out on each flank and were assigned to threaten Early's flanks and cut off his retreat once the infantry attacked. This plan, cobbled together in a few hours, worked excellently (D). Early's army was soon retreating faster than they had advanced in the morning (E). The Battle of Cedar Creek was the final blow to Early's army which reduced it to military ineffectiveness.

more disturbed by the interruption of the Ohio and Chesapeake and the Baltimore and Ohio railroads than he was about the Washington politicians. He saw the interruption in these railroads as a threat to supplying his army.

In each of his battles against Early, Sheridan developed a

brilliant strategy which, if completely successful, would have annihilated Early's army. In the battles of Winchester III, Fishers Hill and Cedar Creek, he won decisively but could not meet his annihilation objective because in each case he ran into unexpected problems and then out of daylight before accomplishing a final annhiliation of his foe. In the combination of the three battles, he destroyed the effectiveness of Early's force and removed all threats to Washington.[4] As ordered by Grant, Sheridan then moved into the southern Shenandoah Valley and burned it, eliminating it as a food source to Lee's army.

Sheridan's victory at Cedar Creek was particularly gratifying to Grant. Sheridan was in Washington and had just returned to Winchester the night the battle began. Confederate troops, led by Major General John B. Gordon, surprised the Union army and drove it back with great losses. On the edge of victory, Early believed no further fighting was required to assure an overwhelming Southern victory. Sheridan arrived on the scene, and by mid-afternoon, his charismatic presence and skill had turned the Army of the Shenandoah around. In the late afternoon, a great defeat was turned into an overwhelming Union victory.

Strategically, Sheridan's victories in the Valley along with Sherman's previous capture of Atlanta and Farragut's earlier capture of Mobile Bay assured victory for Lincoln in the election of November 1864. Without this re-election, McClellan, as President, would probably have negotiated peace-terms that would have allowed the independence of the Confederacy and the continuation of slavery. By the end of 1864, the moves that would have to be made under Grant's leadership by the Union armies against Lee's and the other remaining Confederate mobile armies consisted of a complicated end game.

CHAPTER XXVIII

With Lincoln Elected, Confederate Desertions High and Morale Low, the War Could No Longer Be Won by the South. Why Did Lee Continue a Hopeless Fight?

With Lincoln elected, the chances of a military or political Confederate victory became nil. By March 1865, Sherman would need only fair weather to move the hundred miles to join Grant in the fight against Lee. Lee knew he would suffer defeat by June. Why did he continue the fight? Was the Confederate Secret Service plot against Lincoln part of the reason the Southern leadership decided to continue the war? Did the Confederate Administration plan to conduct a guerrilla campaign? Did Southern leaders make any decision or plan what they should do at all? Why were Confederate lives sacrificed for a now hopeless cause? Did Lee act like an honorable man, as an icon?

The end of the Confederacy was in sight. Grant planned for Sherman to begin his march northward to Virginia as soon as weather allowed, and for Schofield, with the two corps of the Army of the Ohio, to land at Wilmington and New Bern, North

Carolina in mid-January. Grant hoped that part of Thomas's forces would join forces with Sherman while the rest conquered Alabama and Mississippi. Sherman's and Schofield's armies made up the southern jaw of an enormous pincer movement against Lee and the small and weak Southern armies of maneuver in the Carolinas while Grant's armies were the northern jaw.

Sheridan had eliminated most of the supplies available to Lee from the Shenandoah Valley. As soon as weather would allow, Sheridan was prepared to move his now-elite 10,000-man Cavalry Corps into Virginia west of Richmond to destroy another source of Southern supplies. Grant gave Sheridan alternative plans to cross the James River and join Sherman or to participate in Grant's maneuvers to capture the Army of Northern Virginia. The latter was the highly preferable choice to Sheridan since he thought the war would end before he could reach Sherman.

By now, probably as many as half of the Confederate soldiers had voted with their feet to end what they saw as a hopeless war—they had deserted or gone absent without leave.[1] Except for a few leaders and loyal soldiers, the general populace did not accept the reasons for seccession as being adequate ones for sons and husbands to continue to die for the South. They saw no promise and had no confidence in their military leadership since all Confederate army commanders had been thoroughly beaten in the last seven months of 1864. The Union commanding generals in the field in January, 1865 had learned how to fight and how to win. The old experience of the Civil War that a force attacking a strongly fortified defender needed an advantage of 3:1 to assure victory was no longer valid. Under Grant's overall command, Sherman, Thomas and Sheridan had originated and improved offensive tactics that proved effective with a much smaller advantage.

Along with numerous groups of rag-tag militia and cavalry raiders, the Confederacy had three effective armies in the field at the end of July 1864: Lee's, Hood's and Early's. The inappropriate overly aggressive tactics employed by Hood and Early had destroyed their own armies by the end of the year. The Confederacy continued to fight an almost guerrilla-type of warfare in the deep Southern states, and they were trying to organize another field army to defend the Carolinas against Sherman. In addition to the Union armies, disease, despair, defeat and desertion were the Confederate Army's greatest enemies. These factors made it very difficult to build new armies and for Lee to hold together the most effective Confederate field army, the Army of Northern Virginia.[2]

*　　*　　*

In January, 1865, Sherman was 600 miles south of Petersburg in occupation of Savannah; nevertheless, he believed he could join Grant in attacking Lee's army by about May 1st. This was a key planning date for both sides since May 1st had been the approximate starting date for campaigning in Virginia in the two previous years: Hooker began the Chancellorsville campaign on April 29, 1863 and Grant had crossed the Rapidan on May 4, 1864. The Confederate command did not believe an effective attack on the Petersburg-Richmond defenses could be made before April 15th, and every decision they made that spring was based on that date. They turned out to be disastrously wrong. Grant agreed with this timing and did not change his thinking until he was persuaded by Sheridan that they could begin an effective drive against Lee as early as March 30th.

Fort Fisher, guarding Wilmington Harbor, fell on January 15, 1865, and Schofield captured Fort Anderson on the 19th; these actions forced the Confederates to abandon Wilmington, North Carolina on the 22nd. With the capture of Wilmington, one of the few remaining Confederate ports, Schofield moved troops into New Bern, North Carolina which had been in Federal hands since 1862. There, he began to concentrate an adequate force to link up with Sherman's armies when they reached the Goldsboro area.

His efforts would give Sherman a short and reliable supply route from the sea when he was ready to attack Lee.

On his march to the sea, Sherman used new tactics. Since Hood had withdrawn the largest Confederate army in Georgia back into Tennessee, the only way the Confederates might possibly stop Sherman would be to concentrate their troops to delay the advance of his main body. Sherman's plan would not allow successful concentration since he advanced each of his four corps on separate parallel routes over a 50-mile front. This meant that if a Confederate force tried to block one of his corps, the Confederates would almost immediately be outflanked by another Union corps, or by several. The only result for a Confederate force that attempted such a block was being surrounded or destroyed. Sherman's method also made it very difficult for the enemy to identify his next main objective at any time so they could not decide where best to concentrate even if they decided to try. Sherman planned to use the same tactics as he marched north through the Carolinas. [The German panzer divisions used tactics similar to Sherman's when they drove across France in 1940, so Sherman's military ideas were new in 1864 and remained sound for many years into the future.]

Bad weather delayed Sherman from starting north until February 1st. He began with feints against Augusta and Charleston while his real objective was Columbia, South Carolina, which was between these towns. His two armies of two corps each totaled about 60,000 men, and they were supported by 2,500 supply wagons and 600 ambulances. As they had done in Georgia, they would live mostly off the land. His Confederate adversary was Beauregard who had been assigned to lead the defense of the Carolinas. Beauregard's health was never excellent, and after the stress he had faced at Petersburg in June, he was in very poor health. When he arrived on February 3rd, he found he had only 22,500 troops with which to oppose Sherman. These troops were scattered from Augusta to Charleston under various commanders, not all of whom recognized Beauregard's authority over them.

CHAPTER XXVIII

Unable to concentrate his forces on Sherman's route, Beauregard ordered a concentration further north at Cheraw, South Carolina.

On January 23rd, Lee was appointed General-in-Chief of all the Confederate armies; however by this time, it was much too late for him to be of much influence concerning actions in other parts of the Confederacy. Lee still had no replacement competent enough to command the Army of Northern Virginia so he was forced to remain deeply involved in Virginia. One thing Lee did was to recall General J.E. Johnston from inaction on February 23, 1865 to command all troops in the Carolinas, replacing Beauregard.

*　　*　　*

In the 20th Century, it seems clear to all who read about the Civil War after the fact, that the cause was lost by the Confederacy by the end of 1864. Probably, it was lost sooner, after Farragut's, Sherman's and Sheridan's victories in August, September and October 1864 which assured Lincoln's re-election in November 1864. By the end of November, the votes had been counted, and Lincoln's re-election became a fact. December 1, 1864 was the last possible date that any realistic hope could be held for a Confederate victory and this would have to be based on a political, not a military action. How then, could men like Lee and other key leaders continue to spend blood on a war they must have known they would lose?

It is difficult to say these men were so immoral or callous that they could continue to kill thousands of their countrymen for what had by then become a "Lost Cause." If they were in fear of their own lives, it is hard to see how extending a war by six months longer would change their personal situations one way or another. It was also reasonable to think that a negotiated end of the war rather than a surrender forced by military action would probably be more likely to include more personal security guarantees for

Confederate leaders, provided the Union was restored and slavery was abolished.

The obvious reasons for the Confederate leaders to continue the war - hope of military victory, hope of foreign intervention- had become invalid by then. Their soldiers were deserting, which showed many no longer supported the war, and the populace at home was tired of war and no longer supported it. Things like personal security could be solved. So, why did they continue the war? Even remotely, not many possibilities of victory existed, but one remote possibility was the plot to kidnap Lincoln being carried forward by the Confederate Secret Service.

The Confederate plot and a basis to believe it existed is outlined in detail by Tidwell.[3] Two things had to fall into place for a Lincoln kidnap plot to be the basis of continuing the war by Davis and Lee: exact timing and the state of their minds. They had to think it was a possible ploy that might end the war with a settlement favorable to the Confederacy or, at least, shift things into their favor so they might still win somehow. Self-critical thinking and planning was never prevalent in Davis's and Lee's approaches to strategy so they might have been dealing only in ill-considered hopes and remote possibilities.

Timing was critical since the plot must succeed before Grant began a spring campaign which Lee thought would drive the Confederates out of the defenses of Richmond and Petersburg. In the two previous years weather had not allowed the spring campaign to start before the last week in April. Confederate Secret Service agents, Thomas Nelson Conrad and John Wilkes Booth, with their respective underlings, were in place in Washington ready to attempt to kidnap Lincoln by March 1, 1865.

When Lincoln was conducting his duties in Washington and was not in the field surrounded by soldiers, the security given the President was relatively poor. Each team of plotters was sufficiently armed to overcome Lincoln's bodyguards and grab him, provided they could find them alone in a relatively unpopulated place. Escaping the substantial forces that would be mobilized to catch them and recover Lincoln before they could pass into Confederate territory was their greatest obstacle. Tidwell describes how their carefully planned escape route could have worked. On March 1st, it seemed as though they had until about April 20th to find such a position and do the deed. Finding such a time and place was very difficult since the President's schedule was not planned very far ahead and was seldom announced. Sheridan's cavalry had moved into the area north of Richmond astride the planned escape route in mid-March, and this severely interfered with the timing. Lincoln took a well-armed naval transport from Washington to City Point on March 23rd, so all of March was lost to the plotters. Even so, the leaders of the Confederate Secret Service, including Davis and Lee, believed they had the first two weeks of April in which to kidnap Lincoln; after which, they had another four to seven days to move him to a secure place under their control.

Before March 1st Lee, the very intelligent soldier, knew the war could not be won militarily. He had given up offensive operations ten months earlier in the Wilderness. Only his defensive genius as the King of Spades, a description he hated, had kept the Confederacy in the war through 1864. Much of his army and almost all of the other Confederate armies were lost to casualties, defeats, disease and desertion. Supplies were short, and the breadbaskets of the Deep South, northern Virginia and the Shenandoah Valley, were lost to Lee's army forever. To continue to fight and to kill their own countrymen in such a bleak situation required some source of optimism. By this time, Davis was probably irrational when it came to seeing the facts, but Lee was an intelligent and realistic thinker who must have seen the facts.

Hope, however forlorn, had been an integral part of the Confederate policy for some time, as demonstrated in the East by the Antietam debacle and the invasion leading up to the disaster at Gettysburg. In the West, Hood's 1864 campaign into Tennessee was based on hope, not military skill or strength. Even on the last disastrous day before the Battle of Nashville, Hood hoped to take the offensive against Thomas the next day, not recognizing his army was already beaten, and most of his best officers dead or wounded. No chance was available to him that could remotely fulfill his hopes.

Some of this hope was based on the conceit that one Confederate private soldier was several times better than one Union private soldier, i.e., a 20-year-old man from Virginia could fight much better than two 20-year-old men from Ohio. Then, there was the fiction that Confederate generalship was much better than Northern generalship. While this may have been true in 1861 and even during part of 1862, by 1864 and 1865, the positions had reversed, and Northern generals had become superior to their Southern enemies. Even so, these fictions endured and were maintained long after the war. They are sometimes stated as gospel in the 1990s by "experts" who should know better.

Davis and Lee were co-directors of the Confederate Secret Service; therefore, each must have either been part of the origination or approved of the plot to kidnap Lincoln. "Not invented here" has always been a powerful reason to be held against acceptance of a new idea, but the opposite is also true. If the plot was invented by them, or by their underlings with their approval, Davis and Lee probably saw the plot as their own. Because it was probably *their* plot, there would be a great tendency for them to think that the plot was good and to pin their hopes on it. Self-justification excluded most moral considerations for them. This was a result of the Dahlgren-Kilpatrick raid of 1864 which they honestly believed had been undertaken with Lincoln's approval to kidnap or kill Davis and his cabinet[4]. It seems a strong case that Lee's decision to stay in the war in the face of a situation he recognized as very bleak was based on hope the Confederate Secret Service plot to kidnap Lincoln would succeed.

*   *   *

Advancing north, Sherman crossed the Augusta-Charleston

Railroad on February 7th with no opposition. He captured Columbia, South Carolina, the "seed of the rebellion," on the 16th, and the city burned. Whether the fire was the fault of Union or Confederate troops is unknown, but the fire was brought under control by Union troops under Sherman's orders. Hampton claimed Sherman systematically burned the city; Sherman denied this and claimed the fire started when Confederates opened and set fire to cotton bales to prevent them from falling into Union hands.[5]

Sherman's next objective was Cheraw, South Carolina where the Confederates were attempting to set up a defense. Heavy rains slowed this march of 90 miles and he was unable to arrive at Cheraw until March 3rd. Confederate Lieutenant General Hardee was outflanked at Cheraw and withdrew to Fayetteville, North Carolina. On the 16th, Sherman's XX Corps fought at Averasboro, North Carolina, drove the make-shift Confederate forces off and then marched toward Bentonville, North Carolina. Schofield fought another Confederate force at Kinston and joined Sherman at Goldsboro. The combined forces under Sherman were now an imminent threat to Lee since if they took Raleigh, North Carolina, only 40 miles away, they would cut Lee's main supply route from the Carolinas.

Lee ordered Johnston to attack one of Sherman's columns before he could consolidate all of his army. The two forces met at Bentonville, North Carolina on March 19, 1865 where Johnston attacked part of Major General Henry W. Slocum's XIV and XX corps, the left wing of Sherman's force. Approximately 16,000 Federals were attacked by 17,000 Confederates on the 19th; losses were 1,646 Union troops and 2,606 Confederate troops. Slocum withstood and blunted the attack of the 19th, and by 4:00 P.M. on the 20th, Sherman had concentrated his whole army group of 80,000 men against Johnston.

On the 21st, Sherman attacked through difficult swampy ground, threatening to surround the Confederates, and that night, Johnston and the remains of his army retreated to Smithfield,

North Carolina. Rain and mud delayed further movement north by Sherman, who was then 140 miles to the south of Petersburg. There was nothing between him and Lee that could slow him except for mud and flooded streams. Since leaving Savannah, Sherman's army had marched 425 miles in 40 marching days, so he was only about 14 days away from attacking Lee once the weather cleared.

*   *   *

Grant ordered Sheridan to move south, capture Lynchburg, cross the James, move on and join Sherman as soon as weather allowed. Sheridan believed the superior strategy was for him to rejoin the Army of the Potomac and participate in the spring campaign directly against Lee, and Grant changed his orders to give Sheridan discretion to join either Grant or Sherman. Activity in the Shenandoah Valley no longer consisted of clashes between large units; now it was partisan raids; and both sides had withdrawn most of their troops. Only the 10,000 man Cavalry Corps and the small number of West Virginia infantry remained. The West Virginia troops were all that was needed to control partisan activities.

Sheridan's personal status and esteem in the Federal Army was very high in February 1865: he was one of the five major generals who had been appointed to the Regular U.S. Army during the war and who were still active. On February 9th, Sheridan was voted the "Thanks of Congress" for his Shenandoah victories; and he had been appointed an army commander by Grant in the previous September, which had required approval by both Lincoln and the Congress. After the war, many accused Sheridan of excessive ambition, but it is difficult to understand what other ambitions Sheridan could have had. A self-demand for excellence and patriotism, not pure ambition, seems a more reasonable description of his motivation. Sheridan demonstrated his efficiency in leading a large army in combat; further, he had developed a new military doctrine that allowed an attacking force to defeat well-prepared defenders at an advantage of much less than the 3:1 previously necessary.

A general with all the authority to command an army except that he had no army to command, Sheridan was at the height of his abilities and ready to fight. He was dissatisfied with the commander of the Cavalry Corps, Major General Alfred T.A. Torbert because he felt Torbert was not sufficiently aggressive to command the cavalry. Torbert had let him down at Fishers Hill and in a raid on Gordonsville in December, but he respected Torbert's loyalty and efforts and did not wish to embarrass him by relieving him. He solved this dilemma by allowing Torbert to take a two-week leave a week before he planned to begin his move south. When Torbert was not there when the move started, he appointed 30-year-old Brevet Major General Wesley Merritt, the man he really wanted, in Torbert's place. Sheridan recommended that Torbert should become the commander of the remains of the Army of the Shenandoah, by now a small peace-keeping force.

On February 27th, Sheridan with his 10,000 well-trained, experienced and equipped troopers moved out of Winchester in driving rain and snow. The Cavalry Corps captured Staunton on March 2nd, and on the same day, defeated the 2,000-man remnant of Early's infantry at Waynesboro. On the 4th, he captured Charlottesville but decided Lynchburg was too strongly held to be captured and satisfied himself by wrecking the railroad between Charlottesville and Lynchburg.

The cavalry destroyed the James River Canal and railroads for many miles in Virginia west of Richmond. On March 10th, Sheridan reached Columbia, Virginia only to find that all the bridges over the James had been destroyed. This made joining Sherman impossible, so he decided to re-join Grant via White House Landing. Sending word to Grant of his intentions by spies who passed through enemy lines, Sheridan moved out on March 12th, wrecking the Virginia Central Railroad as he moved. Avoiding Longstreet's efforts to intercept him with the divisions of Pickett and Fitzhugh Lee near Ashland, he arrived at White House Landing on the 21st where he rested his men and horses for a week. His losses of men were insignificant, but the horrible condition of the Virginia roads had exhausted his horses. The Cavalry Corps moved into bivouac south of Petersburg on March 28th. On this date, the end of the Confederacy became a certainty, and its collapse followed within less than two weeks.

CHAPTER XXIX

January Through March 1865: With the War Hopelessly Lost, the Confederacy Sends out Peace Feelers on Their Own Terms

The war was irretrievably lost. It was time for a great leader, an icon, to step forward and save the lives the Confederacy would lose in March and April. Knowing the hopelessness of the situation, Lee remained silent. Longstreet met his opposing general, Ord, and they arranged for Lee to talk to Grant. Grant believed negotiating peace was purely political, not a military matter so he would have nothing of it. Lincoln met with Confederate representatives; they still wanted peace only on their own terms so nothing came of these meetings. Grim death for many Civil War soldiers waited for the weather to clear while Confederate leaders did nothing to prevent its coming.

While Sherman was racing north to become a real threat to Lee's army, in Virginia, January, February and March of 1965 were the saddest months of the Civil War. Except for the almost preposterous idea that Lincoln might be kidnaped by Confederate

Secret Service agents, there was no longer any remote hope that the South could win the Civil War. Nevertheless, Confederate leaders stubbornly kept killing their own soldiers while they refused to negotiate peace terms with good faith.

During the first three months of 1865, there were a number of half-hearted attempts made to negotiate peace. By this stage in the war, the North had a substantial military advantage, and their terms for peace were well known: restore the Union and abolish slavery. They had no reason for compromising on these fundamental requirements. An informal meeting between Davis and Francis P. Blair, a former Federal cabinet member, took place. Lincoln and his Secretary of State, William H. Seward, met with Alexander H. Stephens, Vice-President of the Confederacy, Robert M.T. Hunter, a past Confederate Secretary of State and J.A. Campbell. This conference was held aboard a steamer in Hampton Roads on February 3rd. The meeting came to nothing since the Confederacy's price for peace was still independence, and Lincoln would not consider any plan that did not include abolition of slavery.[1]

The exchanges between Lee and Longstreet about Confederate gold shows the degree of moral bankruptcy into which the Confederate States had fallen. In conversations and messages in late February and early March, Lee and Longstreet agreed that when the campaign season opened in the spring, food and supplies would be almost impossible to obtain using payment by Confederate notes or paper currency. Gold was being heavily hoarded by private citizens, but the government had a large supply in its vaults in Richmond. Longstreet proposed sending officers to the vaults and taking what gold was needed for the army to buy supplies in North Carolina. Lee considered this unscrupulous and refused to condone it. Longstreet pointed out that the gold would remain in the vaults while the country perished, waiting for Union officers to claim it. He then dropped the matter when Lee showed no interest.[2] The point of this exchange was not whether the army taking the gold was unscrupulous, or not. The fact was that the Confederate Administration allowed its soldiers to starve while they held onto gold that they would almost certainly lose to the Union. This was reprehensible and beyond understanding.

This exchange between Longstreet and Lee about gold disclosed another disturbing fact. They agreed that supplies and the other things the armies needed existed and were available for purchase in the rear areas of the Confederacy, even now that Union armies occupied much of the Southern states. It was not available for these reasons: paper currency was no good, the central Confederate Government had little power to force states to deliver supplies, the Confederate Army supply system led by Norton was corrupt and ineffective and the people in the rear areas did not have the will to make sacrifices to support central war aims. Lee's relief of the hated Norton was too late to change things.

Longstreet came into contact with Union Major General Ord, his opponent across the line, at a local truce arranged to discuss an exchange of wounded. The two Old Army friends moved off alone and discussed the war and their common hopes of peace. Longstreet suggested to Ord that a military convention be assembled to arrange terms of peace and informed Lee on March 1st he had done so. Ord told Longstreet a few days later that Grant had the authority to meet with Lee if Lee expressed a desire to do so. Lee was not enthusiastic about joining such a meeting since he believed discussing a *general* peace might be considered treasonous by his countrymen, but he did send word he desired to meet with Grant. Ord had apparently been acting on his own, for Grant refused to meet Lee to discuss a general peace, so this hope foundered.[3]

Since early in 1864, many Confederate state governors had become highly dissatisfied with the Richmond government and its conduct of the war. Some did not support the idea that new levies of troops from their states should be sent to Virginia. The governor of Georgia was trying to negotiate a separate peace directly with Sherman, and he withdrew Georgia units from the western armies in order to strengthen local defense forces under his own control.[4] He did not disturb the Georgia units in the Army of Northern Virginia until March 1865 at which time he began to urge the return home of some smaller units.

*   *   *

On March 25th, following the orders of Davis "to attack to shorten Grant's lines," Lee ordered Major General John B. Gordon to attack the Union line at Ft. Stedman. There was vague hope the attack would break through the Union lines and go on to capture or damage the supply base at City Point. For some time, Confederate soldiers had been coming through the Union lines and deserting; between 70 and 100 Confederates were deserting each night across the Petersburg/Richmond lines. These deserters were paid a bounty if they brought their rifles with them when they surrendered. Union pickets were accustomed to a number of "Johnnies" approaching them each night, and friendly conversation occurred between the enemies. When Gordon's troops approached the picket lines acting like deserters, they were welcomed, and the usual offer was made to purchase their arms. Suddenly the "Johnnies" disarmed the pickets, and the Confederate attackers were free to crawl to the base of the fort, which received no warning.

Having moved close to the fort, the few Union sentries were quickly overwhelmed, and by dawn, the Rebels were in control of the fort. Grant had warned his subordinate commanders of the likelihood of a Confederate attack, but those in the attack's immediate path were surprised. Immediately after dawn, artillery fire was concentrated on the captured fort, and soon after 8:00 A.M. the fort was attacked from all sides by Union infantry. It was recaptured with little Union loss, but 5,000 Confederate troops were killed, wounded or captured. Was it surprising that an attack against 100,000 men by just over 5,000 failed?

CHAPTER XXIX

*   *   *

Lee's activities as General-in-Chief of all of the Confederate armies were limited to only two things that were not responses forced upon him by Grant: he ordered J.E. Johnston to attack the left wing of Sherman's army, and he ordered Gordon to attack Ft. Stedman. Both of these actions were doomed to failure before they started, and neither showed skill in generalship. By this time of the war, orders for both Confederate armies to retreat to the mountains, break up into smaller units and conduct guerrilla warfare would have been a remote but the only hope for eventual success. However, guerrilla warfare did not fit with Lee's ideas of soldiering. Besides, the Lincoln plot was running, and based on their actions, Lee and Davis must have held fairly high hopes for its success.

*   *   *

Lincoln arrived at City Point on March 24th at the invitation of Grant. He heard the attack on Ft. Stedman with his own ears from the *River Queen* where he had spent the night. The next day Grant escorted Lincoln to the scene of the battle before all the bodies and wounded had been cleaned up. This depressing experience strongly added to Lincoln's recognizing the true horrors of war. Sheridan arrived at City Point ahead of the Cavalry Corps on the 25th. After meeting with Grant and describing his march from Winchester, Grant assured Sheridan that he would retain his army command status and would continue to report directly to him, not to Meade. The concept Grant and Sheridan discussed was quite "modern." They contemplated forming a "Cavalry Army" which would be the combination of the Cavalry Corps and one or more infantry corps under Sheridan's command. After Sheridan's Shenandoah Valley experience, Grant was fully confident in Sheridan's ability to command such a mixed force and accomplish substantial goals.

On the 25th, Meade was fully occupied, and Grant invited Sheridan to join him in a meeting with Lincoln on the steamer, *Mary Martin*. Sheridan found that Lincoln knew much less about Grant's plans than he did, and that Lincoln had only a vague idea that Grant intended to attack Lee's right. He saw that Lincoln had no idea of the great strength Grant planned to use in the attack. Lincoln was depressed and feared another Ft. Stedman type of attack that would break through the Federal lines and capture City Point with all its supplies. Without disclosing any details of the plan, Sheridan encouraged Lincoln not to worry about such a possibility, since Lee would be far too occupied with his right to make any similar attack.

Grant's orders to Sheridan of the 24th contemplated that he was to try to flank Lee's right. However, if he met severe resistance, he was to break off, destroy the South Side Railroad, the last available to supply Lee from further south, and then ride to join Sherman. Both Sheridan and Brigadier General John A. Rawlins, Grant's Chief of Staff, protested against any movement by Sheridan to join Sherman.

Both believed he could be put to best use against Lee. They recognized Sherman's shortage of cavalry, but they did not like the idea of Sheridan and his cavalry riding over 100 miles to help Sherman attack Johnston and then riding a similar distance back to attack Lee. Whether they persuaded Grant to change his plan or whether Grant was using the idea of sending Sheridan to Sherman as a ruse designed to mislead Lee, Grant soon told Sheridan he was trying to give the Confederates false intelligence and he expected Sheridan to continue in the fight against Lee.

CHAPTER XXX

Worried that Lee Will Abandon His Lines, Grant Hurries to Make His Assault, Knowing He Is Strong Enough to Divide His Forces

Lee knew Sheridan had wiped out the remnants of his opponents in the Shenandoah Valley and was returning to join Grant. Once the fine Union cavalry arrived, Lee knew he could not prevent it from outflanking his right, which would break the siege. Lee lost 10% of his strength in the easily repulsed and futile attack on Ft. Stedman. Desertion was still prevalent in the Army of Northern Virginia, so his manpower was rapidly decreasing while Grant's strength was building every day. Grant's main worry was that on any morning, he would awake to find Lee and his army gone from their lines, and he would never get the chance to attack them.

The Army of Northern Virginia had sixteen days to live on March 25, 1865, the day of their futile assault on Ft. Stedman. In these sixteen days before it surrendered, the army would lose half of its strength.[1] The Confederacy could not long survive this army's destruction.

On that same day, Lincoln had only three weeks to live. He would hear Grant say: "When Sheridan's cavalry arrives, we can end this."[2] He would see the Petersburg defenses broken. He would follow the Union troops into Richmond and sit in Jefferson Davis's chair in the Confederate White House. Lincoln would return to Washington triumphant and keep his appointment with John Wilkes Booth and death at Ford's Theater. He would not live to see the final end of the Civil War and the subsequent peace. And, most important, Lincoln's benign influence and great political skill was lost to the restored Union during the turbulent period of reconstruction.

*　　*　　*

On March 29th, the Appomattox Campaign began. Lee was convinced that the failure at Ft. Stedman and the arrival of Sheridan's cavalry meant that he could not hold the Petersburg-Richmond lines very much longer. Lee planned to move south and link up with the forces of Johnston, who was stuck in the mud along with his opponent, Sherman, only 140 miles to the south in North Carolina. To have reasonable hopes of doing this, the South Side Railroad had to be held.

In anticipation of their needs for supplies when his army moved south, Lee ordered supply depots to be set up at Burkesville, Danville and Lynchburg. A depot of fodder was being accumulated at Stony Creek, 40 miles south of Dinwiddie Court House, and Rosser's brigade of cavalry was assigned to guard it. While preparations for moving out were well under way, Lee was faced with two severe delaying factors: the muddy roads and the debilitated condition of his animals. The horses and mules were just too underfed and weak to haul wagons through the heavy mud. Lee thought he had time to plan and make the move, but Grant refused to give him as much time as he would need.

For months, Grant's greatest fear was that he would awaken one morning and find the Army of Northern Virginia had moved

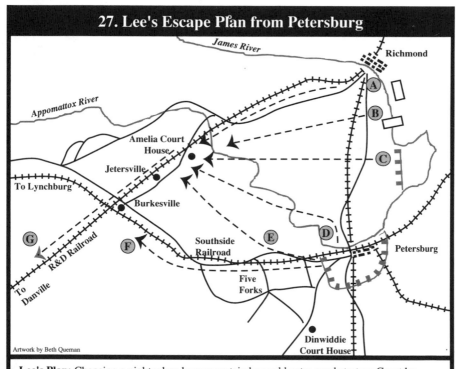

27. Lee's Escape Plan from Petersburg

James River

Richmond

Ⓐ

Ⓑ

Appomattox River

Ⓒ

Amelia Court
House

Jetersville

To Lynchburg

Burkesville

Ⓖ

Ⓕ

Southside
Railroad

Ⓔ

Ⓓ

R&D Railroad

To
Danville

Five
Forks

Petersburg

Dinwiddie
Court House

Artwork by Beth Queman

Lee's Plan: Choosing a night when he was certain he could get a good start on Grant by railroad, Lee planned to move most of his army by rail. He had ordered depots of supplies to be set up at Burkesville Junction, and he believed he would be able to take supplies with him from Petersburg and Richmond. His goal was to join J.E. Johnston's army near Danville; however if he reached Burkesville he could alternatively decide to go to Lynchburg. He planned for the troops near Richmond (A&B) to board the R&D RR, and for most of the troops near Petersburg to move on the Southside RR (F). Rear guards and some of the troops would have to move overland (C&E) to Amelia Court House where they would board trains for the rest of the move. He hoped to be able to take the R&D RR to Danville (G).

out and abandoned its defenses. He was anxious to move, and he wanted to beat Lee to the punch in spite of the generally bad weather.

To add strength to his proposed attack south of the James, Grant ordered Ord and his Army of the James to disengage from Longstreet's forces in Bermuda Hundred and north of the James. Ord was to leave only token forces against Longstreet in an attempt to deceive him about the move. This fooled Longstreet, who had too few cavalry to observe the Union actions efficiently. Unknown to Lee, Ord's divisions crossed the James at night, and backed up the north end of the Army of the Potomac line. This allowed more of Grant's units to shift south to the planned points of attack.

On the 29th, Grant ordered II and V Corps to attack Lee's right. He also ordered Sheridan to lead his enlarged 13,000-man Cavalry Corps around Lee's right and cut the South Side Railroad. Grant spread the cover story that Sheridan was then to proceed south and join Sherman; he hoped this would reach Lee's ears and mislead him into thinking Grant was in no hurry and was planning to conduct a long campaign.

Lee anticipated Grant's plan to move around his right flank and countered it by ordering Pickett, with a force of about 15,000 infantry and cavalry, to move to Five Forks and hold that position "at all hazard." This move further weakened the Confederate Petersburg defenses and made them even more vulnerable to successful attack. Five Forks was a critical point, since its loss would both open the flank of Lee's army to assault and take away the use of the South Side Railroad for supplying his army. Without the railroad, the possibility of an orderly retreat from Petersburg would be greatly reduced and the abandonment of the defense lines might become a rout with many more soldiers being lost.

*   *   *

Grant had learned he could not trust Meade to lead an offensive campaign effectively although he still respected him for his defensive and administrative skills and as a loyal soldier. Grant had every confidence in Sheridan's ability to lead an army in an offensive campaign and continue to take full advantage of opportunities as they arose until the campaign was successful.

Both Grant and Sheridan were innovative and Sheridan had great initiative. As the two generals discussed the coming

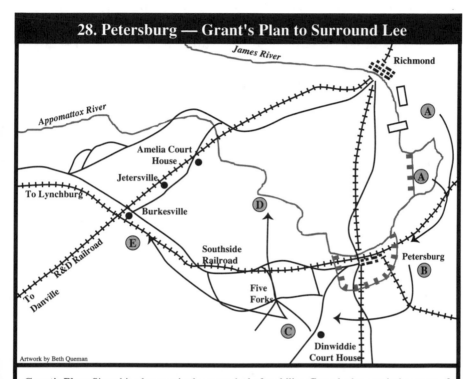

28. Petersburg — Grant's Plan to Surround Lee

Artwork by Beth Queman

Grant's Plan: Since his plan required a great deal of mobility, Grant had to await the return of Sheridan's cavalry and good weather before executing it. Grant ordered Ord's Army of the James to move secretly out of the defenses north of the James (A) and from Bermuda Hundred (A), leaving these areas lightly defended. Ord would reinforce the Army of the Potomac (B) and allow it to move to the south and west of Petersburg so that when he attacked the Petersburg defenses he would put most of his force in the attacks. Sheridan with 10,000 cavalry and with infantry support as needed, would move to Dinwiddie Court House (C). Once there, Sheridan would decide whether to: (1) move directly north through Five Forks (D), cut Southside RR and move into Lee's rear; or (2) move against Amelia Court House or Burkesville Junction (E) which would cut Lee off from all routes of retreat by rail.

campaign, they wished to follow a new concept of war that they had developed over the past ten months: the mobile attack task force. Sheridan would retain his army command status as commander of the "Cavalry Army." The Cavalry Army would be made up of the Cavalry Corps plus infantry corps from the Army of the Potomac that would be assigned to it temporarily while the Cavalry Army pursued a specific task.

Sheridan and his corps marched through heavy rain and mud to Dinwiddie Court House, arriving on the evening of the 30th. The next morning they turned north toward Five Forks. In response, Pickett left his prepared defenses along White Oak Road which runs through Five Forks and attacked the cavalry, driving it back to Dinwiddie.

From his position around Dinwiddie, Sheridan realized that Pickett's advantage in numbers was only temporary, and with the infantry reinforcements that were on the way to join him, he had an opportunity to annihilate Pickett's force if he could fight him in the open swampy land. Pickett's force was such a large part of his army that Lee could not afford to lose it, almost a third of what remained. On the night of the 31st, the rain and mud made conditions so bad that Grant was prepared to postpone the offensive. This was one of the few times in the Civil War that an army commander's attitude was dictated by confidence and opportunity, not weather conditions; it was a great change. Sheridan personally rode 13 miles through the mud to Grant's headquarters, persuaded Grant of the real advantages of the situation and caused him to change his mind. Sheridan wanted infantry support from VI Corps, a unit that had fought under him in the Shenandoah Valley, but it was a two-day march away so he was given Warren's V Corps.[3]

V Corps was only six miles east of Sheridan's cavalry and the movement to join him seemed easy, but flooded streams, washed out bridges and mud slowed its progress. Warren had many opposite attitudes to Sheridan; he was perfectly willing to use the rough weather conditions as an excuse to delay a fight. Sheridan sent Warren an order at 3:00 A.M. on April 1st requiring him "to move quickly as he [Sheridan] planned to [start the] fight at daylight." Warren delayed, and by about noon, Pickett recognized his peril in the open ground and retreated to the prepared defensive positions along the White Oak Road at Five Forks.

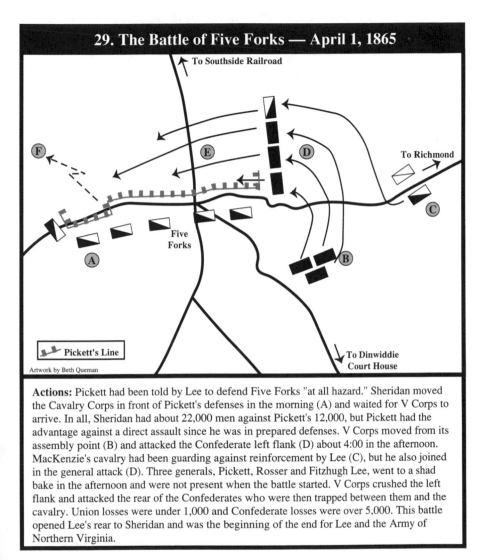

29. The Battle of Five Forks — April 1, 1865

To Southside Railroad

To Richmond

F

E

D

To Dinwiddie
Court House

Five
Forks

A

B

C

Pickett's Line

Artwork by Beth Queman

Actions: Pickett had been told by Lee to defend Five Forks "at all hazard." Sheridan moved the Cavalry Corps in front of Pickett's defenses in the morning (A) and waited for V Corps to arrive. In all, Sheridan had about 22,000 men against Pickett's 12,000, but Pickett had the advantage against a direct assault since he was in prepared defenses. V Corps moved from its assembly point (B) and attacked the Confederate left flank (D) about 4:00 in the afternoon. MacKenzie's cavalry had been guarding against reinforcement by Lee (C), but he also joined in the general attack (D). Three generals, Pickett, Rosser and Fitzhugh Lee, went to a shad bake in the afternoon and were not present when the battle started. V Corps crushed the left flank and attacked the rear of the Confederates who were then trapped between them and the cavalry. Union losses were under 1,000 and Confederate losses were over 5,000. This battle opened Lee's rear to Sheridan and was the beginning of the end for Lee and the Army of Northern Virginia.

Sheridan's battle plan was for two cavalry divisions to hold Pickett's force behind their works while one cavalry division threatened the Confederate right and V Corps crushed their left flank. This brilliant tactic would force Pickett's men to retreat to the west, away from Lee's main force. He sent Brigadier General

297

Ranald S. MacKenzie, an 1862 West Point graduate, east on the White Oak Road to scout for reinforcements coming to Pickett from Lee. MacKenzie stopped weak reinforcement efforts by enemy cavalry and prevented easy communications between Lee and Pickett.

In one of the great derelictions of duty in the Civil War, Virginia generals Pickett, Rosser and Fitzhugh Lee left their men in their defenses in the afternoon to attend a shad bake hosted by Rosser, two miles behind the line. This left the Confederate force under no central command, and the general remaining in command did not know where Pickett could be found.[4] This was a condition of which Sheridan took full advantage. When V Corps attacked at about 4:00 P.M., it rolled up Pickett's left. In an hour and a half, victory was complete, and the remains of Pickett's force scattered and ceased to be effective. The cavalry pursued remnants westward for six miles.

As usual, the courageous Sheridan exposed himself to the same dangers his troops faced. Riding his favorite horse, Rienzi, he leaped over the Confederate works with V Corps troops where the works angled away from the road; this was the key to turning the rebel defenses. Landing among Confederate soldiers who had thrown down their arms and were trying to surrender, his fury turned to humor as he accepted many surrenders and directed the enemy soldiers where to go for their safety. At Five Forks, Pickett suffered over 5,000 killed, wounded and captured while Sheridan's losses were about 800.

Knowing how important the victory at Five Forks was to the rest of Grant's plans, Sheridan made a special effort to get word of the outcome to Grant. When Grant received Sheridan's message that Pickett's force had been destroyed and the South Side Railroad would be cut at dawn, he ordered a general attack on the Petersburg defenses to start at dawn. Because the Battle of Five Forks became a disorganized rout for the Confederates, no one made a great effort to send word of the seriousness of the disaster to Lee. During the night, Lee received many disquieting rumors, but these did not make him decide to begin his retreat that night. This dereliction of duty by Pickett took away the last remote chance for the Army of Northern Virginia to survive for a few aditional weeks. Knowing his only alternatives were to flee or surrender, Lee informed Davis during the early morning of the 2nd that Richmond must be abandoned that night.[5]

Lee began his retreat westward on the 2nd, and the Confederacy abandoned Richmond that night. Union troops accepted the surrender of Richmond at 8:15 A.M. on the 3rd. Davis and his cabinet also began their flight.

CHAPTER XXXI

Lee's Last Retreat; Lee's Last Stand

Lee's army had only sixteen days to live on March 25th, the day of the hopeless attack on Ft. Stedman. On April 1, 1865, Sheridan routed Pickett's large detachment at Five Forks. With only nine more days to live the Army of Northern Virginia abandoned Petersburg and Richmond on Lee's orders, too late to accomplish anything useful for the Confederacy. The division of his forces and leaving the decision to abandon his lines too late doomed the Confederacy's last faint hopes. April 2nd began "Lee's Last Stand."

On the 2nd, Sheridan sent his cavalry westward to engage enemy cavalry while he led V Corps to the South Side Railroad where they captured Ford's Depot without opposition. They rapidly moved eastward toward Petersburg and captured Sutherland's Depot, a position in the flank and rear of the Confederate forces fighting II Corps. These Confederate troops were in serious peril and had to break off the fight and flee. The South Side Railroad had been taken, and all the troops on Lee's right had been broken.[1]

On the 3rd, the cavalry took up the pursuit west, followed by V Corps. They had several skirmishes but overcame all attempts to stop them and reached Deep Creek on Namozine Road by evening.

*   *   *

On the Petersburg lines from Battery Gregg to Hatcher's Run, about half of the whole defensive line, Lee was able to place only one defender for about every 20 feet. By then in a state of near-panic, Lee planned to abandon the lines east of Battery Gregg and establish a new defensive line along Indian Town Creek, west of Petersburg. He would leave only one division north of the James and move all the rest of his troops to strengthen the new defense line.[2]

On the night of April 1st, Lee was very poorly served by Pickett, his staff and his intelligence officers. He did not know the full extent of the disaster at Five Forks; otherwise, he would have ordered the abandonment of the Petersburg lines before dawn on the 2nd. Having missed this opportunity, the only hope of a safe withdrawal and a later concentration was for the army to hold Grant off for just one more day as it had successfully done for the previous nine months. If Grant should turn further behind Lee's right or discover how weak the defenses had really become, Lee knew further disaster would occur. Abandoning the defenses in the face of a strong Union attack *and, at the same time*, saving a substantial portion of the army was near to impossible.

Grant's attack on the Petersburg lines began before dawn on April 2nd. By first light, Federal troops had broken through behind the new Indian Town Creek line from the south and moved a mile and a half northward. When dawn came, Lee could see long blue lines of Union troops advancing toward his headquarters at Edge Hill.

Federal troops had attacked at two points they thought were weak along the line, two miles south and just west of Ft. Gregg. At these weak points, they made wide breakthroughs advancing beyond the Boydton Plank Road. After dawn, a heavy fog held up their advance for a short time, giving Lee's men a chance to reorganize. About 9:00 A.M., Lee saw for himself that he had no line beyond the right of Ft. Gregg so he knew his troops along

Hatcher's Run were isolated, and at this same hour, he learned of the full magnitude of Pickett's defeat. This was disaster followed by calamity.

That day the Army of Northern Virginia was saved by two factors: their own extreme gallantry and the feeling among many attacking Union soldiers that the war was almost over and why die so late in it. Somehow, the Confederates held their lines until night fell, after which a fairly orderly retreat began. This retreat was much more difficult than those Lee had organized after Antietam and Gettysburg due to the poor condition of his men and animals and the terribly muddy roads. They also took some much needed time to destroy the arms they could not take with them.

Lee ordered that all units should move out during the night and converge on Amelia Court House, about 40 miles to the west, where they would try to concentrate into an effective army once again. Only one corps was in a position from which it would not have to cross the flooded Appomattox River and some troops would have to cross it twice. They could not use the South Side Railroad, but if they successfully reached Amelia, they might be able to reach the Richmond and Danville Railroad for more rapid movement. Amelia was about 20 miles from a supply depot that was supposed to be at Burkeville. Once on the R & D Railroad, Lee could move by rail to Lynchburg or to Danville, and he might be able to join Johnston.

Grant also knew the Civil War was ending, and in spite of how much he wanted to move quickly to trap Lee, he allowed his attack to subside during the afternoon. He knew he could take Richmond and Petersburg on the 3rd, without further serious bloodshed.

*   *   *

By the evening of the 4th, the remainder of Lee's army had concentrated at Amelia. After the losses of the 1st and 2nd, Lee could only concentrate a force of about 35,000 men although a few more troops joined him later.

Using a sound pursuit strategy, something few Civil War generals were able to do, Sheridan's objective was to interpose his cavalry and supporting infantry between Lee and his escape route to the south. During the day, Sheridan had ordered cavalry to drive towards Jettersville and tear up the R & D Railroad. At about 5:00 P.M. on the 4th, Sheridan arrived in Jettersville and learned that Lee and his army were in Amelia.

V Corps was brought up to Jettersville to support Sheridan's cavalry, and this eliminated Lee's last good opportunity to escape successfully to the south. If he had attacked the relatively small Union force at Jettersville and then marched promptly to Burkesville, he might have been able to move his army using the railroad to Danville, but Lee chose not to fight at Jettersville.

A dispatch from Lee's Chief of Commissary was intercepted which called for 200,000 rations to be sent to Burkesville from Danville and Richmond. Sheridan immediately informed Grant and Meade that Lee's army was concentrated at Amelia, and he was moving toward Burkesville where the railroads to Danville and Lynchburg joined.[3]

In order to escape and move farther south, time was of the essence to Lee. His total distance to the Roanoke River, the closest place where he could meet Johnston and set up a good defensive line, was 107 miles away, but some of Grant's forces were closer, only 88 miles from that point. Upon reaching Burkesville on the 4th, another disaster struck Lee when his scouts reported the depot there had plenty of arms and ammunition but no food. The fact that Union forces had moved into the area and the lack of food caused Lee to bypass Burkesville. He moved overland to Farmville from where he could move south to the R & D Railroad west of Burkesville.

*   *   *

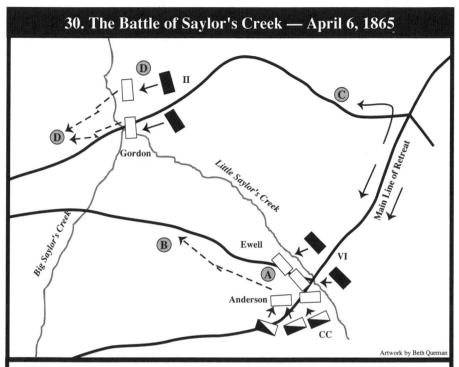

30. The Battle of Saylor's Creek — April 6, 1865

Artwork by Beth Queman

Actions: The pursuit of a beaten army was an imperfect art in the Civil War. Without the necessary mobility, pursuing forces followed their enemy, and whenever they drew close, the enemy rear guard deployed and held up the pursuer while the main body escaped. Sheridan's cavalry had the mobility to attempt two tactics that had not been successful before: (1) find an interval in the escaping column and cut it up; and (2) move around the head of the column, stop and engage it while the infantry caught up with them. Saylor's Creek was an example of cutting an escaping column. The corps of Anderson, Ewell and Gordon, about 17,000 men, were Lee's rear guard, and they were also assigned to protect the army's supply trains. A gap occurred between Longstreet's corps and the rear guard, and Union cavalry general Cook discovered it. The Cavalry Corps (CC) blocked the road near Little Saylor's Creek and trapped Anderson's and Ewell's men between it and VI Corps (A) which was in pursuit. In this action, only a portion of Anderson's corps escaped after hours of bitter fighting. When Gordon saw that the road ahead was blocked, he turned his column around (C). II Corps attacked Gordon near Saylor's Creek, and only a portion of his corps escaped to the west. Union losses were about 1,150 and Confederate losses were about 7,700. These losses and the loss of its supplies doomed the Army of Northern Virginia.

On the 6th, Sheridan ordered his cavalry to move to the left toward Deatonsville. By then, V Corps had been returned to Meade's command so Sheridan no longer commanded any infantry. The cavalry discovered Lee's supply trains, protected by a heavy escort of infantry and cavalry, moving on the road toward Farmville. This made it apparent the whole army was moving toward Farmville.

The cavalry immediately attacked the Confederate escort guarding the supply trains, looking for a weakness. Seeing an opportunity to destroy a large and vital part of Lee's army, Sheridan sent for infantry support and he was pleased when VI Corps was rushed to join him. The cavalry stopped Ewell's and Anderson's vanguard on the road from Deatonsville just south of where it crossed Saylor's Creek. As VI Corps arrived they formed to the east of the cavalry and moved across the road behind the Confederates.

Ewell's Confederate forces were almost surrounded and had no hope of victory. Nevertheless, they fought valiantly in one of the bloodier actions of the war until they could fight no longer. Anderson and about 2,000 men escaped to the west, but 7,000 Confederates were captured, including six generals, and several thousand more men were killed or wounded. The exhausted generals and other officers on both sides had dinner together, and the Union officers shared their blankets with their captives. Some were fellow West Point classmates, some had been comrades in the Old Army. They forgot the bloody day for a little while. Ewell told Sheridan their situation was hopeless and urged him to demand that Lee surrender. Sheridan sent a message to Grant: "We can end it if we press." Grant replied: "Let it be pressed."[4]

With only about 28,000 men in total after Saylor's Creek, Lee could only field about 12,000 veteran infantry riflemen. The physical condition of his army was terrible. Many of its soldiers were unarmed; others had no shoes or inadequate clothing; and many of his men and horses were near starvation. To the south, about half of Johnston's men had deserted by then, and he could field only about 10,000 riflemen. Even if the two armies succeeded in joining, they would only be able to bring an exhausted, pitiful force against two massive Union army groups.

*   *   *

The pursuit continued on the 7th with the main body of the Confederate army in Farmville. Sheridan's and Ord's troops took Prince Edward Court House and severed Lee's last direct route to Danville.

The 8th was the day on which any small chance of escape was finally lost. Using Lee's commissary officer's order which was captured earlier, Sheridan had sent one of his scouts, Sergeant White who was dressed as a Confederate, to deliver the order to a Confederate telegrapher at Appomattox Station on the 7th. The order was delivered; White waited for the supplies to arrive; and on the night of the 7th, he notified Sheridan that four trains had arrived at Appomattox Station loaded with supplies for Lee's army.

Custer and his division led the cavalry to Appomattox Station at high speed, occupied the tracks on both sides of the trains and captured three of them. Confederate cavalry arrived in the vicinity at almost the same time, but Custer won the critical race. He drove them back towards Appomattox Court House. Fighting continued until dark.

On the evening of the 8th, Sheridan notified Grant, Ord and Griffin, commander of the nearby V Corps, that the Confederates were trapped with no means of escape if infantry support could be brought up at once. At dawn on the 9th, Confederate troops tried to break out to the west by attacking the dismounted cavalry. The cavalrymen fell back gradually while Ord's infantry formed lines of battle behind them. When the cavalry moved off to the side, long lines of well-prepared Union infantry were seen to be ready to fight so all Confederate attacks ceased.[5]

The war was over between the Army of Northern Virginia and

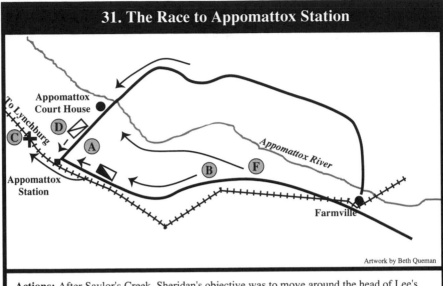

31. The Race to Appomattox Station

Artwork by Beth Queman

Actions: After Saylor's Creek, Sheridan's objective was to move around the head of Lee's escaping column and stop it until the pursuing infantry of the Armies of the Potomac and James could defeat it. He gained intelligence that Lee had ordered four trains of badly needed supplies be sent by rail from Lynchburg to Appomattox Station. In his mind, this established Lee's necessary objective (A) so he ordered his cavalry to gallop to Appomattox Station to capture the supplies before Confederate cavalry could win the race to them; also, if the Army of Northern Virginia could reach Appomattox Station ahead of the Union armies, it might be able to escape by rail to the west. Custer's cavalry (B) reached Appomattox Station first, cut the railroad (C) to Lynchburg and captured the supplies on April 8th. Confederate cavalry (D) arrived soon thereafter, an engagement was fought, but they were defeated. The next morning the infantry of the Union armies came up, and Lee had no chance to escape. Later on April 9th, the Army of Northern Virginia surrendered at Appomattox Court House.

the Army of the Potomac. On April 9, 1865, after an exchange of terse messages between them, Lee surrendered to Grant.

CHAPTER XXXII

Comparing the Confederate and Federal High Commands

On the Confederate side, President Davis was the high command, like a spider in a web. He was frustrated at not being the Confederacy's General-in-Chief, operating in the field. Excepting Lee and the Johnstons, Davis chose poor military leaders. Being very assault-minded, Davis fed these tendencies to his generals to their detriment. Davis interfered with every general's decisions. Lincoln did not consider himself a military expert, but under his tutor, Halleck, he learned quickly. Lincoln's selection process was tortuous, but once he found the right general, he did not interfere with his decisions.

Before appraising Lee as a general, the high commands of the two countries should be considered since they greatly influenced the performance of all generals. Although not in overall command, Lee was an important part of the Confederate high command. How did he influence its decisions?

From the standpoint of basic military prowess, Southerners had an initial advantage over their Union counterparts. Besides enlisting the most experienced officers in the 1861 Federal Army, violence was more commonplace in the hills and society of the

Southern states than it was in the agrarian North. In the South, duels were fought more frequently, and most men knew how to ride. Small farmers were the dominant demographic sector of the North, and they were a relatively peaceful group. To enter into the violent world of combat, many Southerners and most Northerners had to learn and adapt to changes in attitude.

In war, singleness of purpose is critical. The form of government and the idea of states rights made it much more difficult for the South to align its people behind its leadership than the North where a strong centralized government was in place. President Lincoln found himself able to dominate the state governors and other factions soon after his election, but President Davis was never able to accomplish the same ascendancy in spite of much effort on his part. The Confederate Congress was a more powerful organization in opposing Davis's fighting of the war than the U.S. Congress. The latter either chose not to, or was never able to, mount serious opposition to Lincoln's war policies.

The state governments and the state's representatives in the Confederate Congress did not allow Davis to obtain laws that might have helped the Confederacy win the war. The lack of strong enlistment and draft laws that would have prevented the majority of the South's white men from avoiding service, and laws that would have improved their supply situation by severely punishing profiteers and forcing suppliers to ship to the army are critical examples of many such deficiencies. Most Confederate laws in support of the war effort were mere window dressing with so many exclusions and exceptions that they accomplished less than a determination to win the war required.

With a disadvantage in overall population, it was necessary for the Confederacy to use all of its human and material resources to have a chance to win. A large part of the populace was unwilling to make the necessary sacrifices, and their elected representatives were unwilling to pass the laws that were needed to support the sacrifices that those who did serve made so freely.

The South entered the war without understanding that brave

words and self-righteousness alone cannot win a war. They failed to do what was needed beyond these feelings. It is fair to say that those in the halls of the Confederate and Southern State governments did more to lose their war than the Southern soldiers and generals did.

Winning a war is a difficult thing at best; it requires will! In the Southern states, the lack of willingness to make the sacrifices necessary for victory manifested a lack of will in the people and their elected and appointed representatives. In the North this will to win was supplied by President Lincoln who, when faced with similar problems, used his force of character and many skills to assume almost dictatorial powers. Lincoln's strong personality, diplomatic skills and the maintenance of the high moral ground allowed him to impose his strong will upon the Union war effort in spite of all the setbacks along the way.

The South had no such force of will. The populace was too divided on the matter of slavery to exert itself. The state governors held the real power in the Confederacy, and they were most interested in the well-being of their own states as they saw it. As a moral statement, "slavery is good" was untenable. Finally, President Davis shared his countrymen's views on states' rights which inhibited his ability to oppose state governors, and he did not have the kind of forceful personality and qualities of leadership that Lincoln had. Without these qualities, Davis was unable to impose his will on the populace from the top.

Without a will to win, the South had an uncurable weakness in the Civil War. No Southerner found a way to cure this fault!

* * *

The Southern high command became rigid early in the war, in that it proved unable to adapt to changing military conditions. Because Lincoln was a greater disciple of change and because of the frequent infusion of new people, the Northern high command changed its ideas every few months until the last year of the war when its military policies became more stable. Because of its early rigid nature, the Southern high command did not show flexibility in dealing with the many dynamic changes that had occurred in the ten years before the war and then during its course.

For purposes of discussion, the high commands of both countries will be defined as the President, the Secretary of War, the General-in-Chief and the Chief-of-Staff or the Adjutant General of the Army if these positions existed, along with the Commanders-in-Chief of the Eastern and the Western theaters of war. The Confederate high command began the war and ended it with President Davis, Adjutant General Samuel Cooper and Lee as prominent members. The Secretary of War was changed from time to time, but most of these men had little influence on events. Upon his death in battle, A.S. Johnston was replaced by Bragg in the West, and J.E. Johnston was part of the high command at various times. Hood commanded in the West for a short period. The list of individuals that comprised the Confederate High Command is short, and only Bragg and Hood advanced into the group from lower rank than that with which they started.

In the North, only Lincoln began the war as part of the high command and continued throughout its duration. Cameron and Stanton were Secretaries of War. Scott, McClellan, Halleck and Grant were Federal Army Generals-in-Chief. Halleck began the war as Commander-in-Chief in the West, Grant and Rosecrans shared the duty for a year until Rosecrans was relieved, and Sherman ended the war in the position. As Eastern Commander-in-Chief, the Federal list was very long: McDowell, McClellan, McClellan and Pope, Burnside, Hooker, Meade and finally Meade, Ord and Sheridan shared the assignment.

Lincoln was attempting to find a high command that could win the war for him. He recognized that the essential feature of such a high command was an efficient general-in-chief, and after numerous failed attempts, he found in Grant the basis of such a high command. Davis attempted to manage the war effort himself. Besides A.S. Johnston and Lee who were generals of quality, Davis seemed unable to find better generals than his usually inefficient cronies. Davis proved to be a poor strategist and a poor selector of men. Lee had a high opinion of J.E. Johnston and Beauregard, but they did not suit Davis's politics or pre-conceived opinions so he avoided using them except when forced to do so in a crisis. Lee's failure to influence Davis to use J.E. Johnston, a very important consideration, showed that Lee had little real influence with Davis about the overall conduct of the war.

One of Davis's old cronies, General Samuel Cooper, was appointed by Davis to be his General-in-Chief to whom all other commanders would report. When Cooper did not prove effective in that duty, Davis did not replace him. Although Cooper was the highest ranking of all Confederate generals, Davis put him in charge of the army's paper-work as a high ranking clerk. Another of Davis's cronies was Julius Norton whom Davis appointed as the Commissary General of the Confederate Army. Norton proved to be both corrupt and inefficient; every Secretary of War and field commander blamed Norton for the shortage of food that all Confederate armies experienced. Only after Lee was appointed general-in-chief in February 1865 was the combination of his complaints and pressure from the Confederate Congress enough to force Davis to replace his incompetent commissary chief. By that time, Norton had done all the damage to the cause that he could, and it was far too late for a change to help.

The Confederate War Department did not search for younger officers who had proved themselves in combat and might have been qualified to handle high command. Davis and his War Department stood pat with the high command with which it began the war except when death or repeatedly demonstrated bad performance forced them to make a change. The tendency of the Federal administration was just the opposite, and they found numerous high-quality generals who had been in the lower ranks when the war started and who proved fit for high command.

While the North appointed five army commanders under the age of forty, the only army commander under forty the South appointed was Hood. It is reasonable to believe that men of similarly high qualifications to those found in the North were available in the Confederate States. The fact appears that there just was no effort made to find them.

*   *   *

The Federal War Department sponsored the development of new weapons to meet the changing conditions of warfare. Repeating rifles and carbines, stronger rifled cannon, more efficient armored warships, improved ammunition, grenades and even machine-guns were developed during the war, and some of these weapons became widely used in the conflict. No such developments were made in the South so they used captured weapons and followed the North's lead in making improvements.

In 1864, it was still possible for either side to develop new tactics of mobility that would be able to overcome strong, static defensive positions. By mid-1863, the men in the Union cavalry arm and their generals had drawn to equality after the South had enjoyed earlier superiority. The South had the potential to continue their superiority in cavalry, and increase its numbers while improving cavalry tactics. Southerners had a long-standing advantage in their numbers of experienced horsemen, and Northerners had to work very hard to gain the needed experience. The Southern cavalry began to fail in late 1863, to some degree because of a shortage of suitable horses. The normal practice in the Confederate Cavalry was that individual troopers had to furnish their own horses, and when these were killed or broken down, the Confederate establishment was often unwilling or unable to provide replacements. Between the shortage of mounts and the shortage of fodder to feed horses the strength of the Confederate cavalry diminished badly. At the same time, the Union cavalry gained in numbers, strength and in the skill of their leadership. Northern cavalry leaders recognized the potential cavalry had to neutralize strong defensive positions and end the

stalemate that the war had become. In spite of their initial edge
in cavalry leadership and their pride in it, the Southern high
command failed to see the advantages cavalry mobility offered
before the Northern leadership did.

*   *   *

The Confederate High Command was firmly convinced that
their soldiers and generals were superior to their counterparts in
the North on a one-to-one basis. This conceit continued to exist
throughout the war in spite of the fact that the core-strengths of
the opposing armies were farm boys from states like Ohio in the
North and Tennessee in the South. What logic could conclude
that one such boy could be more easily and better trained for war
than the other?

The Confederate high command began the Civil War
convinced that they could win by using only aggressive tactics.
This inflexible tendency continued in spite of repeated failure that
called out for change. They followed this policy of aggression and
never recognized the many signs of its failure until it was far too
late. They never were willing to consider other strategies and
tactics beyond those with which they began the war. Jackson was
a voice for change before he was killed, but the high command
paid little attention to his suggestions to follow new and different
tactics and strategies.

A few younger generals learned from the new tactics some
Union generals were using successfully against them. For example,
Gordon used the same infiltration tactics Upton had used at
Spotsylvania against Sheridan at Cedar Creek, and he might have
won the day if Early had supported him. When young
Confederate generals proposed the use of new ideas, little interest
was shown, and when they were tried, it was usually without the
approval in advance of their superiors.

Much of the responsibility for the continued use of a failed
military policy had to rest with Davis since he acted as the

Confederacy's generalissimo for all but ten weeks of the war. It must have been very difficult for any general to change this fixed structure, but of all Southern generals, Lee had Davis's respect, and a stronger effort on his part might have brought about change. That he made few attempts in this direction indicates that he shared Davis's outmoded views.

CHAPTER XXXIII

How Did the Skills of Leading Union Generals Compare with Those of Lee?

Improved weapons forced Civil War generals to improve their offensive skills. Throughout the war, Lee showed excellent defensive skills. His desire to go over to the offensive never changed, and his offensive tactics did not show improvement as the war progressed as did those of Grant, Sherman and Sheridan. Lee did not know how to use mobility as a weapon as well as Jackson, Sherman and Sheridan. These generals were primary in developing the tactics that eventually won the war. Lee's strategic vision was narrow and weak compared with the master strategic thinker of the Civil War, U.S. Grant.

A basic difference between the Union and the Confederate armies was in their generals' abilities or willingness to make improvements in strategy, tactics and organization. The Confederate generals proved rigid in their strategy and tactics throughout the war. Lee's desire to attack in the face of almost impossible odds at Malvern Hill, Antietam, Gettysburg, and the Wilderness was not very different from Hood's unreal thinking at Atlanta and Nashville.

At the start of the war and during much of it, defenders had substantial advantage over attackers. Crossing open ground in fixed formation with no protection against defenders who fired long-range weapons accurately and who might be comfortably dug-in was difficult to an extreme. Persuading or forcing soldiers to make such attacks was very difficult, especially when they had experienced the failure of almost all previous similar attacks. Innovative commanders on both sides tried to find tactics that might overcome the enormous problem of having to take a strong defensive position.

The generals on the Union side proved more inventive. At the strategic level, Grant developed successful innovations time and again throughout the war. Grant consistently developed strategies designed to work best against whatever enemy general he was fighting at the time. Grant was so original in his strategic thinking that he seldom used the same ideas from campaign to campaign.

Leaders in tactical innovation included Sherman, Sheridan and Emory Upton. Sherman developed two methods to win when on the offensive without enduring heavy casualties. One was the use of imaginative ways to attack his enemy's flank, rear or supply-lines in preference to a direct assault. The other was to mask his intentions as he advanced by threatening many points at once, making it impossible for his enemy to concentrate favorably against him. The latter was a true innovation at the time, and the same idea was followed by Rommel in his sweep across France in 1940.

Sheridan introduced combined infantry, artillery *and cavalry* operations against a strong defensive position in main battle. His enemies were always in danger of annihilation. His plans were excellent and well thought-out, and no Confederate general found a way to stand against him for long.

Emory Upton graduated from West Point in 1861 and rose to major general by the end of the war. Upton developed infiltration attack techniques and first executed them successfully at Spotsylvania. He moved 12 regiments forward silently to the Southern ramparts during the late night darkness. Just before dawn, these men took the Confederate lines and made a wide breach in them. The effort failed because assigned support failed to come forward. Later, Upton's ideas were copied by both sides.

The Confederate army continued to make impossible direct assaults against long odds right up to the end of the war. It is probably not a coincidence that the war turned in the favor of the side which had the most originators as it progressed.

*   *   *

The butchery of their own troops by Confederate generals was enormous. Losses in killed and wounded, stated as a percentage of those engaged, are summarized in the table on page 321 for those generals on both sides who operated as independent commanders. Butchery as a cold conclusion from the numbers shows that Lee, Hood and Bragg averaged over 15% losses in killed and wounded in all their battles. Meade and Rosecrans also averaged over 15%. Only Bragg, of all Confederate commanders, with 15.5%, was able to inflict over 15% casualties on average against his Union enemies. Meade with 22.6%, Rosecrans with 18.7% and Hooker with 18.6% were the only Union generals to inflict over 15% casualties on their enemies. Grant with an average loss of his own troops of 12.2% in his 11 battles was much less a butcher than Lee with 15.4% in his 16 battles.

The table on page 321 suggests numerous additional conclusions besides those involving butchery:

- At age 54-58 over the Civil War years, Lee fought in 16 major battles. The enormity of all this action, concern and responsibility had to have had a strongly negative effect on his mental and physical condition and abilities.
- The Union Army put 11 commanders-in-chief in the field in these 44 battles while the Confederates put 5 in 35. On the Union side, McClellan, Rosecrans, Pope, Burnside and Hooker were relieved of command so only the remaining 6 were in the field at the end of the war.

Only Grant fought his first battle of the war as a commander-in-chief and ended it as such. Of the 5 Confederate commanders, Bragg, Hood and Early were relieved (but only after losing their armies) leaving only Lee and J.E. Johnston still commanding in the field at the end of the war. The latter was relieved and re-instated several times. No Confederate general began as a commander-in-chief and served continuously throughout the war as such: Lee came close.

- The contributing factors to a general's success include: numerical odds, his troops' morale, the commander's confidence in himself, his troops' confidence in him, his military skill, his charisma, his skill in using his resources, his cause, the capability of his enemy commander, the skill of his subordinate commanders, the enemy's morale and which side is attacking or defending. Of these, numerical odds is probably one of the less important factors unless the numerical advantage is overwhelming. Lee's experience shows the validity of this statement: with a numerical advantage he lost at Malvern Hill, with a numerical disadvantage he won at Manaassas II, Fredericksburg, Chancellorsville and held his own at Antietam, the Wilderness and Spotsylvania. In the Civil War, numerical odds had importance in deciding a battle when they reached 3:1 (or 1:0.33), against a commander, or greater. Grady McWhiney's and Perry D. Jamieson's book, *Attack and Die, Civil War Military Tactics and the Southern Heritage*, makes this case well. Before 1864, attacks by either army that were less than 3:1 in the attacker's favor were almost never successful; and in the rare cases when they did prove successful, some other overwhelming factor was in the attacker's favor. Example: the extremely poor engineering of the defensive fortifications by the Confederates at Missionary Ridge.
- Grant was fortunate that he had a numerical advantage

over his opponent in all 11 of his battles; nevertheless, his skills enabled him to use this to his advantage while many generals on both sides proved unable to do so in like circumstances.

SUMMARY OF COMMANDERS-IN-CHIEF'S RECORDS					
UNION COMMANDERS					
Name	Number Battles	Average Odds	Range of Odds	Own	Enemy
Grant	11	1:0.65	1:0.46-1:0.91	12.2	13.6
Sherman	9	1:0.83	1:0.45-1:1.68	7.4	12.3
McClellan	7	1:0.95	1:0.45-1:1.67	9.0	13.1
Meade	4	1:0.82	1:0.65-1:0.90	18.5	22.6
Sheridan	4	1:0.50	1:0.45-1:0.60	8.5	13.4
Rosecrans	3	1:1.02	1:0.85-1:1.14	18.9	28.7
Pope	2	1:0.78	1:0.64-1:2.10	14.0	15.6
Burnside	1	1:0.68	—	10.3	6.5
Hooker	1	1:0.59	—	11.4	18.6
Schofield	1	1:1.04	—	4.3	5.6
Thomas	1	1:0.47	—	5.8	5.4
TOTAL	44	1:0.76	1:0.45-1:2.10	11.7	15.5
CONFEDERATE COMMANDERS					
Lee	16	1:1.34	1:0.60-1:2.16	15.4	12.5
Hood	7	1:1.08	1:0.71-1:2.15	16.9	5.4
J.E. Johnston	6	1:1.13	1:0.77-1:1.67	8.9	9.1
Bragg	4	1:1.18	1:0.88-1:2.30	19.5	15.5
Early	2	1:1.90	1:1.67-1:2.20	11.3	12.8
TOTAL	35	1:1.27	1:0.60-1:2.30	14.9	11.6

NOTES:
1. The above table is derived is largely based on Livermore.
2. Perhaps unfairly, the table ignores commanders who fought west of the Mississippi. Other battles that appeared unimportant to the war's outcome have also been omitted.
3. Odds for Union generals are computed as U/C, for Confederate generals as C/U.
4. Some battles are duplicated on the Union side: for example Grant and Sheridan commanded at Five Forks.
5. Beauregard is not included since he was never fully in command during a major battle.

Other casualty factors besides killed and wounded were also

very important: captured or missing in action, illness and death from illness, suicide, and accident as well as desertion. For the entire war, these were the statistics for the opposing armies:

Casualty Causes	Federal	Confederate
Killed or died of wounds	110,100	94,000
Death from disease	224,580	164,000
Died as prisoner	30,192	29,000
Death from Other causes	24,881	NA
TOTAL DEAD	389,753	287,000
TOTAL WOUNDED	275,175	196,252
TOTAL CASUALTIES	664,928	483,252
Desertions (reported)	200,000	104,000
TOTAL LOSSES	864,928	587,252

These additional conclusions may be made from these casualty figures:

- The almost 2:1 ratio of deaths from disease over deaths in action means that for any period casualty figures (killed and wounded) may be increased by about 72% for the Union and 67% for the Confederacy, excluding captured, missing in action and desertion.
- Desertion in the Federal Army was fairly constant throughout the war. Most desertion as reported by the Federal Army came as a result of a practice which allowed a person to pay a substitute to serve for him if he were drafted or enlisted. Many such substitutes deserted, then substituted again and again. Both sides had a relatively small core number of deserters who left because of cowardice, home-sickness or their inability to cope with military discipline. Desertion increased in the Confederate Army as the war neared its close, as more defeats were suffered and as the private soldiers lost faith that their

generals and leadership could win the war. Records showing the numbers who deserted appear to have been under-stated by both sides, and Condeferate records of all types of losses are often missing after early 1864.

- Two major changes in tactics occurred in the last year of the war. Sherman used parallel infantry columns across a 50-mile front advancing into enemy territory. This made any defending force who chose to attack or block one of these columns open his flank or rear to attack by another of Sherman's columns. It also made it difficult for a defender to discover where to place an effective blocking position since no single objective of Sherman's columns could be identified. This allowed the attacker, Sherman, to move forward offensively with few casualties. At the same time, Sheridan used improved mobility to reduce the advantages defenders had previously enjoyed. He began to use his cavalry as equal partners with the infantry and artillery in main battles. These coordinated attacks always put the defender in fear of the security of his flanks and rear. Sherman's and Sheridan's tactical innovations made it no longer necessary for an attacker to have a 3:1 advantage to win against a well entrenched defender and these new tactics reduced casualties.

*   *   *

There are numerous examples of innovations in military tactics and strategy that came from Grant, Sherman and Sheridan. These were passed on to such generals as James H. Wilson, Thomas, Schofield, Ord and others who also used them effectively. Infantry attacks based on infiltration were developed and used successfully by such Union generals as Ord and Upton.

Confederate generals were not as innovative. With very few exceptions in the many battles they fought, Confederate generals used the same old attack tactics from the beginning of the war to the end. Exceptions do stand out: Jackson was clearly innovative, A.S. Johnston showed promise and John B. Gordon copied infiltration tactics which he used successfully at Cedar Creek and Ft. Stedman. Besides these men, two of whom were killed when they were most needed, it is difficult to find any flair of innovation among Southern generals. Defensively, Lee continued to improve throughout the war, but he showed no change or flair for improving offensive operations.

This differential in innovation proved to be the most decisive factor in the North winning and the South losing the war. In a small period of time (four years) these innovative changes produced an uneven contest. While this may be an exaggeration, it was almost as though an armored division were fighting against 10 Roman legions. Clearly, facing innovative leaders without having many of their own, led the Confederate side to fight a series of doomed battles which brought eventual defeat.

*　　*　　*

The loyalty of soldiers to a cause and a general is a critical factor in the success of any general. In the North, the presidential election of 1864 clearly illustrated the loyalty of soldiers to the Union cause. Because the soldiers in the Army of the Potomac still had great regard for and loyalty to McClellan, the Democratic presidential candidate, many Northern political experts believed they would vote for him, for peace and the end of their killing. In spite of these concerns, Lincoln went out of his way to see that all soldiers be given a chance to vote. This fear was not realized. The veterans talked it over and agreed that the army of 1862 was better and stronger at the time of McClellan than was the army of 1864 under Grant. However, they also agreed that if Grant had been in its command instead of McClellan the war would have been won in 1862. While they still held McClellan in very high esteem, they did not vote for him.

The men of the army showed their loyalty to Grant by voting

overwhelmingly for Lincoln. This was the act of veteran soldiers who knew the value of an excellent commander, not young boys impressed by the flash and words of McClellan. Most important, they were convinced Grant would bring them final victory. In Sheridan's and Sherman's armies the vote for Lincoln was also overwhelming for much the same reasons.

In the Confederate Army of Northern Virginia, loyalty to Lee waned after Antietam when his veterans saw how close he had brought them to disaster. At Chancellorsville, their confidence soared with a great victory which left them convinced that Lee could not lose even in the face of great odds. Before Gettysburg, loyalty to Lee was at its height. This waned quickly after the futile deaths of Pickett's Charge and the army's defeat, followed by near disaster as it tried to cross the Potomac. Many of his officers and private soldiers reached the conclusion that the war could no longer be won under the leadership of Davis and Lee. Some who reached this conclusion decided to keep up the fight as a personal duty. Some began to look for the first opportunity to safely desert. Eventually, one third to half of the major Confederate armies deserted. This led to many veterans being replaced by green recruits so the quality of the Southern armies was reduced as were their numbers. It was the practice of the Confederate Army to allow some soldiers to go home from time to time to tend to their crops. Many who never returned used this privilege to cover their desertion, and their desertion was never recorded.

In writing to his wife in late 1863, the fiercely loyal Brigadier General Stephen Dodson Ramseur probably summed up the feelings of most Confederate soldiers: "our great campaign, admirably planned & more admirably executed up to the final day at Gettysburg, has failed. [insisting that Gettysburg did not necessarily spell the downfall of the Confederacy, he believed other crises would come, and he stood ready] to undergo dangers and hardships and trials to the end." Ramseur died fighting in the Shenandoah Valley in 1864.

*   *   *

Dealing with the problems of an army larger than 15,000 was new to all Civil War commanders. By 1862, most major Civil War armies had over 50,000 men and some had over 100,000. This increase in size brought problems well beyond any single commander, no matter how skillful he was. The solution to these problems lay in the development of efficient command staffs able to support the commander and in his ability to develop good subordinate commanders.

The typical command staff for an army prior to the Civil War consisted of a few young officers, acting as clerks. Frequently, these officers were some important party's son or favorite, and often, they were bright, well educated and ambitious. Lee would have fit this same description when he was on Scott's staff in Mexico. Seldom did these men contribute to the commander's decision-making process. Their duties were usually limited to writing and delivering the commander's orders and gathering information for him. Information gathering was frequently simple, but sometimes it involved coordinating military intelligence gained from many sources which was very difficult to evaluate.

Somehow, most Confederate commanders, including Lee, could not deal with the idea of a high-quality staff. Almost always they continued to use favorites, and while some of these young men developed some skill in specialty areas, none developed overall military skills. Southern generals successfully used engineering officers on their staffs, but they did not add quality chiefs-of-staff to help them in administration or other officers to lead key needed efforts such as logistics, operations planning, intelligence and providing supplies.

At the top, Davis used his old cronies to fill key national staff positions. Samuel Cooper, the highest ranking of all Confederate generals, was originally planned to be Davis's general-in-chief, but he proved inept and suited only to desk-bound administrative duties. Julius Norton was the Commissary General of the Confederacy until 1865 when the Confederate Congress forced Davis to relieve him. Corrupt and bound up in paper-work, Norton could not find ways to deliver the food and supplies that were available in the states to the Confederate armies. Only toward the end of the war did Lee join the effort to get rid of Norton, and the food supply to his army immediately improved, but it was too late.

In the case of Bragg at Missionary Ridge, a very poor engineering staff brought him disaster. Why did Southern commanders fail to develop high-quality staffs in their support? Without any records of their ideas on the matter, any answer involves speculation. Possible answers include: a belief larger staffs were unnecessary, inflexibility due to advanced age, a dedication to cronyism, unwillingness to delegate or a refusal to depend on others for what they thought they could do better themselves. Regardless of the answer, it is clear they did not form quality staffs as well as most Union commanders did.

Lieutenant Colonel Walter H. Taylor served Lee throughout the war as aide-de-camp (ADC) and finally as his chief-of-staff. Taylor had attended Virginia Military Institute and was 23 in 1861. Young and bright, Taylor had no previous combat experience but yearned for action and took part in several engagements without Lee's approval. He remained the officer closest to Lee throughout the war. Lieutenant Colonel Charles S. Venable was an ADC who was occupied with inspections. Lieutenant Colonel Charles Marshall, a lawyer related to Chief Justice Marshall, was Lee's military secretary. These men formed Lee's principal personal staff.

Other officers performed such staff duties as chief of engineers, medical director, quartermaster and commissary, inspector general and chief of artillery. Most of Lee's staff officers were "lightweights" in terms of battle and command experience and authority. No single man worked full-time on intelligence or operations planning. Stuart and his cavalry were assigned to follow the enemy's movements. A fairly large number of other soldiers were assigned to Lee's headquarters as couriers, servants and messengers.

Grant's headquarters staff was also limited in number but was of higher quality. Brigadier General John A. Rawlins, USA, had been with Grant since early in the war. He was a lawyer who provided administrative assistance to Grant, an area in which Grant was weak. This left Grant to develop strategies and manage battles, areas in which he excelled. Chief engineers, an intelligence officer and other officers were also attached to his staff.

It was with its individual army organizations that the Union Army showed its superiority. In 1861, commanders in both armies were hobbled by the old rules of the pre-war regular army. A commander could not draw a piece of ordnance without the approval of the War Department. Similar rules governed manpower, supplies, ammunition and other important needs. No commander could be effective in war under such impediments, which was particularly troublesome if he was over 50 miles from Washington. Early in the Civil War, commanders in the field forced a change in these restrictions, breaking these hobbles. At the same time, those in the War Department found the department did not have enough people or skills to give the needed administrative support to huge armies as they had done easily for small outposts. The pre-war regular army consisted of about 16,000 men in a small number of commands; a single Civil War corps frequently had this many men.

Gradually, the Union armies adjusted their command organizations, staffs, personnel and relationships to meet these new conditions. They maintained the principle that both staff and line functions were responsibilities of the commander. A chief-of-staff, if the army had one, was assigned duties by the commander, not the War Department, and sometimes these duties varied from army to army.

Brigadier General James A. Garfield commanded an infantry brigade at Shiloh and fought in several smaller battles. He was assigned as Major General William Rosecrans's chief-of-staff and served in the Tullahoma campaign and the Battle of Chickamauga. His duties were administrative, to supervise other staff officers and the writing and delivery of Rosecrans's orders as well as to accumulate intelligence from all sources that might help the army. During battle, he managed a campaign map showing the positions of units of both armies as the situation changed. He did an excellent job in the Tullahoma campaign and would have at Chickamauga but for an incredible series of blunders made by others.

After 1862, the Army of the Potomac improved its staff support. Major General Daniel Butterfield, although hated by his fellow officers, was Hooker's chief-of-staff and then Meade's from January 1863 until he was wounded at Gettysburg. Butterfield had previous experience commanding a division and a corps.

Butterfield was not a West Point officer but had been an experienced business executive prior to the war. With this background, Butterfield helped Hooker by handling most administrative and support duties, leaving Hooker to handle operations and battle. Butterfield's duties besides administration were: controlling roads, logistics and needs in rear areas; sorting through the immense number of incoming orders and messages, handling what he could and giving the most important to the army commander; supervising all signal and intelligence traffic. Apparently, he took no large part in planning operations or advising Hooker on battlefield issues.

Major General Andrew A. Humphreys succeeded Butterfield after Gettysburg. He was an outstanding West Point officer who had commanded a division from Antietam to Gettysburg. He had fought in command assignments continuously since 1861. Besides the administrative duties Butterfield performed, Humphreys was an active and valued military confidant and advisor to Meade.

Both Butterfield and Humphreys supervised the staff officers who were chief quartermasters, chief engineers, chief signal officers and those who brought the army intelligence. When appropriate, they handled the matter themselves and gave the commander the necessary information or they took the officer involved to the commander.

In November 1864, Humphreys replaced Hancock as commander of II Corps. In January 1865, Major General Alexander S. Webb returned from leave for wounds he had received at Spotsylvania and became Meade's chief-of-staff. Webb had commanded the brigade that bore the brunt of Pickett's Charge at Gettysburg where he received a Congressional Medal of Honor for his action. He commanded a brigade and then a division until he was severely wounded.

Under the army commander's orders, the chiefs-of-staff of the Army of the Potomac reduced the load of the commander in such a way that would have helped Lee a great deal if such high quality officers had been made available to him.

Sheridan also developed an efficient chief-of-staff, John W. Forsyth, who fought in many Western battles. The innovative Sheridan added a troop of scouts to his staff under an intelligence chief, Major H.H. Young. Young's men usually dressed in Confederate uniforms, mastered Southern accents and spied on enemy activities. While this was very dangerous work, Sheridan's intelligence arrangements were far superior to any other general on either side. Sherman did not believe a chief-of-staff was a necessary post.

*   *   *

Good subordinate commanders were essential to the success of any commander-in-chief. Numerous men in the Union Army began the war at low rank and rose to become army, corps and division commanders. A few examples would be young men like Sheridan, Slocum, McPherson, Howard and Schofield who became commanders of Union armies; one had been a major, two were captains, one a lieutenant and one a civilian at the start of the war. Merritt and Wilson graduated from West Point in 1860 and became corps commanders in 1864. These are but a few of the large numbers of excellent subordinate commanders who were developed by the Union system and by training they received from their earlier superiors.

It is difficult to find similar examples of subordinate officer development in the Confederate Army. John B. Gordon and Nathan Bedford Forrest were examples of excellent soldiers who gained corps command by the end of the war. Hood's record was similar, reaching army command, but he had little success as an army commander.

Commanders like Bragg could never develop good subordinates because much of the time they argued with and unfairly placed blame against most of their subordinates. That Lee did not develop good subordinate commanders is apparent. Longstreet and Jackson were excellent, but Lee did not develop them. When they became corps commanders, Jackson's replacements, Ewell and A.P. Hill, quickly demonstrated they had been promoted beyond their level of skills. Longstreet's temporary replacement, Anderson, did not show himself to be an adequate corps commander.

Lee was amicable, helpful and considerate to all his subordinates. He apparently was unwilling to take the time to tutor any of his subordinates in generalship as Rosecrans did with Sheridan. It may also have been the Confederate system that interfered with the development of good subordinate commanders who might become able to replace their commanders. The older men who began as commanders satisfied Davis, who was of like age, so the question may have been: why waste time in developing subordinates since we can win with what we have? Another system problem the Confederate Army had was a more rigid promotion system that emphasized date of commission first, time in rank second and ability a poor third. The Federal Army had a different situation. Except for Grant, early Union commanders proved unsatisfactory and inefficient so their only option was that they be replaced by their juniors. This made for a dynamic situation that brought hope for upward mobility to junior officers and forced a need to train lower commanders. This proved to be a more healthy situation for the Union Army than did the static approach to leadership development followed in the Confederate Army.

* * *

With the large armies on both sides, the need for them to be supplied over the long distances as they moved made the Civil War one where logistical skill contributed much to the ability to win. In spite of the fact that the South had the advantage of shorter, internal lines, the North clearly won the logistics war.

The North had two great advantages in the logistics war. The first is that they had a superior railroad network and more engineers expert at building, repairing and extending railroads. These engineers were able to continuously extend the railroad to a supply base that moved forward to a changing point close behind an army as it advanced. Northern railroad repair crews were able to keep the railroads operating in spite of the depredations of Confederate raiding parties.

The second advantage was that their leading generals, Grant, Sherman and Sheridan, had been quartermaster officers earlier in their careers. This experience made it easier for them to intimately understand the logistical problems of a large army. They saw to it that their armies were well fed, clothed and shod, and they would not tolerate poor performance by supply troops behind their lines. They knew what their logistical limits were. For example, Grant knew sending more soldiers to Sherman was fruitless since the logistical network could not adequately support more men, and Sherman also recognized this fact.

Grant was conscious of the advantages he could gain by changing his base at appropriate times. In the Virginia Overland Campaign he changed his base from Acquia Creek to Port Royal to White House Landing to City Point over a two month period.

Only a general who fully understood the problems and advantages associated with logistics would have had the nerve to order such frequent and difficult changes. An idea of what was involved in such changes is shown by the fact that City Point was one of the ten largest deep water ports in the world while Grant was using it as his base.

Lee was an officer who had engineering training and experience. He was never able to keep his army well fed, well clothed and well shod. He tolerated the poor performance of Norton and other commissary officers to the severe deficit of his army. Was this because Lee did not understand supply logistics himself or because he was powerless against a Davis crony? His horses were underfed and he could not obtain adequate replacements. He did not enlist the aid of a quartermaster officer skilled enough to help him solve the problem as an addition to his staff. From studies of what was available in rear areas, there was no shortage of the needed items in the Confederate States; they simply could not develop efficient ways to acquire and move these items to the armies.

*   *   *

The weapons and ammunition used by Confederate infantry, artillery and cavalry were of great variety. To keep all these different weapons supplied with the appropriate ammunition was an enormous problem, a logistical nightmare. Often this need was not met, which produced idle guns and men or forced soldiers into making costly bayonet charges.

While Stuart's cavalry used over six different types of pistols, rifles and carbines, mostly single shot, Sheridan had different ideas for his cavalry corps. When he took it over, one of his major goals was to provide each of his 15,000 troopers with a Spencer repeating carbine. This standardization using the first servicable, breech-loading, multi-shot carbine was mostly accomplished in his first month in command and was completed soon thereafter. This step not only standardized his corps' weapons and ammunition but provided his troopers with a far superior weapon to anything available to Stuart's troopers. The technical and production superiority of the North contributed to this and similar advantages. Similar steps were taken by the Federal infantry and artillery. No similar effort could be taken by the Confederacy.

They did not have the industrial capability to produce the technically more difficult repeating carbine. Their sources of weapons were so varied that standardization could not be practiced by the South.

*   *   *

The leading Confederate army commanders averaged 55-59 years of age during the Civil War. Their directly competitive Union counterparts averaged 40-44 years. Besides the health problems men frequently encounter between 44 and 55, there is no doubt that war is a young man's game. In those days, health expectancy at birth was under 40 years, but if one lived through the rampant childhood diseases, he had a good chance of living into his 50s. Nevertheless, if we compare ages in the 1990s with the 1860s for general health and well being, the Confederate Civil War commanders would compare with men in their late 60s in the 1990s. These considerations show that the Union commanders had a considerable health advantage over their Southern competitors. One of many such favorable examples is that Lee spent eleven days in his tent, ill, during the Virginia Overland Campaign, while Grant spent only one day.

Jack D. Welsh, M.D., has recently published two books on the medical histories of Confederate and Union generals. Dr. Welsh used only medical records, the observations of qualified medical experts and sometmes letters written by the patient himself describing his symptoms in compiling his medical histories. He has ignored anecdotal descriptions by unqualified lay observers of the health of another person. Such observations have often been wrong, but this has not prevented many lay historians from repeating these misconceptions time after time until they have been accepted as real history.

Dr. Welsh's books do two things: they illustrate the terrible health, sanitation and medical conditions that existed during those times, and they give accurate details of individual generals' health. This allows a historian to deduce how medical problems affected a general's efficiency and whether a health deficiency in a commander affected the outcome of a particular battle. There is much for a historian to learn from these volumes. Looking at health generally, the generals on both sides were very tough and had survived many health problems before the war. Most had re-occurring malaria from infection they had obtained earlier in their careers; many had survived one or more of these diseases or disorders: yellow fever, cholera, smallpox, typhoid fever, body damage from accidents, severe wounds and resulting infections and many other problems.

With respect to Robert E. Lee, health problems did interfere with his performance. He did have some kind of heart disorder about the time of Chancellorsville; this was probably rheumatic heart disease resulting from some infeciton. By the time of Gettysburg he was complaining of symptoms, extreme fatigue, lack of motivation, inability to perform the acts he wished; these symptoms are consistent with what we now call "congestive heart failure." Doing the things a commanding general had to do with these symptoms would be very difficult, indeed, and would require an iron will even to try. His request to be replaced at this time probably represented his true wishes in these circumstances. Health problems continued to trouble Lee throughout the rest of the war.

On the other side of the line, Grant's health was excellent. His worst problems resulted from several falls he had from horses. As a result, he had joint problems, rheumatism and what we would now call arthritis from time to time. Grant's medical records never mention alcohol as affecting his health. In a private letter to the author, Dr. Welsh believes Grant could not have been diagnosed an alcoholic since this condition was not considered as a disease in those times, and there were no standards for it. He also said liver disorders from alcohol were not a problem in the Cvil War and points out that cancer of the throat and tongue, probably brought on by heavy smoking, caused Grant's death with no mention of alcoholism. This is not to say that Grant did not binge on occasion; however, the indications are that the problem of alcohol was exaggerated by his detractors.

*   *   *

Politicians on both sides offered their generals plenty of interference. On the Union side, a huge change occurred when Grant was appointed General-in-Chief. Lincoln took the position that he, Stanton and the other politicians had done a poor job so far in trying to win the war so now they had to let Grant do it. Not only did Lincoln not interfere with Grant's decisions himself, but he would not tolerate Stanton or others doing so.

The big test of Lincoln's resolve in this matter was when Early threatened Washington. Under personal threat, all the politicians wanted Grant to return to Washington and save their lives. Grant successfully resisted this pressure, Lincoln supported him, and Lincoln allowed Grant to take other steps to save Washington.

Under Federal law, Grant could not arbitrarily appoint a corps or army commander since this required Presidential and Congressional approval, but never did the politicians thwart his desires. The incompetent and very senior Major General Benjamin Butler presented Grant with a serious military problem. In view of his many military failures and the threat his incompetancy made against any operation with which he was involved, Grant wanted to be rid of him early in 1864. The politics of doing so might cause the loss of Butler's large Democratic war constituency that supported Lincoln in the 1864 election. Grant was not allowed by Lincoln to dismiss Butler until after the 1864 election, but soon after it and Butler's failure at Fort Fisher, Lincoln allowed him to dismiss Butler quickly.

Political interference with commanders of Confederate armies was much more severe and remained so until the war's end. Davis acted as *de facto* general-in-chief until Lee was appointed to this position less than two months before the end of the war. Davis actually went to battles and gave orders until Lee took command. Lee prohibited this behavior, probably giving Davis the choice of commanding himself or having Lee do it. Davis continued to interfere with his generals throughout the war. In Lee's case, this interference was probably less severe since both men shared the same aggressive spirit and a conceit which said Southern privates and generals were better than those of the North. Both seemed oriented towards hope rather than reality.

One must conclude that by the end of the war, the level of expertise of Union army commanders was far above that of any Confederate general, including Lee. This difference in skill level contributed greatly to the eventual Union victory.

CHAPTER XXXIV

The True Phenomenon of the Civil War: The Development of Grant, Sherman and Sheridan

Although all were West Point graduates, Grant, Sherman and Sheridan were insignificant officers in the Union Army at the end of 1861. During 1862, all three were promoted to major generals based solely on their highly efficient performance. Grant proved to be one of the best military strategists the United States has ever developed. Highly flexible, Grant showed he could win by maneuver or by attrition, and he always had dogged determination. Sherman and Sheridan were excellent leaders of men; both developed new tactics and fighting doctrines with which older, more inflexible generals could not cope.

Before the Civil War started, it could hardly be imagined that Grant, Sherman and Sheridan would end the war as the North's leading generals. Since being forced to resign from the army for drunkenness, Grant had failed at many things before the Civil War started. Sherman had resigned as a captain in 1855 and became president of a military school in Louisiana. Sheridan had served as a second lieutenant in Texas and Oregon for seven years and was promoted to captain in May of 1861.

Grant had performed well during action in the Mexican War. In 1860, he applied for positions on Scott's and McClellan's staffs but was rejected. After other rejections, he was finally appointed colonel to organize an Illinois infantry regiment. Later when the War Department desperately needed generals, he was one of a group to be appointed brigadier general to rank from May of 1861. This gave him early high seniority. Without reasonably high seniority, Grant would have fought the war at the division or corps commander level. At these levels which require administrative skills as well as fighting leadership abilities, his lack of patience with administrative details might have limited his promotion or even caused him to fail. Early good fortune and the help of his local Congressman, Elihu B. Washburne, had much to do with Grant receiving an opportunity to reach the Union army's highest rank.

Sherman's family had great political influence. His brother, John, was a Senator, and his foster-father had been a cabinet officer and a judge. Early in the war, he was offered a clerkship in the War Department which probably would have led to his soon becoming Assistant Secretary of War. Because he despised politicians and Washington, Sherman rejected the offer, an action that put him in bad graces with Lincoln and the War Department.

Sherman was appointed second in command to Major General Robert Anderson for the Military District of Kentucky, and because of Anderson's poor health, Sherman soon succeeded him to command. His great respect for Southerners and a sense of military reality made him one of a few Northern generals who believed the war would last long and be very hard to win. When he voiced this opinion as he frequently did, it made him very unpopular. Albert Sidney Johnston gulled Sherman into thinking he was far stronger than was the fact. Sherman began to doubt his ability to defeat Johnston; he became indecisive; and this made him mentally depressed. The newspaper reporters, whom he also hated, said: "Sherman is crazy!" All this led to his relief as a department commander. But for Halleck's respect for Sherman and patience with his problems, his military career would have been over.

At age 30 in 1861, Sheridan had served in Oregon with some distinction and had gained experience in engineering, as a quartermaster and in leading small numbers of soldiers in combat. His engagements with Indians in Oregon showed promise as a strategist, tactician and leader, but he was little noticed by the War Department. Recently promoted to captain and unwilling or unable to leave his command to a Southern successor, he remained in Oregon until after Manassas I had been fought. He had little going for him beyond a boyhood acquaintance with Sherman and a network of old friends and acquaintances from West Point and the Old Army. One of his helpful acquaintances was Halleck.

*   *   *

After the war, Southern historians not only glorified Lee, but they put down Union generals to make Lee appear better in comparison. In most of their writings, Grant was presented as a "butcher, continuously battering Lee's army" which implied he was not fighting fairly, thus deprecating Grant's skill. Sherman was a rapacious burner of Southern cities beyond meritorious comment. Dowdey, a leading Southern historian, limited his remarks about Sheridan to saying that he "was a small man with a big head who brought his rough and tumble cavalry tactics with him to the East." Nothing could have been farther from the truth, since Sheridan had been an infantry division commander in the West through five major campaigns. These are but a few of the comments made by Southern historians, and very few had anything good to say.

Mostly, they ascribed the successes of Union generals to factors other than skillful generalship or the failings of Confederate generals. Freeman, one of the leading Southern historians, was an exception; although sometimes overly pro-Lee, he limited himself to praising Lee, not often putting down soldiers on the other side.

It is true that Grant, Sherman and Sheridan received many honors after the war. Grant became President, although a poor one, and Sherman and Sheridan were considered for the office. Both refused. In his colorful fashion when notified he would be nominated in 1884, Sherman instantly telegraphed his reply: "If nominated, I will not run; if elected, I will not serve." All three men died as four star generals and were highly respected during their lifetimes. In spite of all this, history places them in much lower esteem than it does Lee.

Lee did not share these low opinions of Grant. After the war was over, he was most complimentary about Grant's generalship. Among other things, he said: "We all thought Richmond, protected as it was by our splendid fortifications and defended by our army of veterans, could not be taken. Yet Grant turned his face to our Capital and never turned away until we had surrendered. Now, I have carefully searched the military records of both ancient and modern history, and have never found Grant's superior as a general. I doubt that his superior can be found in all history."

*   *   *

Grant became a field commander in Halleck's Military Department early in the war. His first battle at Belmont, Kentucky was the only one he fought in which he proved somewhat inept. The addition to his staff of John A. Rawlins did two very important things for Grant: Rawlins kept him off the bottle, as was his tendency when Grant became depressed or stressed; and Rawlins performed Grant's administrative duties well. This allowed Grant to concentrate on strategic and tactical planning and decision-making, skills Grant had at a very high level. Rawlins provided a trusted and confidential ear and opinion for Grant. Except for periods of sick-leave for tuberculosis, Rawlins was at Grant's side throughout the war.

A man of exceptional military vision, Grant saw the western

rivers, the Mississippi, the Tennessee and the Cumberland, as broad supply roads running deep into Confederate territory. As a former quartermaster, Grant understood that these rivers could move large numbers of men quickly and efficiently bring up the huge quantities of supplies they would need. As a soldier, he saw the great advantages of having available the navy's floating batteries of heavy guns and mortars. In the West, he designed a strategy to use these rivers as a means to destroy Southern armies and cut the Confederacy into smaller pieces, each too ineffective to offer strong resistance by itself.

Not only could Grant design a good strategy, he could execute it well. In the West, Grant showed his tenacity after recovering from shock and disadvantages of the fighting on the first day at Shiloh, coming back from preliminary defeat to victory. In the Vicksburg campaign he showed great skill at maneuver and siege warfare. In a very short time at Chattanooga, he turned a grim situation into an offensive victory against a seemingly impregnable defensive position.

Grant always showed an indomitable will to win. In the Virginia Overland Campaign, he used many strategies and fought most possible types of tactical engagements. At the same time, he conceived and directed the nation-wide strategy of the entire Union war effort, giving strategic orders to generals all over the country. His ability to use different strategies and to develop tactics to take advantage of success or meet threats was outstanding. Grant was among the most flexible of Civil War generals. He listened to and often took the advice of men he respected: particularly Sherman, Rawlins, and Sheridan.

Above all, Grant was a winner.

*   *   *

Sherman was blunt, over-sensitive, brilliant, hyper-active, opinionated and often withdrawn, but on other occasions, he was warm and friendly. A very complex individual, he was frequently depressed and insecure in spite of his great ability. To many, all these character flaws made him a poor candidate to become a leading general. The country was fortunate that Halleck saw through these negatives to Sherman's real values, was patient with him and decided his career was worth saving. Grant and Sherman recognized each other's great capabilities so Sherman became Grant's closest friend, colleague and confidant.

After Sherman's recovery from what may have been a nervous breakdown, Halleck assigned him as one of Grant's division commanders in the planned Tennessee River campaign. As senior division commander, Sherman was second in command. In fact, Sherman waived the seniority rights he held over Grant.

Left in command of the army at Shiloh while Grant was meeting with other officers ten miles away, Sherman performed badly when he allowed A.S. Johnston to surprise his army in a lightly protected camp. Grant and Sherman were lucky to recover from this disadvantage and defeat the Confederates on the second day of the battle; probably the death of the skillful A.S. Johnston on the first day had much to do with the Union victory. Subsequently, Sherman performed poorly in an attempt to capture Vicksburg at Chickasaw Bayou. Once these failures were behind him, Sherman's performance for the rest of the war was nearly impeccable.

Without repeating descriptions of Sherman's battles, there were common threads in all of them. He coordinated the actions of his subordinates and could depend on them to follow his orders. This resulted in his battles being well conceived, multi-directional and varied from one to another. Whenever possible, he avoided the direct assault for more subtle indirect moves against his enemy's flank, rear and supply line. His multi-column movements through Georgia and the Carolinas were both innovative and efficient. He used the military assets he had available to his best advantage. All these features in his attacks made it very difficult to mount a defense against him. He found ways to reduce the advantage defenders would have held against his attacks if they had been made earlier in the war.

As an independent army group commander, Sherman successfully directed the actions of three armies in coordinated attacks and maneuver. Through 1865, only Grant and Sherman had successfully managed the difficult business of commanding and maneuvering such a large unit as an army group.

*   *   *

Sheridan is much more difficult to assess as a general than Grant or Sherman. He bore the brunt of more criticism by Southern historians than Grant or even Sherman. The picture they tried to paint was that of a rash, obscene, spoiled favorite of Grant who made his reputation as a result of favoritism, not skill in generalship.

To become a favorite of Grant, a general had to demonstrate a few clear qualifications: he must be loyal to Grant and not self-seeking; he must support and follow Grant's strategic plan; he must be able to adapt and develop sound tactics that made Grant's strategic plan successful; he must have initiative since Grant's lack of interest in detail required him to make many important decisions; he must speak out if he has a better idea, but if he does not speak out in advance, he should not be critical later; and he must win battles. Failure to meet these criteria would cause Grant to find a replacement, and this meant the end of one's career since Grant never assigned a later command to a general he had previously relieved. Hence, Grant's favorites became the leading Northern generals by the end of the Civil War. These generals earned their positions through merit; by no other means could they gain and keep Grant's support. Sheridan earned the highest place among Grant's favorites following Sherman.

Sherman was a man who spoke the truth as he saw it, often whether it hurt or not. He was also as good a judge of generalship as could be found. He had known Sheridan since boyhood and commanded him for years after the war. After Sheridan's death, Sherman commented about him: "So much stress has been laid upon his [Sheridan's] dash as an officer that the public did not give him credit for the mental concentration he was capable of. He was a man of brains as well as heart, of thought as well as action. He did not read much but did his thinking from an original basis and with excellent results. I tell you Sheridan had a great head well stored with useful knowledge... General Sheridan's services to his country could scarcely be overestimated. He was a man of quick perception, and as a commander had the faculty of grasping the whole situation on a field of battle intuitively, and history already records the valuable work he did in the country's defense."[1]

The picture Sherman verbally drew of Sheridan is not that of a rash, impetuous and callous man as is drawn by Southern historians. Another view of Sheridan can be paraphrased from letters by a VI Corps soldier written home when his unit became part of Sheridan's Army of the Shenandoah. At the time, the morale of VI Corps was at an all-time low following its heavy losses in the Virginia Overland Campaign. He said that when they marched in the Valley, Sheridan was always near the front taking personal charge. When traffic jams or roadblocks occurred, the officer galloping up to clear it was often Sheridan himself. If the private soldiers were ordered to march through the rough fields in order to leave the roads available for the use of the artillery and supply wagons, Sheridan dismounted and marched with them.

An officer of VI Corps wrote: "he [Sheridan] often stormed and swore, but when others were upset and excited, he was soft spoken, calm and controlled. Either way, he struck sparks and got action."

Soldiers of VI Corps also wrote of other changes for the better when Sheridan commanded them. They received food, clothing, shoes and other supplies when they needed them. Within a month, the pesky little annoyances of being a soldier began to disappear. Marching and camp life changed; they knew someone was in charge, Sheridan. They appreciated his modest quarters and how he lived after they had seen Meade's elaborate personal arrangements. When the also modest Grant first saw Meade's headquarters, he asked Rawlins: "Where is the Imperial Caesar?" Is it any wonder that common soldiers quickly grew to love Sheridan and would do anything for him, no matter how dangerous or difficult?

Sheridan developed strong personal loyalties from his officers and men by seeing to their needs and being a common man, far from the stiff, pompous commanders they had previously experienced. As they became confident in his strategic and tactical ability, he used this loyalty and his strong charisma to get the best possible effort from his troops.

He was more difficult with his subordinate generals than with his private soldiers. If generals disobeyed or disappointed him, they were in for a tongue-lashing; if this failure continued, he would replace them. Sheridan was just as demanding on himself as he was on his subordinate generals. After battle management, organization was Sheridan's strongest point. This was illustrated many times in the Civil War. Examples are: (1) when he had commanded a cavalry brigade for only a month, it defeated a force several times its size; (2) he took command of the Cavalry Corps which was in a state of disarray, and reorganized it in five weeks into the best cavalry force of the war; (3) he organized the polyglot Army of the Shenandoah and made it into a crack fighting army in only six weeks.

Like Grant and Sherman, Sheridan was an innovator. He developed and proved the effectiveness of a new attack doctrine. This used the cavalry's mobility combined with the brute force of infantry and artillery to overcome static defensive positions that had dominated the war until Sheridan's rise. Many of his methods are still used in the 20th century.

Fighting Sheridan had to be most difficult for a Confederate opponent, who always had to look to his escape route and be in fear of annihilation. To mount a coordinated attack against such an opponent must have been very difficult, and at the same time, enemy generals had to begin to realize that a static defense against Sheridan would also prove ineffective.

*   *   *

That these three men rose to prominence at all is surprising. For the Union it was fortunate that they did, for no other general appears qualified to replace any of them at the same level of ability. For the Confederate States, it was very unfortunate since their rise spelled defeat.

A key to the successes of the Federal armies toward the end of the Civil War was that Grant, Sherman and Sheridan worked so well together as a team. Neither Sherman nor Sheridan were in awe of Grant or his position, and while they respected his skill as a man and soldier, they never hesitated to state their positions, strongly if necessary, even if they were contrary to Grant's. The mutual trust the three men displayed for one another made a great contribution to their success. Their relationship was a reversal of that of many earlier Civil War generals where hatred was a commonplace basis for some relationships. All three of these men knew the importance of their subordinates and insisted that they be the most efficient available.

The rise to prominence of Grant, Sherman and Sheridan and their development into extraordinary generals was the greatest phenomenon of the Civil War and was a great contribution to Union victory.

CHAPTER XXXV

Appraisal of Lee as a Commanding General

The burdens placed on Lee by others were enormous, including a political system that failed to bring about a complete mobilization of the Confederacy against its enemy. His President was inept militarily and interfered with most important decisions. The corrupt supply system failed to move needed, available supplies to his army. Lee did not fight adequately to overcome these burdens. Throughout the war, Lee failed to see what was necessary for the Confederacy to win with logistics or the most suitable strategies and tactics. Lee spent the lives of his men too liberally, lost their loyalty and thus failed his country.

*T*he burdens heaped upon Lee in his attempts to win a war were enormous. Most important, the Confederacy was never willing to make the sacrifices necessary to fully mobilize its strength behind the war effort. Being a loose confederacy, the states had various ideas of just how important it was to fight for a poor cause, slavery, and a vague cause, states rights. The Congress representing these states did not pass laws that would ensure the armies would receive sufficient men and other needs to fight a strong and determined foe. In short, the South lacked the determination to win for many reasons. At the same time, many Southerners had the conceit that they could win by merely appearing on the field. This was a combination that assured defeat if it were not changed. Lee protested against both of these defects but was unable to change them.

The "offense at all costs" syndrome was shared by Davis and Lee. Men like J.E. Johnston, Jackson and Longstreet were more for maintaining a defensive strategy until the opportunity for a "sure-win" offensive opportunity presented itself. In the face of Davis's opposition and without Lee's support, no one could successfully propose more likely to be successful defensive strategies. One of the characteristics of an outstanding general is his ability to cast aside whatever burdens are thrust upon him. Clearly, Lee accepted the burdens put upon him by others with only minor protest.

* * *

For some people, human nature is at its most unfortunate when a man has a great talent but prefers to use a lesser skill in the face of severe difficulty. This seems to have been the case for Lee: he was a defensive military genius, but he preferred to use offensive strategies and tactics, areas in which he did not exhibit much expertise.

Until mid-1864, Civil War generals had not yet developed offensive tactics that were effective against the superior weapons that were introduced into serious combat in 1861. The conventional offensive tactics of previous years no longer worked against these longer range and more accurate weapons. Lee's record clearly shows that because he was not an innovator competent to develop new tactics, he was poor to mediocre as an offensive general.

To be effective, a sound and strong defense must include some offense: counter-attacks, flanking actions and taking advantage of the enemy's exhaustion or mistakes. After Lee's initial experience in the Peninsula Campaign and his subsequent reorganization of his army, he forged a great defensive team with his principal subordinates, Jackson and Longstreet. On the Peninsula, Lee had almost no staff support, no corps-level commanders and lots of interference from his civilian, political superiors. These were problems he began to bring under control before Manassas II.

The three-man team of Lee, Jackson and Longstreet showed great defensive skill at Manassas II, Antietam and Fredericksburg when they defeated or held off a poorly led but numerically superior Federal army by remaining largely on the defensive. However, they missed a great opportunity to destroy Pope's army by a counter-attack Jackson had set up for Lee and Longstreet, and this missed opportunity was one of Lee's greatest mistakes of the war.

McClellan and Burnside showed little skill in planning their attacks against the Confederates at Antietam and Fredericksburg, but there is no question as to Lee's and his subordinate's skills in defending against Union attacks. At Antietam, Lee's decision to fight a 130,000-man Union army with a force of only 50,000 was rash to say the least. His back was against the Potomac River, and a competent Union commanding general would surely have destroyed his army and probably ended the war. Even without victory, meeting a more numerical Union force at Antietam and avoiding catastrophe was as impressive a success as defeating Burnside's larger army at Fredericksburg since Burnside had no chance of success.

Compared to his predecessors, Hooker proved to be a superior strategist at Chancellorsville, but he lacked the tactical skill and nerve to execute his good plan or to take advantage of the opportunities Lee gave him to win even late in the battle. For the South, it was unfortunate that Longstreet and two-thirds of his corps were absent at Chancellorsville, but Lee and Jackson gave excellent performance in what was essentially a defensive battle. The addition of Longstreet's force may well have turned the

Confederate victory at Chancellorsville into an even greater Federal disaster. Such a disaster could have been war-ending in the favor of the Confederacy; but this did not happen; and Chancellorsville proved to be Davis's and Lee's last opportunity for a Confederate military victory.

These successes apparently led Lee to believe he was invincible and could make any move, no matter how rash, against the numerically superior Army of the Potomac. In fighting these battles as he did he ignored the fact that he was receiving more casualties than the South could afford. He failed to understand that these successes resulted from poor enemy leadership in situations which allowed Lee to fight on the defensive. It did not logically follow that Lee would also be successful when he made a frontal assault against the same army in a well-prepared defensive position. He was to discover this bitter truth at Gettysburg on July 3, 1863, as he had already seen it at Malvern Hill!

Lee moved into Pennsylvania in June 1863 before he had reorganized his army after the loss of Jackson and while his health was at its poorest level of the war. This was a combination of two handicaps that no able commander should have accepted and then proceeded as if they did not exist. It was a self-imposed invitation to disaster, and the inevitable debacle happened quickly at Gettysburg. Lee's decisions to attack a superior Union position on the afternoons of July 2nd and 3rd were poor in the face of both the situation and the fact that his army had never before mounted a similar large attack successfully.

Meade was a good leader, his position was well-chosen and he had slight numerical superiority. When Lee failed to defeat Meade's army on the first day, and failed to renew the fight on the second morning of the battle when he still had a chance to win, Lee should have gone over to the defensive and moved around the Union army's left flank that night. This would have allowed Lee to choose a strong defensive position between Meade and Washington and allowed Lee and Longstreet to use their best skills.

Instead of taking defensive steps that might have led to his winning the campaign, Lee ordered two impossible frontal assaults. Lee may have been intoxicated with past successes and believed these justified such rash action in spite of the fact that he had no precedent on which to base any hopes of success. Lee was the same man who had personally observed Union troops fail while assaulting a Confederate position of similar strength at Fredericksburg. He had failed himself at Malvern Hill. He ignored his own observations. Why? It seems likely that Lee believed his generalship and soldiers were superior and could succeed where the Union Army and its generals had failed. Apparently, he also ignored the huge losses he had suffered throughout his officer corps and the problems presented by untrained, inexperienced replacements. Even the super-aggressive Hood blamed Lee for the defeat because Lee refused to make the opportunistic move around the Army of the Potomac's open left flank.

Lee continued to show his high degree of defensive skill at Mine Run, the Wilderness, Spotsylvania, North Anna and Cold Harbor. The attempted offensive in the Wilderness was not only ineffective, it used up most of Lee's reserves and ended his ability to counter-attack when opportunities later developed. Except for the futile and damaging Wilderness attack, Lee found his best generalship skills in 1864. Unfortunately, it was too late since by this time he had lost his best subordinates to death and wounds. Without Jackson, Stuart and Longstreet, Lee and his second-rate subordinates were no match for Grant and his subordinates. The Union generals of the Army of the Potomac in 1864 were greatly improved over the leadership at any earlier time in the Civil War.

Lee held a numerically superior Union army at bay before Petersburg for nine months. While this was an accomplishment, Lee missed several opportunities for more positive results. Petersburg was never fully surrounded, and full corps of Confederate troops operated as many as thirty miles south of Petersburg undisturbed by Union forces in the summer of 1864. Grant's army never had adequate protection on its southern flank.

In addition, every item of supply came to the Union armies through City Point, which was less than ten miles from the Confederate forces on both sides of the James River.

Although there were concerns among Union generals that an attack against the Union left south of Petersburg would be attempted, no such attack was mounted by Lee. Its feasibility was demonstrated by Hampton's successful raid which captured most of the Union cattle herd. Neither did Lee make a serious attempt to disrupt Grant's supply arrangements at City Point. An aggressive and confident general would not have missed attempts at these targets. Instead, Lee used up his reserves in many small and inconsequential actions that summer.

Whether influenced by Davis or not, Lee's actions around Petersburg seemed to be based on an obsession to protect Richmond at all cost. All Grant had to do to draw Lee's scanty reserves north of the James was to make a minor threatening move in that area. Eventually, Grant became aware of the effectiveness of this ploy and used it to his advantage many times. From Lee's standpoint, this concern about defending Richmond eliminated the possibility of a major offensive south of the Appomattox River which might well have been successful.

*   *   *

Davis was undoubtedly a strong negative influence that reduced Lee's ability to use his best skills. In selecting commanders, Davis's skills were very poor as is shown by his appointment of Bragg, Pemberton and Hood to top commands in the West. In every theater but Virginia, Davis's poor appointments to command led to virtual military collapse. Lee was by far the most competent of Confederate field commanders, but Davis's agreement with Lee about the desirability of offensive strategies and tactics hurt Lee's generalship. Instead of being encouraged to follow his "offense at all costs" ideas, Lee needed a superior who supported his defensive genius. If this had happened, Lee's generalship might have proved quite remarkable and the outcome of the war different. As it was, the tendency for Lee and Davis to agree on a faulty offensive strategy mitigated against any possible success of the Confederacy.

Lee had overall military responsibility for all Confederate armies for only the last six weeks of the war. Before this assignment when he was commander in only part of Virginia, he made decisions he thought best for his area of operations. Some of these decisions severely damaged Confederate operations elsewhere, and Lee may have made different decisions had he been in overall command. Examples of such local decisions were: Lee's decision to move into Pennsylvania rather that to reinforce Bragg, and Lee's decision to send Early to the Shenandoah Valley instead of reinforcing J.E. Johnston in Georgia. One might properly say that troops sent to Bragg might have been wasted, but substantial reinforcement of J.E. Johnston might have stopped Sherman before he reached Atlanta. This was a time when the political situation in the North was extremely tenuous, and any delay in further Union advances might have changed the outcome of the war. It is also questionable that these parochial decisions should be held as black marks against Lee's generalship; clearly, Davis was more at fault in not over-riding Lee's inappropriate decisions.

*　　*　　*

A general may be gentle or harsh with his subordinates and soldiers and still be competent, but to be successful, he must demand, obtain and maintain their loyalty and support. From Manassas II until he lost at Gettysburg, Lee received the intense loyalty of his men. This loyalty was somewhat damaged at Antietam where only luck and McClellan's incompetent and timid leadership saved Lee's army, but it was fully restored at Chancellorsville.

Private soldiers know they are in trouble when they cannot trust their generals to take care of them. Taking care of them means seeing that they are fed, clothed and above all not wasted in battle.

Private soldiers will accept any hardship, even heavy losses in battle, if only they are victorious. Lee was never able to feed and cloth his army adequately, and at Gettysburg, he gave them huge loss of life and defeat, not victory. Pickett's Charge was directly observed by almost all soldiers in the Army of Northern Virginia and most saw its futility. This severely eroded his soldiers' loyalty to Lee. He did not lose the loyalty of all of his soldiers, but along with the many casualties, there were enough who were no longer loyal to greatly reduce the effectiveness of his army. For many who had to continue to fight, Lee's lost battles and high casualties took any romance out of a dirty business, *war*. Without romance and glory, war showed itself in its true colors: a business of random, cruel death and maiming. As a result of disillusion, some of Lee's soldiers just lost interest in the cause.

*　　*　　*

Before the Civil War, an assignment to be a quartermaster was considered the lowest posting a West Point graduate could receive, while an engineering assignment was by far the most prestigious. The Civil War changed all this since logistics became more vital than in all previous wars.

Compared to all previous U.S. war experience, Civil War armies were far larger, weapons fired further with more rapidity and accuracy, and steam powered ships and railroads were able to transport large numbers of men and supplies quickly over great distances. All these men had to be supplied with food, fodder, clothing, shoes, equipment and ammunition, and the total amounts needed were enormous. This was the work of quartermasters who were under far greater strain than ever before, and there was no longer a place for the corrupt among them. Weeding out corrupt quartermasters was an almost never ending problem for both sides, but the North proved more efficient in this difficult process.

An army stops functioning when it runs out of its needs. An

example shows the enormity of the supply problem. When the Army of the Potomac crossed the Rapidan, without counting IX Corps which was independent, it had almost 100,000 men and 50,000 animals. The duty of its supply train was to move supplies, food and fodder from the supply base on the railroad to the army as it advanced. According to Quartermaster General Rufus Ingalls, the Army of the Potomac supply train had 3,476 wagons, 591 ambulances, 4,076 horses, 20,184 mules and it was 32 miles long when it was in a single line. In all, the horses in the Army of the Potomac required 500 tons of fodder per day to maintain their needed strength.

The basic reason the Union Army's quartermaster system was efficient was that its importance was recognized by army commanders. It was no coincidence that the most successful Union commanders, Grant, Sherman and Sheridan, all had substantial quartermaster experience personally. On the other side, Confederate soldiers were seldom adequately fed or clothed. Frequently, Stuart reported his horses were in poor condition and only a portion were suitable for combat. The Confederacy had food and fodder available, but it was far behind their lines and could not be brought to the army where and when it was needed. Confederate Quartermaster General Julius Norton showed little skill in developing an efficient supply system, and Davis, Lee and other commanders did not choose to address the problem seriously until near the end of the war when it was too late.

Of the leading Confederate generals, only J.E. Johnston had extensive quartermaster experience. Some Confederate commanders had earlier U.S. Army field commands and had to deal with the supply problem, even though it would have been on a smaller scale. Lee had no such opportunity until he became a Confederate army commander. This was one of the reasons why his army was poorly fed and clothed and why he did not stand up to the supply problem with Davis and Norton. This deficiency hurt Lee as a commander since his men eventually became worn down and were convinced that Lee did not care about their needs.

The manpower shortage of the Confederacy was stated by Lee to be a fiction. He said that the Confederate Congress and public were not sufficiently dedicated to gaining their independence. These groups allowed laws to be passed that exempted many able-bodied men from military service and allowed many to remain comfortably at home. In the absence of a complete mobilization of all able-bodied white males, Lee wanted to use slaves in support positions behind the fighting lines. He proposed that they be given their freedom in exchange for service. This use of the South's huge black population to support the war effort was only begun in the last few months of the war.

*　　*　　*

In conclusion, what were the basic reasons for Lee's failure?

1. Lee failed to throw off the burdens imposed upon him by his superiors and a political organization not sufficiently dedicated to the cause.

2. Lee failed to become expert in logistics in a logistical war. He might have gained the needed expertise through previous experience, through extensively studying the problem himself or by adding a really expert quartermaster to his staff. Lee had no previous quartermaster experience and he did not choose either of the other two approaches.

3. Lee remained bound to old, out-moded offensive tactics that were not effective against the new weapons both sides were using. He ignored the fact that enemy commanders like Grant, Sherman and Sheridan were developing new offensive tactics that could defeat static, defensive positions. He failed to improve his skills, and thus, he fell below the skill level of these and other Union generals.

4. Lee became intoxicated with his successes against poor Union commanders like McClellan, who allowed him to perform even rash acts without retribution. Succeeding against poorly led but larger armies made Lee believe his men and his own generalship

were superior to the men and generalship of the Army of the Potomac. Regardless of the fact that Lee had never been successful in such a direct frontal assault, this self-delusion led him to attack Meade at Gettysburg under impossible circumstances. Lee never came to grips with the facts of the war, and as a result, wasted his magnificent army and lost his men's loyalty.

5. Human nature is often perverse: frequently, some people do not wish to do what they perform best. Lee's failure was a variation of this kind of perversity. As a genius on the defensive which he hated, he most wanted to assume the attack where he was an ordinary commander, at best. Lee insisted on offensives in the face of situations he could not overcome, and he did not develop new offensive tactics that had a chance to win against the overwhelming advantage of defenders; instead he remained bound to old, failed tactics. Lee did not choose to act within his genius. Lee failed because he acted outside of his genius, and this probably also brought failure to the Confederacy.

Lee was a talented man given a great opportunity, but for these many and complex reasons, he failed his country.

NOTES

PREFACE

1. *The War of the Rebellion (Official Records)*. 128 vol. Washington: Government Printing Office.
2. Dowdey, Clifford, and Manarin, Louis H., Editors. *The Wartime Papers of R.E. Lee*. Boston: Little, Brown and Company, 1961. P. 589-90.
3. Alexander, Bevin. *Lost Victories: The Military Genius of Stonewall Jackson*. New York: Henry Holt & Company, 1992.
4. Nesbitt, Mark. *Saber and Scapegoat, J.E.B. Stuart and the Gettysburg Controversy*. Mechanicsburg, PA: Stackpole Books, 1994.
5. Fuller, J. F. C. *The Generalship of Ulysses S. Grant*. Bloomington: University of Indiana Press, 1929.

    _____. *Grant and Lee*. Bloomington: University of Indiana Press, 1932.
6. Nolan, Alan T. *Lee Considered: Robert E. Lee and Civil War History*. Chapel Hill: University of North Carolina Press, 1991.
7. Connelly, Thomas L. *The Marble Man: Robert E. Lee and His Image in American Society*. New York: Alfred A. Knopf, 1977.

CHAPTER I

1. Freeman, Douglas S. *R.E. Lee*. (Charles Scribner's Sons. New York: 1934.) I:550-78.
2. Freeman. II:74-76.
3. Freeman. II:409-414.
4. A review of the states from which generals and colonels came shows a great majority came from Virginia.
5. Jones, Archer. *Confederate Strategy from Shiloh to Vicksburg*. (Baton Rouge: Louisiana University Press.) Chapter XI. Freeman. III:19.
6. Bridges, Hal. *Lee's Maverick General, Daniel Harvey Hill*. (Lincoln, NB: University of Nebraska Press, 1961.) Hill was negotiating with *Century Magazine* for articles he wished to write. The editor

pressed him to comment on many things about which he had knowledge concerning Lee: Did Lee overrule Jackson in ordering him to leave the army and capture Harpers Ferry? Who was responsible for the lost message at Antietam? What was the real relationship between Lee, Jackson and Longstreet? Hill could have shed light on these and many more mysteries of the Civil War. Instead, in a letter to the editor of *Century* of January 28, 1885 he wrote: "I cannot criticize Lee now [after his death]."

7. Pickett made this statement to John S. Mosby after both visited with Lee shortly before his death. In fact Pickett lost 500 killed, 2007 wounded and 375 captured, 67% of the 4300 men of his own division who participated.

8. Wigfall Papers, Longstreet-Wigfall letter of August 18, 1863. Longstreet, James. *Manassas to Appomattox.* p. 434.

9. Lee, Fitzhugh. *General Lee.* (New York: DaCapo Press.) p. 299-310.

10. Livermore, Thomas, L. *Numbers and Losses in the Civil War in America, 1861-65.* (Dayton, OH: Morningside Books.)

11. *The War of the Rebellion: Official Records of the Union and Confederate Armies* (hereinafter known as "OR"). Series I. XXVI:2:1265.

CHAPTER II

1. Lee was 2nd of 46 graduates in 1829 and was assigned to the engineers. Meade 19/56 in 1835 to artillery. Grant 21/33 in 1843 to infantry. Sherman 6/42 in 1840 to artillery. Sheridan 34/52 in 1853 to infantry. J.E. Johnston 13/46 in 1829 to artillery. A.S. Johnston 8/39 in 1826 to infantry.

2. Sheridan, P.H. *The Personal Memoirs of P.H. Sheridan.* (New York: DaCapo.) I:29-57.

3. Gibbon, John. *The Artillerist's Manual.* (New York: 1860.) p. 249. Wilcox, Cadmus M. *Rifles and Rifle Practice.* (New York: 1859.) p. 247.

4. Scott, Winfield. *Infantry Tactics.* 1861 Edition. McWhiney, Grady and Jamieson, Perry D. *Attack and Die.* (University, AL: University of Alabama Press.) p. 1-41.

5. Freeman. I:170-263.

CHAPTER III

1. Grant, U.S. *Personal Memoirs of U.S. Grant.* (New York: DaCapo.) p. 363-67.

2. McWhiney, Grady and Jamieson, Perry D. *Attack and Die: Civil War Military Tactics and the Southern Heritage.* University, AL: University of Alabama Press, 1962. p. 13-24.. p. 13-24.
3. Livermore. p. 140-45.
4. Wiley, Bell Irvin. *The Life of Johnny Reb.* (Indianapolis: Bobbs-Merrill, 1943.) p. 244-69. Long, e.B. *The Civil War Day by Day; an Almanac 1861-1865.* (New York: DaCapo paperback edition, first published by Doubleday in 1971.)
5. Alexander, Porter. *Military Memoirs.* p. 42. Henderson, G.F.R. *Stonewall Jackson and the American Civil War.* (New York: DaCapo Press.) p. 131-32
6. Boteler, A.R. "Southern Historical Society Papers." Vol. 40:165
7. Alexander. p. 94. Freeman. II:84. OR II:I:32.
8. Henderson. p. 397-98. Freeman. II:260-61.

CHAPTER IV

1. Freeman. II:79-80. There was also no question that at the time Davis looked at Lee's command as a temporary appointment.
2. *O.R.* 5:2:775, 781-85, 788-9. 5:2:21.
3. Freeman. II:492.
4. *Battles and Leaders of the Civil War.* John B. Imboden I:111 ff.
5. Freeman. I:545-9, 551, 554, 560-76.
6. Freeman. I:574.

CHAPTER V

1. *O.R.* XIX:2:633-34.
2. Alexander, Bevin. *Lost Victories, the Military Genius of Stonewall Jackson.* (New York: Henry Holt & Co.) p. 111 nt.8.
3. McWhiney. p. 41-47.
4. Hoffman, John. *The Confederate Collapse at the Battle of Missionary Ridge.* (Dayton, OH: Morningside Bookshop Reprint, 1985.)

CHAPTER VI

1. Livermore, Thomas L. *Numbers and Losses in the Civil War in America, 1861-65.* (Dayton, OH: Morningside Books, 1986 (reprint).) p. 84-85. Livermore reports that the total number of soldiers engaged in the period June 29 through July 1, 1862 (Malvern Hill) was 83,345 for the Union and 86,748 for the Confederacy.

2. Freeman. II:236. *O.R.* XXII:2:493.
3. Alexander. p. 97.
4. *O.R.* XI:1:1039.
5. *O.R.* XI:2:489-99, 552-53.
6. *O.R.* XI:2:492.
7. Livermore. pp. 84-85.
8. Alexander. 167-71. Henderson. 393-94.
9. B. Alexander. p. 100.
10. *O.R.* XI:1:51.
11. Freeman. II:132-35. *O.R.* XI:2:834-40.

Chapter VII

1. Alexander, Bevin. p. 156-7.
2. *OR.* 12:2:185. Henderson. 420. Alexander. *Military Memoirs.* p. 182, 185.
3. OR. 11:3:674-76.
4. Alexander, Bevin. p. 158. Henderson. p. 424, 426.
5. *OR.* 12:2:553-54, 642-3. Freeman. *Robert E. Lee.* 2:284, 300-301. Henderson. p. 424.
6. *OR.* 12:2:67, 260, 333. 12:3:654-55. Henderson. 420, 434-35.
7. *OR.* 12:2:35-6, 71-2, 337, 360-61. Henderson. 441-42. Freeman. *Robert E. lee.* 2:259, 328.
8. *OR.* 12:2:321, 556, 565. 12:3:681. Henderson. 458-60, 463. Freeman. *Robert E. Lee.* 322-25, 327-28, 347.
9. Livermore. 88-89. Only 45,000 of Pops's army were engaged on the first day.
10. Freeman. *Lee's Lieutenants.* 2:125-6. *Robert E. Lee.* 2:331-34.
11. Freeman. *Robert E. Lee.* 2:328-29.
12. Livermore. Union: 10,200 killed and wounded, 7,000 missing. Confederacy: 9,100 killed and wounded, 81 missing.

CHAPTER VIII

1. Dowdey and Manarin. p. 312.
2. Jackson and Longstreet were informally appointed corps commanders in June 1862; the appointments were confirmed by the Confederate Congress in October 1862. Longstreet was appointed lieutenant general on October 9, 1962 and Jackson on October 10th. *OR* 19:2:698-99. Freeman. *Robert E. Lee.* II:345. *Lee's Lieutenants.* II:250-69, 297-8,

3. *OR* 19:1:835, 981. 19:2:646ff, 697.

4. The reasons behind McClellan's foolish decision not to use Porter's V Corps at Antietam are unclear. The facts are that Porter had been arrested as a result of a complaint by Pope that he had "willfully disobeyed orders." Porter was found guilty of the charge the following January and the sentence of the court was reversed in 1878.

5. McClellan formed three sub-commands (wings) which were to be headed by Franklin, Sumner and Burnside. This organizational plan fell apart before it started. Catton, Bruce. *Mr. Lincoln's Army.* (Garden City, NY:Doubleday & Co., Inc. 1950.) pp. 200-201.

6. Henry J. Hunt was promoted by McClellan to brigadier general and his chief of artillery just before the Battle of Antietam. He had no real authority until later.

7. Alexander, Bevin. p. 207-213. Henderson. p. 131-33. OR. 12:3:374.

8. *OR* 19:1:145, 19:2:603-4. Freeman. *Robert E. Lee.* II:363.

9. *OR* 19:1:140. Freeman. *Robert E. Lee.* II:373-74.

10. *OR* 19:1:140. Freeman. *Robert E. Lee.* II:375-76.

11. Henderson. p. 541.

12. Livermore states that 51,844 Confederate troops were engaged and 75,316 Union troops. pp. 92-93.

13. Alexander, Bevin. p. 216.

14. *OR* 19:1:140.

15. McWhiney and Jamieson.

16. *OR* 19:2:988. 19:1:891.

17. Livermore. pp. 92-93.

18. According to Arthur Ducat, one of Grant's staff in Mississippi at the time, in a letter to Rosecrans of April 24, 1885, Grant's headquarters received a dispatch from Cairo, Illinois on the night of October 18, 1862 which stated that McClellan had "exterminated" Lee at Antietam. About midnight a second dispatch was received saying: "Longstreet and his division were captured, A.P. Hill was killed and the whole rebel army was trapped against the flooded Potomac."

19. Baster, Roy P. *The Collected Works of Abraham Lincoln.* (New Brunswick, NJ: 1953-55.) 5:537. Freeman. *Robert E. Lee* 2:419.

20. Livermore. p. 82-93.

CHAPTER IX

1. Livermore. p. 92. (Killed and Wounded only)

	Manassas II	Antietam	South Mountain	All
Union	10,096	12,410	1,813	24,320
Confederate	9,108	13,724	2,685	25,517
TOTAL	19,214	26,134	4,498	49,837

2. Jackson wrote D.H. Hill before the battle. "We will whip the enemy but gain no fruits of victory."
3. Alexander, Bevin. p. 265.
4. Livermore. p. 96.
5. Comment by Jackson to Heros von Bork at Fredericksburg, December 13, 1862.
6. *OR.* XXI:140, 453-54, 510-13, 646-48, 661.
7. *OR.* XXI:633-34.
8. *OR.* XXI:222-23, 227-29, 263, 311-12, 430-33, 583-90.
9. Longstreet. p. 316-17.
10. Comment by Alexander to Longstreet on December 13, 1862.

CHAPTER X

1. *OR. The Official Military Atlas of the Civil War.* Plate XXXIX:No. 3.
2. Henderson. p. 650-51. Livermore. p. 98-99.
3. *OR.* XXV:2:702. This means Early's division of about 10,000 men and 26 artillery pieces were left on Marye's Heights above Fredericksburg so the force moving against Hooker had about 48,000 men and 144 guns.
4. *OR.* XXV:1:850.
5. Henderson. p. 654.
6. *OR.* XXV:1:941, 956, 966-67.
7. *OR.* XXV:1:193, 198-99.
8. Alexander, Bevin. p. 329, note 3.
9. Henderson. p. 665, 694-95. (Henderson's source was a personal letter from Jedediah Hotchkiss, Lee's Chief Engineer, who was an eye-witness.)
10. *OR.* XXV:1:386.
11. *OR.* XXV:1:941.
12. Henderson. p. 674.

13. Alexander, Edward P. *Military Memoirs.* p. 340-41, *Fighting for the Confederacy.* p. 204-6. *B & L* III:209-12. Captain James Power Smith, CSA.
14. *OR.* XXV:1:941, 1004.
15. *Report of the Joint Committee on the Conduct of the Civil War.* 1865, I:130-35. Report of Major General Joseph Hooker.
16. Black. *Above the Civil War.* pp. 101-102.
17. *OR.* XXV:1:386.
18. Livermore. p. 98-99.

CHAPTER XI

1. Doubler, Michael D. *Closing with the Enemy.* (Lawrence, KS: University of Kansas Press, 1994.) pp. 1-10.
2. Same. This is one of the major and very well supported conclusions of the book.
3. Luvaas, Jay and Nelson, Harold T. *The U.S. Army War College Guide to the Battles of Chancellorsville and Fredericksburg.* (New York: Harper and Row 1988.) pp. 3-121.

CHAPTER XII

1. Livermore. (Killed and Wounded only):

	UNION			CONFEDERATE		
	Killed	Wounded	Total	Killed	Wounded	Total
Cedar Mountain	314	1,445	1,759	231	1,107	1,338
Manassas II	1,724	8,372	10,096	1,481	7,697	9,178
South Mountain	325	1,403	1,728	325	1,560	1,885
Antietam	2,108	9,549	11,657	2,700	9,024	11,724
Fredericksburg	1,284	9,600	10,884	595	4,061	4,656
Chancellorsville	1,575	9,594	11,169	1,665	9,081	10,746
SUB-TOTAL	7,330	39,963	47,293	6,997	32,530	39,527
Death from disease			14,660			13,994
TOTAL			61,953			53,521
*Estimated at twice the number killed: some say this should be thrice.						

2. *O.R.* 20:1:698-99. 20:2:674.
3. *TWCD.* 325. O.R. 25:2:843.
4. Dowdey, Clifford and Manarin, Louis H. *The Wartime Papers* of *Robert E. Lee.* (Richmond, VA: 1961.) p. 589.

5. Nolan, Alan T. *Lee Considered.* (Chapel Hill: The University of North Carolina Press 1991.) pp. 30-58.

6. *O.R.* 17:2:599, 601.

7. Woodworth, Steven E. *Jefferson Davis and His Generals.* (Lawrence, KS: University of Kansas Press 1990.)

8. Warner, Ezra J. *Generals in Gray.* (Baton Rouge: University of Louisiana Press, 1959.) This volume indicates that of 425 Confederate generals, 77 (18%) were killed or mortally wounded in action and 235 (55%) were killed or wounded.

9. Cozzens, Peter. *This Terrible Sound.* (Chicago: University of Illinois Press, 1992.) Chapters 27-30.

10. The conversation between Lee and Longstreet regarding maintaining a tactical defense is disputed but seems logical in view of the men's actions and the known facts.

CHAPTER XIII

1. Meade replaced Hooker as commander of the Army of the Potomac by order of President Lincoln on June 27, 1863.

2. The actions of the "Lee cult" after the Civil War and Lee's death in 1870 against Longstreet, Stuart and others and in support of their own positions are detailed in: Connelly, Thomas L. *The Marble Man.* (Baton Rouge: Louisiana State University Press, 1977.)

3. *U.S. Military Academy Monthly Class Reports and Conduct Rolls.* 1831-1866. Welsh, Jack D., M.D., *Medical Histories of Civil War Generals.* (Kent, OH: Kent University Press, 1995). pp. 99-100.

4. Fremantle, Arthur F.L. *Three Months in the Southern States.* (London: William Blackwood and Sons, 1863.) p. 260.

5. Freeman. *Lee's Lieutenants.* p. ix, 90-100.

6. *O.R.* 27:3:943. 27:2:444.

7. Freeman. *Lee's Lieutenants.* pp. 1-19.

8. Dowdey. *The Wartime Papers of Robert E. Lee.* p. 589. Welsh. pp. 134-136.

9. *Life and Letters of George Gordon Meade.* Vol. I:351-54.

10. Robertson, Jr., James I. *General A.P. Hill.* (New York: Random House, 1987.) p. 205-6.

CHAPTER XIV

1. Catton, Bruce. *The Glory Road.* (Garden City, NY: Doubleday, 1955.) pp. 289-345.

_____Coddington, Edwin B. *The Gettysburg Campaign.*
(Dayton, OH: Morningside Bookshop (reprint), 1989.)__
_____Gallagher, Gary W. (ed.) *The First Day at Gettysburg.*
(Kent, OH: Kent State University Press, 1992.)
_____Gallagher, *The Second Day at Gettysburg.* (Kent, 1993.)
_____Freeman. *Robert E. Lee.* III: 29-162.

2. Nesbitt, Mark. *Saber and Scapegoat.* Mechanicsburg, PA. This book is a careful study of Lee's orders to Stuart and their interchanges during the battle. One must conclude that Stuart followed Lee's orders. Either the orders were at fault, or the more than 50% of the cavalry Stuart left with Lee failed them both.
3. Welsh. p. 135.
4. Parrish, T. Marshall (ed.). *Reminiscences of the War in Virginia by David French.* (Austin, TX: 1989.) pp. 19-21.
5. Gordon. *Reminiscences of the Civil War.* pp. 153-59. Freeman. *Lee's Lieutenants.* III: 90-100.
6. Coddington. p. 388-96. Fremantle. pp. 267-69.
7. Fitzhugh Lee. p. 289.
8. Alexander. *Fighting for the Confederacy.* pp. 280-85.
9. Longacre, Edward G. *Pickett, Leader of the Charge.* (White Mane Publishing Co., Inc., 1995.) pp. 128-9.
10. Same. p. 179. Mosby, John S. *The Memoirs of Colonel John Singleton Moseby.* (Boston: Little, Brown & Co., 1917.) pp. 380-1.
11. Cozzens, Peter. *That Terrible Sound.* (Champaign, IL: University Of Illinois Press, 1993.) pp. 368-70.
12. *O.R.* XXVII:2:320, 359.
13. Nesbitt. p. 87.
14. Nesbitt. p. 68-9. *O.R.* XXVII:3:927-28.
15. Nesbitt. pp. 57-84.
16. Nesbitt. pp. 65-67. H. McClellan. p. 317-18.
17. *O.R.* XXVII:1:658-59. Longstreet. p. 344.
18. Little Round Top was occupied by only a Union signal party until noon of July 2nd; its capture by Confederate troops, which would have been very easy until this time, would have unhinged the whole Union defense line.
19. Hood, John B. *Advance and Retreat.* (New York: DaCapo Press (reprint), 1993.) pp. 57-59.
20. Same. pp. 59-60.
21. Sedgwick communications and papers. Cornwall Historical Collection, No. 400, Cornwall, CT.
22. Longstreet. pp. 334-36.

23. *O.R.* XXVII:1:658-59.
24. Freeman. *Robert E. Lee* III:108-114. *Lee's Lieutenants.* III:180-88.
25. Meade, George G. *Life and Letters of George Gordon Meade.* (New York, 1913.) II:135. *O.R.* XXVII:1:73-4.
26. Livermore. pp. 102-3.
27. Dowdey and Mandarin. pp. 589-90.
28. Same.
29. Woodward, Steven E. *Davis and Lee at War.* (Lawrence, KS: University of Kansas Press, 1995). pp. 249-50.
30. Davis, Jefferson. *Rise and Fall*, II: 447-49.
31. Randolph McKim was a physician working for the Confederate War Office at the time.
32. Wade Hampton letter written in 1867 to J.E. Johnston.
33. Longstreet. pp. 385-91.
34. Pollard, Edward. *The Southern History of the War: The Third Year of the War.* New York, 1865. pp. 15-6. Author quotes previous newspaper writings in *Richmond Examiner.*

CHAPTER XV

1. Alexander. pp. 439-40. Sorrel. p. 171.
2. Humphreys, A.A. *Gettysburg to the Rapidan.* (New York: Charles Scribners Sons, 1883.) p. 6.
3. Humphries. *Gettysburg to the Rapidan.* p. 6-8.

CHAPTER XVI

1. Dowdey and Mandarin. pp. 589-90. Welsh. p. 135.
2. Livermore. p. 103. Lee had 77,054 effective soldiers before Gettysburg and lost 28,063 killed, wounded and missing, leaving 46,991.
3. Freeman. *Lee.* III:254-6.
4. Dowdey and Mandarin. August 8, 1863 letter to Jefferson Davis.
5. Cozzens, Peter. *This Terrible Sound.* (Urbana, IL: University of Illinois Press, 1992.) This book describes the great influence of Longstreet and his corps on the Confederate victory. See especially pp. 357-477.
6. Cozzens, Peter. *The Shipwreck of Their Hopes.* (Urbana, IL: University of Illinois Press, 1994.) This book is a very good general description of the battles of Lookout Mountain and Missionary Ridge.
7. Cozzens. *Shipwreck.* For the poor design of the Missionary Ridge defenses, see pp. 257-342.

CHAPTER XVII

1. Graham, Martin F. and Skoch, George F. *Mine Run, A Campaign of Lost Opportunities.* (Lynchburg, VA: H.E. Howard, Inc., 1987.) pp. 3-4. Agazziz, George R. (ed.). *Meade's Headquarters, 1863-65.* Boston, 1922. pp. 36-37.
2. Humphries. *Gettysburg to the Rapidan.* p. 12-32.
3. Same. p. 37.
4. Graham and Skoch. p. 59.
5. Catton. *Grant Takes Command.* p. 139. Church, William Conant. *Ulysses S. Grant and the Period of National Preservation and Reconstruction.* (New York, NY, 1897.) pp. 248-49.

CHAPTER XVIII

1. Piston, William G. *Lee's Tarnished Lieutenant.* (Athens, GA: University of Georgia Press, 1987.) p. 89.
2. The bill restoring the rank of lieutenant-general was signed by Lincoln on February 26, 1864. Lincoln immediately submitted Grant's nomination to the post to the Senate, and it was confirmed the following day.
3. Sword, Wiley. *Shiloh: Bloody April.* (New York, NY: William Morrow & Co., 1974.) This book describes the battle well.
4. Welsh. pp. 118-119.
5. Livermore. pp. 79-80.
6. Grant. *Memoirs.* p. 192.
7. Catton, Bruce. *Grant Moves South.* (Boston, MA: Little, Brown & Co., 1960.) pp. 471-89. This section of this book gives a description of the surrender in detail.
8. Cozzens. *Shipwreck.* pp. 42-78. This is a good description of the Brown's Ferry ("Cracker Line") operation.
9. Same. This book is an excellent description of the battles around Chattanooga.

CHAPTER XIX

GENERAL NOTE: For the best available exposition on the last year of the Civil War, I recommend highly Don Lowry's four-volume series. These books not only describe actions throughout the world, but Lowry weaves into the chronology such things as the Confederate Secret Service involvement in the Lincoln-kidnap plot and their attempt to burn New York. All four of these excellent books were published by Hippocrene Books of New York

between 1992 and 1995. Lowry titled the books: *No Turning Back, Fate of the Country, Dark and Cruel War* and *Towards an Indefinite Shore.*
1. Piston. p. 89.
2. Steere, Edward. *The Wilderness Campaign.* (Harrisburg, PA: The Stackpole Company, 1960.) This is a good work on this very complicated battle.
3. Livermore. pp. 110-11.

CHAPTER XX

1. Starr, Stephen Z. *The Union Cavalry in the Civil War.* (3 vol.) (Baton Rouge: Louisiana State University Press, 1979.) I:47-61.
2. Same. I:58.
3. *OR.* XXX:1:184-88.
4. There are few good general works describing the Battle of Spotsylvania, but a good description appears in: Catton, Bruce. *A Stillness at Appomattox.* pp. 93-137.
5. Livermore. pp. 112-14.
6. Welsh. pp. 63-65.

CHAPTER XXI

1. *OR.* XXXVI:1:812.
2. Starr. pp. 101-8.
3. Two Confederate generals, Stuart and Gordon, were killed, and other Confederate casualties were estimated at 1,000; Union casualties were about 500.

CHAPTER XXII

1. Miller, J. Michael. *The North Anna Campaign: "Even to Hell Itself."* (Lynchburg, VA: H.E. Howard, Inc. 1989.) This book gives a comprehensive view of the Ox Ford action.
2. Numbers calculated from Livermore. pp. 112-114.
3. *Southern Historical Society Papers.* XIV (1986). p. 535.

CHAPTER XXIII

1. Freeman. *Robert E. Lee.* III:389.
2. Same. pp. 373-83. Cat ton. *Stillness at Appomattox.* pp. 145-149.
3. Same. pp. 149-80. This is a good general description of the fighting at Cold Harbor.

4. Livermore. p. 114. There are no records of Confederate losses so Confederate losses are estimated.
5. Grant. *Memoirs.* pp. 444-45.

CHAPTER XXIV

1. Good descriptions of Grant's strategy are to be found in these books:

Grant, Ulysses S. *Personal Memoirs of U.S. Grant.* (1885) (New York: DaCapo Reprint.)

_____Catton, Bruce. *A Stillness at Appomattox.* (Garden City, NY: Doubleday & Co., 1953.)

_____Howe, Thomas J. *The Petersburg Campaign: Wasted Valor* (Lynchburg, VA: H.E. Howard, Inc., 1988.)

CHAPTER XXV

1. Howe.p. 21-42.
2. Smith, W.F. *From Chattanooga to Petersburg.* (Boston: Houghton Mifflin Co., 1893.) p. 27.
3. *O.R.* LI:2:265-66. LI:1:721.

CHAPTER XXVI

1. Early's performance at Chancellorsville and Gettysburg was considered poor by most Confederate generals, with only Ewell coming to his support. His later poor performance in the Shenandoah Valley supported this contention. Lee must also have not been impressed since after Early lost his army, Lee found no place for him.
2. Grant. *Memoirs.* p. 369.
3. These books best describe Sheridan's operations in the Shenandoah Valley:
    _____Starr. II:245-326.
    _____Wert, Jeffry D. *From Winchester to Cedar Creek, the Shenandoah Valley Campaign of 1864.* (New York: Simon & Schuster, Inc., 1987.)
4. Grant. *Memoirs.* II:313.
5. Powell, William H. "The Battle of the Petersburg Crater," in *Battles and Leaders.* IV:545.

CHAPTER XXVII

1. Calculated from Livermore. pp. 119-21.

2. *The Medical and Surgical History of the War of the Rebellion.* Washington, 1875. Medical Volume, Part First and Appendix. p. XLIII. Of 360,222 Union deaths from all causes, 224,580 resulted from disease. The most accepted numbers of Confederate killed or mortally wounded in battle was 94,000, and deaths from disease were 164,000.
3. Sherman, William T. *Memoirs.* (New York: DaCapo Edition, 1984.) II:15. Sherman reported the strength of the Army of the Cumberland at about 50,000 effectives, the Army of the Ohio at about 15,000 and the Army of the Tennessee at about 35,000. These figures are slightly different from those in Livermore.
4. Wert. The battles of Winchester III, Fishers Hill and Cedar Creek.

CHAPTER XXVIII

1. Freeman. III:497-9, 516-7, 541-2.
2. Freeman. III:233-4. *OR.* XLVII:2:1320.
3. These two books have advanced the real history of the Confederate Secret Service and Davis's involvement in the plot to kidnap Lincoln enormously during the past ten years:
    _____Tidwell, William A., Hall, James O. and Gaddy, W. G. *Come Retribution: The Confederate Secret Service and the Assassination of Lincoln.* Jackson: University of Mississippi Press, 1988.)
    _____Tidwell, William A. *April 1865.* (Kent, OH: Kent University Press, Ohio, 1995.)
4. Whether the documents implicating Lincoln in a plot to kill Davis and other Confederate officials that were found on Dahlgren's body were real or planted, the fact remains that Kilpatrick received his first instructions about the raid directly from Lincoln. *OR.* XXXIII:552.
5. Sherman's *Memoirs* are a good primary source of information about his passage through the Carolinas. See also: Clatthaar, Joseph, T. *The March to the Sea and Beyond.* Baton Rouge: Louisiana State University Press, 1985.

CHAPTER XXIX

1. In January and February of 1865, Lincoln's representative, a former Cabinet Officer, Francis Blair, Sr., met with Davis twice, and a high-ranking Confederate Commission met with Lincoln and Seward at Hampton Roads.

2. Longstreet, James. *From Manassas to Appomattox.* (New York: Mallard Press (reprint).) pp. 588, 641, 646 and 649.
3. Same. pp. 583-5.
4. Sherman. *Memoirs.* pp. 137-40.

CHAPTER XXX

1. Livermore. pp. 135-39. This covers period from March 29 through April 9, 1865 added to which were 5,000 men lost in the Ft. Stedman attack on March 25.
2. Grant. *Memoirs.* pp. 531-2.
3. Porter. *Campaigning with Grant.* pp. 428-9.
4. Freeman. *Lee's Lieutenants.* III:665-6.
5. Freeman. *Lee.* IV:41-47.

CHAPTER XXXI

1. *OR.* XLVI:1:1106.
2. Treudeau, Noah Andre. *The Last Citadel.* (Baton Rouge LA: Louisiana State University Press, 1991.)
3. Sheridan. *Memoirs.* pp. 334-5.
4. *OR.* XLVI:3:595-98, 610. XLVI:1:1161-69.
5. Sheridan. II:190. Freeman. *Lee's Lieutenants.* III.723 *OR.* XLVI:1:1132, 1136-7, 1120, 1126.

CHAPTER XXXIV

1. O'Connor, Richard. *Sheridan, the Inevitable.* (Indianapolis IN: Bobbs-Merill Company, Inc., 1953.) p. 355.

BIBLIOGRAPHY

The War of the Rebellion (Official Records). 128 vol. Washington: Government Printing Office.

Battles and Leaders of the Civil War. 4 vol. (1884-88) New York: Castle Books Edition.

Papers of the Military Historical Society of Massachusetts (1895-1918).

National Archives: Papers of U.S. Grant, P.H. Sheridan and others.

Albright, Harry. *Gettysburg, Crisis in Command.* New York: Hippocrene Books, 1991.

Alexander, Bevin. *Lost Victories: The Military Genius of Stonewall Jackson.* New York: Henry Holt & Company, 1992.

Ambrose, Stephen E. *Halleck: Lincoln's Chief-of-Staff.* Baton Rouge: Louisiana University Press, 1962.

Boykin, Edward. *Congress and the Civil* War. New York: The McBride Company, 1955.

Cadwallader, Sylvanus. *Three Years with Grant.* New York:Alfred A. Knopf & Co., 1956.

Cannan, John. *The Wilderness Campaign, May 1864.* Conshohocken, Pennsylvania: Combined Books, 1993.

Catton, Bruce. *Mr. Lincoln's Army.* New York: Doubleday & Co., 1955.

_____. *Glory Road.* New York: Doubleday & Co., 1955.

_____. *A Stillness at Appomattox.* New York: Doubleday & Co., 1955.

_____. *Grant Moves South.* Boston: Little, Brown and Company, Inc., 1960.

_____. *Grant Takes Command.* Boston: Little, Brown & Co., 1968.

Chamberlain, Joshua L. *The Passing of the Armies.* (1915) Dayton: Morningside reprint.

Cleaves, Freeman. *Meade of Gettysburg.* (1959) Dayton Ohio: Morningside Bookshop reprint, 1980.

Coddington, Edwin B. *The Gettysburg Campaign, A Study in Command.* New York: Charles Scribner's Sons, 1968.

Connelly, Thomas L. *The Marble Man: Robert E. Lee and His Image in American History.* New York: Alfred E. Knopf, 1977.

Connelly, Thomas L. and Bellows, Barbara, *God and General Longstreet, The Lost Cause and the Southern Mind.* Baton Rouge, Louisiana: The University of Louisiana Press, 1982.

Cozzens, Peter. *This Terrible Sound.* (Chickamauga). Urbana, Illinois: University of Illinois Press, 1992.

Davies, Henry E. *General Sheridan.* New York: D. Appleton & Co., 1912.

Davis, Burke. *JEB Stuart: The Last Cavalier.* New York: Rinehart and Company, 1957.

Davis, Jefferson. *The Rise and Fall of the Confederate Government.* (Vol. II, 1881) New York: DaCapo reprint.

Dowdey, Clifford. *The Seven Days, the Emergence of Robert E. Lee.* New York: The Fairfax Press, 1964.

Lee's Last Campaign. (1960) Lincoln, NB: University of Nebraska reprint.

Dowdey, Clifford & Manarin, Louis H. (Ed.) *The Wartime Papers of Robert E. Lee.* Boston: Little, Brown & Co., 1961.

DuPont, H.A. *The Campaign of 1864 in the Valley of Virginia.* New York: National Americana Society, 1925.

Early, Jubal. *Memoirs.* (1912) . Baltimore: J & A Publishers Reprint.

Eckenrode, H.L. & Conrad, Bryan. *James Longstreet, Lee's War Horse.* Chapel Hill: University of North Carolina Press, 1936.

Freeman, Douglas S. *R. E. Lee* (4 vol.). New York: Charles Scribner' Sons, 1943.

Lee's Lieutenants (3 vol.). New York: Charles Scribner's Sons, 1944.

Fuller, J. F. C. *The Generalship of Ulysses S. Grant.* Bloomington: University of Indiana Press, 1929.

_____. *Grant and Lee.* (1932) Bloomington: University of Indiana Press.

Gordon, John B. *Reminiscences of the Civil War.* (1874) Civil War Times reprint.

Grant, Ulysses S. *Personal Memoirs.* (1885). New York: DaCapo Edition Reprint.

Hallock, Judith Lee. *Braxton Bragg and Confederate Defeat.* (Vol. II) Tuscaloosa, Alabama: The University of Alabama Press, 1991.

Henderson, G.F.R. *Stonewall Jackson and the American Civil* War. (1989) New York: DaCapo reprint.

Hood, John Bell. *Advance and Retreat.* (1880) New York: DaCapo reprint.

Horn, John. *The Petersburg Campaign.* Conshohocken, Pennsylvania: Combined Books, 1993.

Horn, Stanley. *The Robert E. Lee Reader.* New York: Bobbs Merrill Company, Inc., 1949.

Kidd, J. H. *A Cavalryman with Custer.* (1908). New York: Bantam Books (slightly abridged) 1991.

Lee, Jr., Robert E. *Recollections and Letters of General Robert E. Lee.* New York: Kenecky & Kenecky reprint.

Leech, Margaret, *Reveille in Washington, 1860-1865.* Alexandria, Virginia: Time-Life Books, Inc., 1962.

Livermore, W. R. *Numbers and Losses in the Civil War* (1913). Dayton: Morningside Reprint.

Long, A.L. *The Memoirs of Robert E. Lee.* (1886) Secaucus, N.J.: The Blue and Grey Press reprint.

Longstreet, James. *From Manassas to Appomattox.* (1888) New York: Mallard Press reprint.

Lowry, Don. *No Turning Back: The Beginning of the End of the Civil War, March-June 1864.* New York: Hippocrene Books, Inc., 1991.

_____. *Fate of the Country, The Civil War from June-September 1864.* New York: Hippocrene Books, Inc., 1992.

Luvaas, Jay & Nelson, Harold W. *The U.S. Army War College Guide to the Battles of Chancellorsville and Fredericksburg.* New York: Harper & Row, 1988.

_____. *The U.S. Army War College Guide to the Battle of Antietam.* New York: Harper & Row, 1987.

_____. *The U.S. Army War College Guide to the Battle of Gettysburg.* New York: Harper & Row, 1986.

Lyman, Theodore. *Meade's Headquarters, 1863-65.* Boston: The Atlantic Monthly Press, 1922.

McCartney, Clarence E. *Grant and His Generals.* New York: The McBride Company, 1953.

McKinney, Francis F. *Education in Violence* (1962). Chicago: Americana House, 1991.

McWhiney, Grady. *Braxton Bragg and Confederate Defeat.* (Vol. I). New York: Columbia University Press, 1969.

McWhiney, Grady and Jamieson, Perry D. *Attack and Die: Civil War Military Tactics and the Southern Heritage.* University, AL: University of Alabama Press, 1982.

Nolan, Alan T. *Lee Considered: Robert E. Lee and Civil War History.* Chapel Hill: University of North Carolina Press, 1991.

O'Connor, Richard. *Sheridan, the Inevitable.* Indianapolis: Bobbs-Merril Company, Inc., 1953.

Palumbo, Frank A. *George Henry Thomas, The Dependable General.* Dayton, Ohio: Morningside reprint, 1983.

Pollard, Edward A. *The Lost Cause, A New Southern History of the War of the Confederates.* New York: E.B. Treat & Co., 1867.

Porter, Horace. *Campaigning with Grant.* (1897). Secaucus, N. J.: The Blue and Grey Press.

Robertson Jr., James I. *General A.P. Hill.* New York: Random House, 1987.

Sears, Stephen W. *George B. McClellan, The Young Napoleon.* New York: Ticknor & Fields. 1988.

Sheridan, Philip H. *Personal Memoirs.* 2 vol. New York: Charles L. Webster & Company, 1888.

Sherman, W. T. *Memoirs* (1884). New York: Da Capo Reprint.

Sorrel, G. Moxley. *Recollections of a Confederate Staff Officer.* (1905) Dayton, Ohio: Morningside reprint, 1978.

Stackpole, Edward J. *The Fredericksburg Campaign.* Harrisburg, Pennsylvania: Military Service Publishing company, 1957.

Stern, Philip V.D. *An End to Valor.* Boston: Houghton Mifflin Company, 1958.

Starr, Stephen Z. *The Union Cavalry in the Civil War.* 3 vol. Baton Rouge: L. S. U. Press. 1979.

Steere, Edward. The Wilderness *Campaign.* Harrisburg, Pennsylvania: The Stackpole Company, 1960.

Stewart, George B. *Pickett's Charge.* Boston: Houghton, Mifflin Company, 1959.

Sword, Wiley. *Embrace the Angry Wind.* New York: Harper Collins Publishers, 1992.

Symonds, Craig. *Joseph E. Johnston.* New York: W.W. Norton & Company, 1992.

Thomas, Benjamin P. and Hyman, Harold M. *Stanton, the Life and Times of Lincoln's Secretary of War.* New York: Alfred A. Knopf, 1962.

Tidwell, William A., Hall, James O. and Gaddy, W. G. *Come Retribution: The Confederate Secret Service and the Assassination of Lincoln.* Jackson: University of Mississippi Press, 1988.

Trulock, Alice R. *In the Hands of Providence (Chamberlain).* Chapel Hill: University of North Carolina Press, 1992.

Welsh, Jack D., M.D. *Medical Histories of Confederate Generals.* Kent, Ohio: The Kent State University Press, 1995.

_____. *Medical Histories of Union Generals.* Kent, Ohio: The Kent State University Press, 1996.

Wert, Jeffry D. *General James Longstreet.* New York: Simon & Schuster, 1993.

Williams, Kenneth P. *Lincoln Finds a General.* (5 vol.) New York: The MacMillan Company, 1950-54.

Williams, T. Harry. *Lincoln and His Generals.* New York: Dorset Press, 1952.

Wilson, James H. *Under the Old Flag.* 2 vol. New York: D. Appleton & Co., 1912.

Woodworth, Steven. *Jefferson Davis and his Generals.* Lawrence, Kansas: The University of Kansas Press, 1990.

_____. *Davis & Lee at War.* Lawrence, Kansas: University of Kansas Press, 1996.

Index